NIGHT FEVER

NIGHT FEVER

CLUB WRITING IN THE FACE 1980-1997

EDITED BY RICHARD BENSON

BOXTREE

First published in 1997 by Boxtree, an imprint of Macmillan Publishers Ltd
25 Eccleston Place, London SW1W 9NF and Basingstoke

Associated companies throughout the world

ISBN 0 7522 2214 7

9 8 7 6 5 4 3 2 1

A CIP catalogue record for this book is available from the British Library

Cover design by Craig Tilford
Cover photograph by Elaine Constantine
Book design by Tim Lewis

Printed and bound in Great Britain
by Mackays of Chatham PLC

00 CONTENTS

FOR GAVIN

01 **INTRODUCTION**

Writing a thesis on dance clubs is not as easy as it may sound. So I was wondering whether FACE readers would write to me to help me with my research. The question I'm puzzling over, which perhaps proves that sociology is the study of the bleeding obvious, is why do you, or don't you go to clubs? What is their appeal? The music, the crowd, dancing, drinking, drugs, hiding out, watching or being seen? What has been your best club or warehouse experience?

Extract from a letter from reader Sarah Thornton, FACE letters page,
June 1990

OF ALL THE THOUSANDS of readers that have ever written to The FACE to express their opinions on clubs, on club culture, or on Culture Club come to that, Ms Sarah Thornton of Glasgow must stand alone in her ability to summarise the club-centric questions that FACE writers and editors have spent the last 17 years attempting to answer. The frank bewilderment of her letter certainly made it stand out to me as I found myself working my way through 200-odd back issues of the magazine at the start of 1997. Charged with making a compilation of all the club-related writing published in The FACE since its inception in 1980, I was desk-deep in the tales and details of lost weekenders and wee-small-hours and next-big-things that make up the history of our glorious, notorious club culture. And I was finding there is nothing quite like that particular experience for raising the questions: what are we doing in these places? And: why on earth are we doing it? What is it that has made people dress up and look forward and go back again and again to these places in search of the best of times? Just the lust for life, the pleasure principle? Or more than that? Or less?

Sarah wrote the letter in the summer of 1990, at a time when a major new wave of club culture – usually referred to as post-acid house, or just house, or rave – was growing from subculture to mass lifestyle in an unprecedented way. Clubbing – by which I mean going out with the idea of the club as your primary destination, rather than as an available drinking and pulling venue once the pubs have shut – was transforming itself into a multi-million pound leisure industry, turning the youth markets for commodities such as drinks and clothes and pop music on their heads in the process. For a significant proportion of the population, the club was edging out the pub as the favoured house of fun for the weekend. Curious observers like Sarah, and indeed some curious participants who were wondering what was happening to their lives, were beginning to ponder the possible motivations that were at work. To contemplate why clubbing could mean so much to so many people; to ask what was created and achieved through this strangely brilliant and brilliantly strange activity that some claim makes their lives, and others say makes them a living, and many people can't for the life of them understand. Why do you, after all? Or why don't you? And did you ever?

Fortunately for the curious, background research had already been in progress for many years. Because since The FACE was launched in May 1980, it has employed the most gifted young journalists from each successive generation to put these questions

11

to themselves, and to the promoters and clientele of the clubs that have kicked. Indeed, some of the writers had been contemplating the issues before 1980. That's why they were able to contribute the retrospective accounts of the more important Seventies club capers – Northern Soul, New York disco and London's pre-Blitz scene – that appear in this collection.

The premise which made – and still makes – The FACE unique was that youth and pop culture should be treated with the sort of reverence and critical intelligence that prior to May 1980 was almost exclusively associated with the highbrow. From the outset its editors made a point of recruiting bright, sharp and smart kids from British clubland to write about it; they were encouraged to think seriously about the clubs that strove to provide alternatives to the mainstream, and to chronicle the lives of the people who went to them. From month to month, and then from year to year, they not only documented what was happening underground, but also asked if sometimes those clubs might not have bigger meanings that went beyond just drinking and dancing. The writers and editors shared two unspoken beliefs. First, that our clubs are places in which the young and creative try on new ways of expressing and enjoying themselves that feel right for the times. And second, that this means clubs can be the best places in which to hunt out the new music and ideas that may eventually infiltrate everyone's everyday lives. This whole approach, and the love of clubbing that sustains it, has become a cornerstone of The FACE tradition; and the writing in this book shows that those beliefs have been proved over and over and over again.

The first mentions of clubs in Britain come from the 1600s, when people who gathered for parties in taverns began to speak of themselves "clubbing together" (so far as anyone knows, they used the words because they likened the collective mass they formed to the thick end of a wooden club). By the end of the seventeenth century, many of these revellers had begun to organise their gatherings by agreeing rules and membership arrangements – establishing the basic principle that clubbing is the gathering of revellers linked by a common idea of how to have a bacchanalian good time, and their shared intention to have it. That many of these early organisations developed into the rigidly-formalised gentlemen's drinking clubs of the eighteenth century is evidence enough that shared tastes on clothes, conduct and stimulants have been important from the very beginning too. It was, however, the new class of rich bright young things who grew up in the 1920s and 1930s, and who built the jazz age of that period on the foundations of their heightened sexual interplay, female emancipation, demonstrativeness, and style consciousness, that mapped out the modern dancefloor as we know it. They also generated the belief, promoted by contemporary observers like F Scott Fitzgerald, that their new, decadent leisure pursuits could be seen as forms of expression that were as relevant as works of art or literary debate. Although ridiculous excesses would be committed in its name in the 1960s, that argument became more convincing with the social changes of the war and post-war years. The advent of the teenager, the rise of the dancehall, and the increasing wages of the working class brought the People to the new, modern dancefloors, and that meant that the intelligent observer could then look out on those floors, and see changes that were sometimes indicative of changes in society at large. Once Nick Logan launched The FACE, the world had a magazine that went looking for the clues all the time. And once the clubbing boom of the early Eighties had given us the now commonplace one-nighter, whereby a promoter takes over a venue to run a singular event on a weekly, monthly or one-off basis, the changes became more and more frequent, the clues more and more entertaining, as the years went by. This book is a selection of those clues and conclusions which recounts the history of this strange, brilliant, often absurd and also important pleasure pursuit over the last two decades.

If you wanted to take a serious moral from looking back at this history, you could perhaps start by thinking about the rather weighty idea of freedom. About what gets created – and what gets wasted – in the great pockets of liberation that nightclubs become to many of their habituées. Since clubbers look at their clubs as places in which they can express themselves, and since a good time will often be felt more keenly when it's being had in new ways, clubs will every once in a while be places in which people try out new ways of doing things – dressing, dancing, making music and carrying on generally – for the first time. And although the end result of this will often amount to little except memories and potentially embarrassing photographs, every now and again what people do in these clubs, these laboratories of our leisure time, will eventually affect our whole culture. That so many of the pieces of writing in this book begin as straightforward reports on clubs and end up articulating shifts in the way that generations thought about themselves is testament both to the perception of FACE writers, to the creativity of the people in those clubs, and to the potency of this particular pleasure.pursuit.

Together, the features included here tell a story of 17 years in which clubland has won more friends, and influenced more people, than anyone would have predicted in 1980. They tell the story of how the DJ has come to play as important a role as the people who make the records that he or she plays. They tell the story of how underground clubbing, once a tiny, disorganised sub-sub-sector among leisure industries, has developed into a major concern whose favours are courted by multi-national corporations. In a way they tell the story of The FACE, which has grown alongside that underground. But most of all they tell the stories of how successive generations of our clubland's citizens have explored all the avenues that were open to them, and then gone down all the ones that weren't; how they have innovated, imitated, lived, loved, schemed, and seemed and dreamed; how they have dressed up and dressed down, fallen out and made up, stayed up, played up, looked after their own, taken on the world, been ludicrously exclusive and lovingly inclusive, sometimes burnt out, occasionally even faded away, but more or less always kept on keepin' on in this great two-decades-and-counting disco inferno. These stories mostly have no end, because the impulses that drive them have no end; they serve best as preludes to future dancefloor adventures still to come. And as for an answer to Sarah Thornton's question (which itself lead her to write a book), there can be no one definitive response, just millions of different ones, changing from time to time and from place to place. That's why it all becomes interesting in the first place.

If you don't recognise any truth in all this, then it may be that you've led a commendably well-balanced life in which going to a certain club at a certain time has never seemed all that important. If so, congratulations, but read on; you'll find the stories interesting anyway. And if you're one of those to whom going to a certain club at a certain time has at some stage in your life seemed as important as anything else ever has – well, to a greater or lesser extent reader, this is your life.

Richard Benson
Editor, THE FACE
London, April 1997

ACKNOWLEDGEMENTS

A big shout goes out, as they say in some clubs, to all the writers whose work appears in the following pages, and indeed to all the contributors who have helped to create The FACE over the last 17 years. For their editorial contributions to this book, special thanks are due to Elaine Constantine, Trish Farley, Matt Fiveash, Charles Gant, Sheryl Garratt, Tim Lewis, Peter Lyle, Paul Murphy, Simmy Richman, Chris Stocks, Craig Tilford, and Nina. A special acknowledgement is also due to Gareth Grundy, the current FACE clubs editor, who commissioned several of the latter pieces in this collection. For their support and/or advice, I would like to thank Stephen Armstrong, Gordon Benson, Pauline Benson, Guy Benson, Helen Benson, Michelle Boon, Robert Black, Anna Chapman, Laura Craik, Ben Clissitt, Johnny Davis, Ekow Eshun, Karina Givargisoff, Carole Harris, Ashley Heath, Chris Heath, Jamie Hewlett, Gavin Hills, Darren Hughes, Sarah Jacombs, Dylan Jones, Nick, Julie and Christian Logan, Craig McLean, Emma Moore, Geoff Oakes, Michael Oliveira-Salac, Jo-Anne Smith, Susanna Paz, Jacqui Pinto, Mark Ratcliff, Nancy Rohde, Miranda Sawyer, Rod Sopp, Stuart Spalding, Lee Swillingham, Irvine Welsh, Kelly Worts, and Clare Hulton, Jake Lingwood and Sarah Bennie at Boxtree.

THE CULT WITH NO NAME

NOVEMBER 1980

Nightclubbing and the quest for a life of style by Robert Elms

----

TURNING LEFT HALF-WAY down Wardour Street on a Tuesday night in the autumn of 1978 meant going to Billy's; a subterranean other-world of diamanté and occasional drag, where sharp dress meant everything and to be out was to be literally outside.

The invitation cards called it a Bowie Night and boasted Rusty Egan of the Rich Kids as DJ. The turntables were dominated by the Thin White Duke and the air was thick with an atmosphere of stylish and extravagant sleaze.

The underground club scene which was to lead to Steve Strange, Spandau Ballet and mass media talk of "Blitz Kids" was under its flamboyant way as London's young night people found a home in the heart of Soho.

Billy's had originally been just one of the myriad of basement nightspots which dot the backstreets of central London like so many sleazy pot-holes. Frequented largely by gays, it became known for the high level of import soul available within, and for the fact that the management and clientele were able to accept the shock of immaculately if extraordinarily dressed young socialites invading their premises. The word spread; Billy's was in, and everybody turned out.

It was Rusty Egan, the Rich Kids' young drummer about town, who decided to transform a chance gathering of fashionable young things into an evening specially set aside for those with an abiding interest in all things Bowie and beautiful.

Tuesday night became the night to look right as the still dominant black leather of the post-punk depression was rejected in favour of gold braid and pill-box hats. It was toy soldiers, cossacks and queens to the outsider, an odd fantasy world down the stairs; to the participants it was a mutual admiration society for budding narcissists, a creative and competitive environment where individualism was stressed and change was vital.

Billy's wasn't a place for those who dressed up for the occasion but for those who dressed up as a way of life. A small incestuous group numbering no more than a couple of hundred kids in search of a life of style.

Looks came and went as fast as the innovators could construct them. Some opted for then-radical Sixties chic while others scoured eras past and ideas future. The aim was to create a look, then go out and enjoy it, dance and pose the night away amidst like minds and good music.

Good music had originally meant David Bowie, but just as the style progressed so did the sound. Marlene Dietrich competed with the theme from *Stingray* while Iggy Pop's "Nightclubbing" represented a suitably decadent and danceable anthem.

Kraftwerk provided the first signs of the move towards electronic disco as "Trans-Europe Express" and "Man Machine" because Tuesday night classics. Obscure British bands operating within the same sphere were discovered and danced to. "Warm Leatherette" by The Normal and "Being Boiled", the first single by the then unknown Human League pointed the way to the electronic explosion about to occur.

Gary Numan was a regular observer, lurking in dark corners amidst all the other Bowie-Boys.

Billy's was a vital beginning, yet the roots of a scene which has since grown out of its Soho confines and into newspaper headlines and television documentaries can be traced back some three years earlier and 200 yards further up Wardour Street.

Wednesday night at Crackers in 1975 was Bowie Night, attracted Siouxsie and Severin, pre-punk Nazi-Chic and plastic trousers, clothing by Acme Attractions and a King's Road shop by the name of Sex.

Wednesday night at Crackers was for people with coloured hair and nowhere else to go and was the start of a scene which was to move on to other gay clubs, Louise's and Chaguaramas, and was finally to be spotted and exploited by Sex shop proprietor Malcolm McLaren.

In autumn 1976 Chaguaramas closed down, re-opening in December under a new name, The Roxy. Neal Street, Covent Garden's famous "birthplace of punk" was thereby born.

The dominance and growing commercial clout of punk interrupted the more obscure, more elitist nocturnal scene for a full two years. 1977 was for the most part a quiet time. Displaced souls tired of a Punk Rock world diluted and distorted by mass acceptance, clung to old Bowie and Roxy albums and posed quietly at Banshees gigs. Some returned to soul clubs while others waited until the time was right and the underground line could continue; then came Billy's.

By the early months of 1979 Billy's had become well known, and demands of space necessitated a policy of selection at the door. Steve Strange, sales assistant at PX, a Covent Garden clothes emporium of radical repute, friend of Rusty Egan and all-purpose style setter, took on the job of Billy's doorman, and thereby all-round arbiter of chic. The elitism which had always been inherent was now institutionalised and the pattern which was to become famous at the Blitz was set.

It was on Tuesday February 6, 1979, that the Bowie Night as it was still called moved from Soho to upmarket Covent Garden, from Billy's to the Blitz. Rusty Egan was still DJ, Steve Strange controlled the door, and admission was £1 for those who had been granted membership (for which they had paid £2). The move had occurred largely due to the simple desire to move on, an ever-present need for change.

It was still a very small, closed world of some 300 young devotees, among them clothes designers, artists, hairdressers and musicians. The looks there ranged from shoulder-padded futurism to fringed outlaw revivalism, ideas later to be taken up and exploited by ageing fashion moguls, destined to end up on the racks of the mass marketeers.

The creative atmosphere was obviously a vital part of the Tuesday night gatherings, yet for those involved it was primarily a night out. Drinking and dancing until the early morning, ensuring perfection in front of the crowded mirrors of the ladies toilets and revelling in the belief that they were all special, every one a star in their own right as the flashes of voyeur photographers regularly exploded in front of eager eyeballs.

The music was always geared for dancing and as the club scene progressed so it became more specialised. The term "Electro Disco" was coined to cover records ranging from Giorgio Moroder's "The Chase" to "Moskow Disco" by Telex who, along with the Yellow Magic Orchestra, were discovered directly through their regular appearances on the Blitz turntables. Bowie was almost silenced as Sparks played their Number One Song both in Heaven and at the Blitz and the Bowie Night tag was dropped as the club and its extravagant commissionaire became known in their own right.

By the time of the winter of 1979 there began a move in clothing away from the futur-istic and geometrical styles which had already reached the high street. The cold weather brought out hats and gabardine coats, Frank Sinatra stood next to Oscar Wilde, and tuxedoed Joel Greys looked on; the time was right for another move, a sharp reaction against everything electronic.

The result of this swing towards the classic was two months of Mondays back in Soho as the St Moritz in Wardour Street became an immaculate modern version of Berlin in the Thirties.

As usual the new style had originally emerged via the clothes people wore and, as usual, the music followed. Billie Holiday and Frank Sinatra set the basis for nights which moved on to *Cabaret*, swing, Edith Piaf and bossa nova. Dancing was cheek-to-cheek and "formal dress" a must as flowing gowns swayed gently to "These Foolish Things" or "Lili Marlene". St Moritz was the perfect spot for posing and the *Sunday Times* and the *London Evening Standard* quickly grasped the headline potential of decadent youth decked out in full Edwardian dress. Word spread too quickly and St Moritz was sud-denly stopped. Short, sharp and purist; a vacation away from a tired and ageing Blitz.

Tuesday nights in Covent Garden continued and continue to exist, still providing good music and good company. Yet the expectant excitement of Blitz a year earlier is no longer there.

Outside of London the story is just starting. You might think this kind of thing couldn't happen in your town but you'd be wrong. The idea of commandeering a local club for one night of fashion and fun has already spread to Cardiff (The Tanschau) and Birmingham (at The Rum Runner). Embryonic scenes are also happening in Liverpool and Southend.

As for the London scene, this has now transported itself quietly to Hell, deeper in Covent Garden, a move back underground to a small nightspot away from the gaze of a world alerted to a scene which, resisting a label, has found itself ludicrously dubbed "Blitz Kids".

Directed by Egan, Strange and Chris Sullivan, one of the minds behind St Moritz, the music policy at Hell gives turntable space to rockabilly and salsa as Puerto Rican styles and stances creep slowly into vogue.

Hell is now the home of a scene which for two years has provided a spark to a London otherwise slipping back into the early Seventies greyness. A colourful, exotic world which has set the styles to be copied both in terms of look and sound. Artists as diverse as, say, Grace Jones, Spandau Ballet and The Skids have all been influenced by late nights spent amongst sharp youth, while a whole new generation of young clothes designers is beginning to emerge from this nocturnal existence. Above all, though, for two years those involved have dressed and danced and laughed the night away while amazed onlookers simply stared and reached for their cameras •

03   BRINGING ON THE CLONES

The Bowies of Pips Disco, Manchester by Mick Middlehurst

PIPS DISCO, LOCATED behind Manchester Cathedral, is a huge commercial complex boasting seven dancefloors and four different types of music. As you walk through the dimly lit corridors of Pips you pass by a perfect cross-section of Mancunian nightlife.

One room may house a works party of insurance secretaries, neatly dressed and giggling, enjoying a break from routine. The next is packed with baggy jumpers and sneakers, bodies that cavort to standard supermarket disco. (This is the most popular of the four rooms and effectively typifies the standard Mancunian youth.) From the next you will hear a barrage of Northern Soul and a swift glance inside will reveal a vision of crazed dancing and floor-length leather coats.

Deep at the back of Pips is the most interesting room of all, a place that hasn't changed at all in eight years, the infamous Roxy room. This is the breeding-ground for extremes in fashion; a throng of caricature figures that make the dance scenes from *Cruising* look like Emily Bishop's wedding reception. Heads are tilted, eyes glare and stare at the faces of any newcomer. Elitism runs high.

The Roxy room started to operate in the heyday of glitter pop and served as a lifesaver for the sadly declining Manchester club scene. In the late Sixties the city boasted the finest clublife in the country with legendary nightspots like The Twisted Wheel, Oasis, Rowntrees Sound, Jackies Explosion and the smooth Nice 'n' Easy.

Pips was born out of the ashes of Nice 'n' Easy and, as the other clubs closed down, Pips won the hearts of the expanding Bowie generation. In those days the music played in the Roxy room was Bolan, Glitter, Bowie, Roxy Music, New York Dolls, Iggy and Lou Reed. Everyone tried as hard as they could to imitate their own particular idol, and most people believed these new-found glamorous fashions would last a short time before dying out. A lot of them did. The Roxy fans metamorphosed into smooth lounge lizards and then into hip, smartly-dressed newlyweds. The Bolan/Glitter fans stayed with pop and eventually turned to disco. The Iggy/Dolls set went on to punk. (Generally speaking of course.)

But the Bowie fans, they remained loyal and through the dark years of '75 and '76 they continued to frequent the Roxy room. Even the '77 punk apocalypse couldn't deter their enthusiasm. Although the Roxy has had its thin spells, it survived all this and last year's mod/ska revival to emerge once again this year, stronger and more outrageous than ever.

The music now played is a neat mixture of the old stuff plus the electronic sounds of the Human League, Gary Numan, Kraftwerk and even Throbbing Gristle. The Bowie influence is still the strongest, however, and it is interesting to note that not only have the Bowie fans successfully fought off all short-lived fashions but they have remained themselves hyper-fashionable, a fact which surely pays tribute to the shrewdness of the man himself who has managed to stay in vogue for over nine years.

Intrigued by the phenomenon, I spent a night at Pips slyly observing the action. A trained mime artist repeatedly stumbled into imaginary brick walls and broke off into an intricate dance routine every time "Sweet Thing" poured from the speakers. Two matching Rita Hayworth clones strolled elegantly past clutching exotic cocktails. An exaggerated Bryan Ferry told me how he'd spent the past five years trying to speak with a mild Geordie accent.

The bouncers kept a watchful eye on the disco kids who occasionally wandered in to gloat and laugh at the "freaks". The disco kids also sometimes stood by the toilet entrances and verbally threatened the Bowies as they passed. Apparently this was a typical night.

I asked six separate Bowie fans why they dressed to such extremes. The standard reply was "Because it makes me feel different and special", with the odd "Because it's a laugh" thrown in for good measure. Thankfully, most Bowie clones use their own creative ideas to add to the normal Bowie figure. It's usually the ones with a passing resemblance to Bowie who seem most content to merely imitate their idol. Then again, at Pips it is admittedly the ones who look the closest to Bowie who are regarded as the elite.

Paul McVeigh looks like Bowie. His hair, dyed red, rises in spikes at the top and flows smoothly down his neck in the classic Ziggy Stardust style. Paul is an almost-wed 21-year-old who earns his keep by cleaning aircraft at Manchester Airport.

I met him at his flat which is just half a mile from the "noisy" end of the runway. Every ten minutes some unconcerned pilot would just manage to clear the top of the flats and produce a din so loud it caused the room to visibly shake. Not surprisingly the area is run down, with house prices here being the cheapest in Manchester. On the wall of Paul McVeigh's flatblock is a huge spray-painted Bowie slogan. I didn't ask him if he was the culprit.

He talks with the halfway posh accent of most dedicated Bowie fans. "I've been a Bowie fan for six years actually, which isn't all that long. Everyone was into Bowie in those days and we used to regularly go to Pips and the Ranch Bar before it turned punk. I stopped going to the Ranch after I was beaten up one night by a group of teddy boys. As you know, it got really heavy in those days and for some reason the Bowies always used to bear the brunt of it. After that we started going to gay bars just because they were safer for us. They were, and still are, much friendlier places and we like the atmosphere there."

Paul has a collection of over 40 Bowie albums and every one of his singles, official and unofficial. "I have 20 bootlegs, and actually I'm lucky because there are so many Bowie bootlegs on the market. My favourite is the recording of Bowie's last-ever concert with the Spiders at the Hammersmith Odeon. That was his best period, the Ziggy Stardust period, although I have never heard a Bowie song that I dislike. Even the electronic sides to 'Low' and 'Heroes' are great to relax to with a bottle of wine at night.

"I've had some great experiences as a Bowie fan, like the time we went to his Earls Court gigs in London and stayed in a top hotel. In the morning we came down to breakfast still wearing the heavy make-up from the night before. I had an Aladdin Sane flash and the other guests just stared in amazement. The entire room went quiet. It was incredible."

Paul's bedroom at home is, not surprisingly, covered from wall to wall with posters, screen prints, photographs and various other mementoes of Bowie. His scrapbooks dutifully record every music-press article about the man ever been printed and, for the casual observer, they add up to probably the best history of Bowie one could wish for. It almost goes without saying that Paul's girlfriend is named Angie. He assured me that this was purely coincidence. They have a three-month-old daughter named, you guessed it, Zoewie (with an extra E). Paul's main ambition is to meet David Bowie.

Nick Greenwood is a Gary Numan fan. He met his wife, Beverley, at Pips some 18 months ago and they were both into Numan from the early Tubeway Army days. Nick looks like Gary Numan in his "Are Friends Electric" incarnation: the white hair, black eyes, black-boiler suit look. I talked to him at his mother's house in Timperley, Cheshire, and was surprised to hear of his dislike of the newer Numan albums and images.

"I liked Numan at first because he was quiet, shy and very honest, but I feel he has gone against the whole concept of those early days. He's sold out, just a little, and all this giving up touring bit is silly. It's a smack in the face for the fans who have made him what he is today. I still like him actually, I must admit, although it is difficult because he is no longer hip. It's really hard to tell someone that you are a Numan fan. I get embarrassed because I know that they instantly tag you as a teenybopper and that's just not true. I think Numan's made some superb music although I doubt if he has Bowie's ability to change.

"It's getting really heavy round our area [Oldham]. I can't go into a pub any more and it's bloody dangerous just walking home when dressed like this. Not just from other kids, but blokes and everyone. Even Beverley has been attacked in the past just because she dresses a bit different."

I wondered what kind of music he liked before Numan. "Ultravox, Human League, Japan. All those bands who have a bit of class and something to say. Or rather, something different to say. Really, Britain is wide open for a huge pop hero at the moment. Sooner or later someone is going to take the teen market by storm, it must happen."

I think of the Police as I ask the nature of the gold record that I breezed past in his mother's hallway. His answer floors me. "That is a real gold album, not a fake. It is Jethro Tull's or rather one of Jethro Tull's. It's Ian Anderson's, y'see, I'm his cousin."

Nick Greenwood is considering forming a band. He believes, as I do, that Manchester has a ready-made audience impatiently waiting to latch on to a band who represent the Pips set. I'm amazed it hasn't happened yet.

David Roles is one of Manchester's better-known Bowie fans. Four years ago he had his story told in a large *Manchester Evening News* article. His outrageousness has calmed a little since then. Gone are the glittery costumes; his current look is mellower Bowie (circa-"Station To Station"). David is the classic example of a Bowie. He is a hairdresser, an occupation that has always been related to Bowie and one of the most effective ways of being accepted into the elite.

"I remember in the Ranch Bar days when I cut a lad's hair in the toilets. I was well out of it at the time, beer and drugs and things, and I created the most hideous mohican cut on a friend's hair, at his request, and on the night he loved it. Well so did I on the night but I woke up the next morning thinking, 'God, what have I done?' I didn't see my friend for a long time after that, nobody did.

"I used to be a lot more outrageous in those days, an extreme Bowie if you like. I've always been completely fanatical. I have thousands of albums by him. I wasn't at all happy with 'Lodger' though. After that I thought it could be the end but luckily 'Scary Monsters' is one of the best and has restored my faith, as it were."

David's faith is not in question. He has 13 copies of "Ashes To Ashes", each in a different-coloured sleeve. He had to buy them all just to remain able to boast that he has everything and anything on David Bowie.

It's a crazy world, that of the Bowie fans. Rebellious only through the medium of fashion, but it is certainly artistic and it is, above all else, a lot of fun. Whatever you think of Bowie and the Bowies, there is no denying that they have left their mark all over rock music and fashion, past and present. From Spandau Ballet to Slaughter And The Dogs, from Japan to Talking Heads. Without Bowie and the Bowies we could all be still sweating away in dirty denim •

BLITZ TO THE STICKS

MAY 1981

New Romantic goes to the country. Extract from FACE club news

----

THE IRREPRESSIBLE (not to mention talkative) Rusty Egan informs us that he's itching to return to regular DJing but that London is to be denied any immediate access to his legendary taste and technique. "The London thing's gone bloody stupid, all lah-de-dah, wanting to be elite and all that nonsense. It's the people out in the sticks who matter," he told The FACE Showbiz Desk without a hint of provincial condescension.

Rusty's strategy is two-pronged: to get out of the capital, and to consummate a union between electronic dance music and disco/soul. He wants to hear Spandau Ballet, Visage and Ultravox played at the soul clubs, and we don't doubt him when he says that electro's canoodling with funk and soul can change the face of UK clubland.

From Monday March 30, and weekly thereafter, Rusty will be dominating the turntables at Flicks, famous soul establishment in Dartford, Kent, playing 50/50 soul and electronic dance cuts to what he hopes will be an equally mixed audience. He has his slogan all worked out, "From the Blitz to the Sticks – Mondays at Flicks".

As well as Rusty's peerless technique the first night will also feature videos, and appearances by Basildon's very own Depeche Mode •

GET INTO THE GROOVY

JUNE 1981

The new psychedelia by Deanne Pearson

AMONGST DRUIDS, EXECUTIONERS, impaled human bodies and victims of the plague, cages of rats (literally the size of cats), dank, dripping archways and slimy walls, the stark organ sound of early Pink Floyd blasts forth, and a collection of gaudily clad people, with limbs propelling, hair flying and eyes revolving, shake and shimmy through bright streams of light.

This is the London Dungeon, these are the new psychedelics. Well it had to come, didn't it?

As yet there are probably only 300-400 people in the whole country involved, a cross-section of older, closet psychedelia freaks, who have been keeping their chains and beads, their paisley shirts and their hairspray in mothballs for the last 12-15 years, to younger kids who freely admit they either got bored with punk or mod, or were just looking for something "new".

There are coachloads from Southend and Birmingham, even a few from Scotland, and most have come via the same source, a psychedelic clothing stall in Kensington Market, The Regal, which is owned by Graham Pettitt. A soft-spoken clothes designer with a slight West Country accent, Pettitt is partial to multi-coloured corduroy regency jackets, and has collar-length hair gently teased at the crown.

According to Graham, who has organised most of the parties, the new psychedelia is not a movement as such: "It's just a collection of people who have been brought together, largely because of their taste in clothes." (His stall, by all accounts, is the only one selling such designs in the country.) "But it's also because they love having fun, going to parties, and listening to similar sorts of 'fun' music, such as the Electric Prunes, early Pink Floyd, the Byrds, Love, the Clockwork Watch Band, and loads more."

He only vaguely remembers psychedelia the first time round, at the end of the Sixties. "My older brother was very involved in it, and I remember that he and his friends always seemed to have such a good time. And the clothes – they were in the wildest fabrics, designs and colours you can imagine, you could really go over the top, do absolutely anything you liked."

After finishing college in Devon, and becoming frustrated at working for a very straight, commercial designer in London for a while, he decided to take a gamble and start up on his own, making the kind of clothes he liked. "That's all there is to it really – my partner and I never really sat down and planned a set look for our stall and designs – we just did what we liked – it was all based on a feeling."

Coincidentally or not their stall opened about the time the term "new psychedelia" first appeared in the music press (about a year ago), in connection with bands such as Echo And The Bunnymen, Doll By Doll and The Teardrop Explodes. Graham, however, barely acknowledges these bands. "The people who are into psychedelia now like fun music, bands they can go wild to and dance to. They don't want the hollow gloom and despair of the Bunnymen.

"And it's only been in the last four or five months that it's really taken off," he continues. "A lot of mods, particularly, have started coming in to the shop – especially since Paul Weller began wearing our gear."

Graham has made clothes for people like The Jam, The Revillos, small local bands, and recently Jenny, the Belle Stars' vocalist, for whom he made a tiny polka dot mini-skirt (about six inches long) in pink and mauve, a suit and a pair of flared hipsters (with a rise of about three inches).

The Regal is, however, predominantly a man's shop, although women often buy the shirts, priced at £12.50-£15 for a multitude of designs – paisley, Dr Kildare's, frilled, ruffled, full-sleeved, giraffe-collared, turn-back cuffs and glass buttons, all in a dazzling confusion of bright and often clashing colours. "There's a real art to teaming up two or three clashing colours though," Graham insists.

There will, though, shortly be a range of girls' clothing, just as soon as The Regal gets established in its new and larger premises in Newburgh Street, near Carnaby Street.

The opening of this shop, coupled with the fact that Graham has just started Psychedelic Nights (which include caged go-go dancers) at the Phoenix and Planets clubs in London's West End, suggest a growing trend, although Graham insists he hopes "new psychedelia" doesn't take off in a big way.

"I would like to keep it on a small scale, just as a collection of friends attending word-of-mouth gigs, parties and club nights. At the same time I don't want it to be an elitist thing, as the New Romantics were when they started. We're not snobs, we don't gather to admire and compete with each others' looks and clothing; we're trying to create an atmosphere where anyone can walk in and have a good time and feel comfortable. Really the only qualifications you need to come to any of our parties is to want to enjoy yourself," he sums up. Sounds easy enough •

06   GOLD! ALWAYS BELIEVE IN THE SOUL

AUGUST 1982

Ten years of the Canvey Island Gold Mine by David Johnson

SOME SAY THE whole of today's style scene has its roots here... The Gold Mine, Canvey Island, has passed into countless legends for the trends it has set and on August 14 manager Stan Barrett pulls the cork to celebrate his club's tenth birthday.

Mind you, feet have pounded its original sprung maple dancefloor since the Thirties. Southend and the towns of the Essex triangle have reared cults since the word was invented, so when in 1972 the Gold Mine began playing what rivals then called "silly music" – "My Guy" and all that soul stuff – the local hipsters took their cue. It was that wild man among DJs, Chris Hill, who, as the only man south of Wigan playing soul, put Canvey Island on the map and ushered in the soulful new Age of the Dance.

Then in 1975, for a reason no more obscure than a simple father-to-son legacy, came a Glenn Miller revival.

Stan Barrett says: "Chris played 'Singin' In The Rain' one Saturday and of course even kids who couldn't remember the original knew the words to it. Everyone started being Gene Kelly on the dancefloor, dressing as GIs and Betty Grable. So he played 'Moonlight Serenade' then the Andrews Sisters 'Boogey Woogey' – that's when they all started to jive and to dress up."

The *Sun*, which has a remarkably consistent record for picking up trends first, featured the Gold Mine. "Coaches came from Newcastle, Wales, everywhere," Barrett remembers. The rest is undisputed history, for the influence of Essex stylists on the emergent London nightlife scene has been visible, from Chagueramas and the Vortex to the Blitz and beyond.

The key to the Gold Mine's success? Impossible selectivity at the door, which may sound over-familiar today. Barrett says: "Nobody too old. And only people into style – which means your own style, not Gary Numan's. It costs you at first but look how it pays off in the end. People have never come to the Gold Mine for a good drink-up, always the music and the scene."

Right now, the south-east is a musical ball of confusion with the electronic camp of Depeche Mode and Talk Talk holding sway. Drinking with Talk Talk drummer Lee Harris at the Gold Mine the other night was clubrunner-about-Southend, Steven Brown, who sports a £100 PW Forte Sixties suit and reckons that psychedelia is still big there, heaven help us.He's also done time with a non-psychedelic local band of jokers called Doodle Sax: "It's had about 35 people in it at various times but we're not very serious." One of them, synthesiser doodler Andy Norton, says the vibes are already about for much heavier rhythms. "Music has to turn much more macho."

And if there are any visual indicators at the Gold Mine today, they are less fancy, more free. A regular called Andy "from Stanford-No-Hope" said "Make-up is so out of date, it's like watching old crows trying to pull. The Gold Mine is much better now that we don't get all the arty students down" •

07 HARD TIMES

SEPTEMBER 1982

The new young soul rebels by Robert Elms

BEAR WITH ME for a while: this first bit may be hard but it is important. Read it twice if you have to because there is something that you are going to have to grasp before we can go any further. And that is the notion that Youth Culture now represents not a rebellion but a tradition, or rather a series of traditions that date back to the advent of the teenager and continue to grow along a compound continuum of action and reaction.

Imagine a spiral that begins with a birth out of affluence and post-war liberation, and moves through time propelled by its own mythology and its own contrariness and is affected by technology and whimsy and economics. It is cyclical, but the circle is never completed because it is also revolutionary; therefore patterns repeat but they are never quite the same.

Now you must also accept that there is no such thing as a "generation gap" any more; how can you rebel against the generation of Coltrane or Brando or MacInnes? What we have is a heritage that you can draw succour and inspiration from; and there are those who do and those who don't. That's the only gap.

In the mid-Seventies there was really only Northern Soul with its sparse, functional uniform, its £30 singles and its clenched-fist plea to keep the faith which kept alive the tradition of a mobile, underground lifestyle that demanded commitment and pledged enjoyment. But in recent years we've experienced a dramatic revival in the colour and clamour of what was once called Youth Culture but is now in drastic need of redefinition.

Right now every kid is a dressed-up kid, every home has a hipster. Just how that occurred and where it's all leading takes us neatly into A Tale Of Hard Times.

It's more than just a feeling now, more definite than the presence of denim where once was silk; it's definitely a cycle reasserting itself, but we'll return to that much later.

Suffice to say things are changing. What began as a desire to shed the clinging, depressive old skin of post-punk monotony and replace it with a set of bold, bright new clothes is slowly evolving into an entrenched, die-hard mentality where "Good Times" is replaced by "Money's Too Tight To Mention". But the dancing at least doesn't stop.

It's still easiest to describe as a hardening of attitude. Somehow the atmosphere when you walk into a club today is different: gay abandon has evolved into a clenched-teeth determination where precious lager cans are cradled to stop them disappearing and sweat has replaced cool as the mark of a face.

Surely everybody knows by now that it was never a chintzy-cocktail set whirl of debs' do's. That only ever existed in the minds of a paranoid rock press and the parties of a few Funkapolitan flunkies. But misunderstanding and misrepresentation of the kind that labelled those who wanted to dress and dance as "little Lord Fauntleroys" and even "escapist middle-class Fascists" turned too often into self-fulfilling prophecy as too many people got the wrong end of the stick and then toyed with it.

But if we take a look at how things stand right now, literally take a look, you'll see that clothes at least are definitely getting harder. Ubiquitous Levi's worn into holes, sweatshirts serving their purpose and losing their sleeves, leather dominating everything – sandblasted for effect if you're rich and Italian, genuinely old and ragged if you're not. Leather caps, leather jerkins, big boots or no socks and espadrilles. Trousers are getting tighter, T-shirts ripped and torn.

The reference points are numerous but the look is new. Brando on a motorbike in the American Fifties that never made *Happy Days*. There's the ever-present rockabilly input, only now pink pegs have made way for stained drainpipes and checked shirts have been ripped to shreds. A touch of Bolshevism here and there with flat caps and red flags, still a glimpse of beatnik angles and shades, and an awful lot of macho gay icons. And what you have is London in the winter of 1976.

Fashion has always had its own very internalised mechanism of change based on action and reaction: you know, someone wears something, so everyone else wears it, so he wears something else. But in recent times that process has been speeded up to an almost indecent pace by a media that's been alerted to the fact that something's going on and is more than willing to tell everybody. And indeed the latest change was a reaction against scores of kids in their grandfathers' suits and their mothers' make-up, against idiot dancers on *Top Of The Pops* dressed up in cast-offs from auntie's last pantomime, a reaction against Bucks Fizz dressed as New Romantics and Pete Shelley in a suit.

Sure, suits followed frills and jeans followed suits because that's the way things happen, but it is more; it's a sign of the times if you like. For a start it's all very functional: hot funk in crowded clubs makes a mess of any designs that lean towards dandyism. If you go to the Beat Route on a Friday night you sweat. Perhaps that's one of the places we really ought to visit.

At the moment there are two definite trends at work in London after eleven o'clock, and if you're looking for examples, one of them resides at The Palace and one at the Beat Route. The Camden Palace, hugely popular, glossy, efficient, is the equivalent of ABC: taking the ingredients that have added the spice to the last couple of years, dressing it up nicely and selling it to a million smiling customers.

ABC and The Palace both bear impressive witness to the fact that a wholesale revitalisation of mainstream pop culture has resulted from the natural tendencies of a few dancers in the wilderness. Steve Strange very genuinely hosts evenings of good honest entertainment where bank clerks mingle with milky-bar dreads and everybody believes they're in Studio 54 for a night.

But just as ABC soon dropped their original "Radical Dance Faction" tag, so The Palace is just a disco. They are both signs that England has been turned into a swinging place again, both signs that the oh-so-derided attitude which re-emerged in places like The Blitz a few years ago has had a much wider influence than many people like to admit. There is a new orthodoxy now, but there is also a new front line.

The Beat Route has been going for more than a year now; some say it's not what it was, but it has certainly played its part. Its uncompromising, often uncomfortable atmosphere has kept away painted faces and prying eyes, so things have had the rare luxury of time to develop.

What has emerged is a more aggressive hedonism, where sex and dancing and stimulants represent a back-against-the-wall defiance. The Beat Route attracts people from all over the country, and the age range is right across the board. That's vital, for this whole new feel isn't just that of a new generation: that concept simply doesn't apply any more. It's 15-year-olds and 35-year-olds dancing defiant steps side by side. People who've learned to dance to Gil Scott-Heron have learnt that age doesn't mean a thing.

But there's also a dark side, victims of an all-out lifestyle. For some, hedonism has turned to cheap heroin as depression creates one of its ugliest panaceas. But just as hard times leave scars on some, so others become hard enough to beat it.

Just as the idea for once-a-week clubs where you use their space to create your environment originally rose out of a black soulboy tradition of warehouse parties where you literally do everything yourself, so the Palaces and the Ultratecques which cater six nights a week for the new electropop creamed off the ideas and the energy which arose out of the once-a-week clubs, to stuff the pockets of financiers. So young and old, those who care, move back to warehouses and create their own space. Enter the Dirtbox.

The increase in the number of warehouse parties of late is a sure sign that something is happening, and the other thing happening is the Dirtbox: a tradition builds on itself.

Situated above a chemist's in Earls Court, the Dirtbox will almost definitely have ceased to exist by the time you read this. But its policy of £1.50 entry, bring your own drink in a cramped claustrophobic room with a fan, some settees and a sound system produced a series of wild nights. All organised by two decidedly post-Blitz kids and DJ'd by a rockabilly who shopped in Sex before the Pistols did.

Built to self-destruct, it bore all the hallmarks of the times, dancing on the edge of illegality. They've already got another place to move to: move fast, hit hard guerilla tactics. I may be a bit romantic, but the Dirtbox is a return to the soul. Now that's a word for the times.

Just as mainstream pop culture becomes more and more produced, safer, predictably bright and danceable, so the reaction occurs. The spiral moves on by looking back, looking for some roots, searching for a little soul in a soulless world.

If Kevin Rowland is still searching for soul rebels then now is the time when he could just find them. For just as people will now draw selectively from the wardrobes of the past, so they'll live and learn from a musical heritage that stretches right back. The immature, myopic desire to reject things because of their age has been resigned to an acne'd past. Soul is about depth and it's the new rebels with torn jeans who are digging deep.

Jazz, soul, funk, rockabilly, cajun. You can go out for a night and hear The Last Poets, Gil Scott-Heron, King Pleasure, Ann Peebles, Warren Smith, Clinton Chenier. Culture Club, quite simply, aren't all that's going on. Music no longer plays a central and really rather damning role in everybody's lives. It has its place, and that place is filled from as wide a source as possible.

And just as looking back has led to a "discovery" of neglected talents, so looking forward has meant "Shoot The Pump", "How We Gonna Make The Black Nation Rise?", "Money's Too Tight To Mention". Hard sounds when everybody else wants to sound like Dollar. Without the likes of Steve Lewis some of the best records of the last two years would have gone almost unnoticed. Steve Lewis is a political man. That's another topic.

Political awareness is a personal thing, but everybody who can feel is feeling pain right now. People are getting angrier, the optimism that once led to bluff and bravado is now an optimism that you'll be able to hold on, an optimism that you can defy and you can dance. An awful lot of the music is directly political, but it isn't The Clash: listen to Curtis Mayfield and see how deep politics can go. Political awareness now runs deep indeed. Robert Wyatt is a star on the scene.

Northern Soul is spinning quietly back, old unemployed steel workers next to young unemployed school leavers. Jazz both here and in America is beginning to mean jazz again: Wynton Marsalis at 20 years old playing be-bop to teach us all. Funk and soul are finally creeping back into the funk and soul racks where once lay little but forgeries. And in Britain black leather and torn jeans are walking up the streets again.

Punk is now part of the heritage. In 1976 a small offshoot of the club scene broke away from bright clothes and increasingly bland music to become something angrier, something wilder.

Things are changing again only this time we know a lot more than three chords. With any luck there's even harder times ahead •

08   OUT ON THE FLOOR

SEPTEMBER 1982

A Northern Soul Primer by Neil Rushton

PART ONE: THEN

Veteran soul writer Dave Godin coined the phrase "Northern Soul" after a trip to Manchester's famed Twisted Wheel all-nighter in 1970 for Blues&Soul magazine. The tag successfully summed up the lifestyle and individuality of north of Watford post-Mod Soul freaks doggedly into their own underground based on deleted Soul 45s and specialist clubs around the industrial wastelands of the Midlands and the North. Four years later the term had become a bankable commodity – with the startling overground success of Wigan Casino and a series of chart hits, notably on Pye's Disco-Demand label.

Topping the sales list was Wigan's Chosen Few's "Footsee" – ironically the most untypical of the true Northern genre that could have been dug up. The sales led to Pye chartering coaches for the London music press to slum it at Wigan, and they duly turned out vivid pieces about back-dropping, baggie trousers, holdalls, embroidered Soul patches – and a bit about the music to boot. Not surprisingly the mass publicity led to wall-to-wall dances at the Casino Saturday-night-through-Sunday-morning all-nighters, which was obviously gratifying to club owner Gerry Marshall but diluted the spirit of a culture that till then managed to hang on to most of its identity.

The next generation of Casino-ites jumped on the bandwagon with a vengeance and seemed to be as much into the idea of travelling to Wigan as being Soul fans. Crass maniacal "stompers" took over the turntables to turn the dance floor into a mass of macho dervish spinners and back-droppers.

All this was truly a world away from the "roots" – the late Sixties "Rare Soul" clubs in Droitwich, Wolverhampton, Stoke, Leicester, Nottingham, Leeds, Manchester and Liverpool. These clubs developed from the example of the "ace face" frenetic Mod R&B clubs livening up Soho in the Sixties, driven on by adrenaline, amphetamine, a handful of US imports, the latest Tamla, Stax or Atlantic releases and sweat-drenched live shows from the likes of Geno Washington, Jimmy James, Herbie Goins, Alan Price and Georgie Fame. After peaking, the Soul craze lost mass appeal – being elbowed aside by Heavy Rock, Psychedelia and (gulp) Flower-Power.

Soul clubs still survived in some shape or other of course – North and South. But the London clubs were falling to the hypnotic early street funk of James Brown, Bobby Byrd, Simtec and Wylie and Kool & The Gang. "Up north" tastes were funnelling into a growing appetite for rare Motown. And as soon as the clubs had exhausted the repertoire of Brenda Holloway, Barbara McNair, The Contours, The Elgins, The Velvelettes, Earl Van Dyke and Barbara Randolph the chase began for import Soul 45s that hadn't been released in the UK before.

A typical shopping haunt was F.L. Moore's in Leighton Buzzard – imports started there at 1.6d and 60 miles further up the M1 had developed a £2 price tag. The Soul press made success certain for the "Rare Soul" craze by criticising it as unhealthy and elitist. The original Soul rebels took time off from back-dropping (with just one

"Right On" glove carefully worn on the right hand) to give the London establishment a quick V-sign.

As a fifth former at a grammar school in 1969 I can vividly remember a sizeable section of the year totally ignoring Zeppelin, Dylan and Hendrix and entering into bitter rivalry to see who could get the first copy of Billy Butler's "The Right Track" or track down a demo of Rufus Lumley's "I'm Standing" on mint Stateside. A scooter-riding army of 16- to 18-year olds threw themselves wholeheartedly into the Soul world of Shermans, 2-Tone flares, carefully tailored blazers with £15 individually-made gold wire club badges and braided slits and collars and illogical arrays of buttons up the sleeves.

This really was the key to the future mass-market Northern scene – many keen collectors desperate for an acetate of Earl Harrison's "Humphrey Stomp" or The Vibrations "Soul A Go Go" were too young to get into the clubs and instead took the rhythm to the small youth clubs. From there the grapevine spread and Soul music – the rarer the better – became the lifestyle for growing numbers. By the time the "apprentices" successfully made it to an all-nighter – where they found the beat was aided not just by Coca-Cola but liberal dashings of speed as well – the movement was unstoppable.

The Twisted Wheel closed following aggro with the drug squad but was soon replaced by Up The Junction at Crewe which found itself overtaken by Chris Burton's The Torch in Tunstall, Stoke-on-Trent. By 1972 the market was so big that John Abbey's Contempo/Mojo label was able to invest some of its profits from 250,000 plus sales of Tammi Lynn's "I'm Gonna Run Away From You" on recording Major Lance live at the Torch. The resulting album reflected all the frenzy and none of the great music qualities of the all-nighter circuit.

Records were no longer just obscure, they were like gold dust and Torch jocks Alan Day, Keith Minshull, Tony Jebb and Martyn Ellis were forking out £40 for the likes of the The Triumphs "Walkin' The Duck", Eddie Parker's "I Love You Baby", Tony Clarke's "Landslide" and Jimmy 'Soul' Clarke's "Sweet Darlin". Bootlegging suddenly became a nifty way of fabricating a fortune with enterprising dealers getting around legal restrictions by changing the names of labels and (sometimes) artists and composers.

At Blackpool Mecca, the eccentric Ian Levine had teamed up with Colin Curtis to create an even more esoteric groove and when the inevitable drug squad pressure forced The Torch to close after an expensive legal battle, "The Mecca" took over as number one. Other clubs soon rushed to fill the gap – Whitchurch Civic, Nottingham Palais, Bolton Va-Va's and Hanley Top Rank and the bootlegging had got so serious that a group of DJs tipped off the BPI about one deal that resulted in a £10,000 damages settlement being paid out. Jocks had also taken to "covering up" the labels of their records – to stop rivals also getting a copy and to prevent mass bootlegging.

Soon came Wigan Casino – but by then the underground was about to go well and truly over the top.

PART TWO: NOW

And so Northern Soul is in The FACE. Instead of being dismissed as some extinct tribal ritual revolving around "baggies and the footsee" (thanks NME) it is suddenly being taken seriously by outsiders.

Northern Soul is why I'm in the Cavendish Suite at the Old Vic Hotel in Wolverhampton on a sweaty Friday night. Wolverhampton has a Northern Soul tradition stretching back to the "Rare Soul" nights (and Sunday afternoons) at the long demolished cramped Catacombs Club in Temple Street. Out on the floor tonight the kids, to quote Dobie Gray, are groovin', yeah. You could have watched Dobie's hit get the same instant reflex rush to the dance floor at the 'Cats' back in 1969. It's not entirely

31

deja-vu, though. The fashions owe little to those days of button-collar Ben Shermans, Levi Sta-Prest and dashes of Brut. Instead it's pegged trousers and bowling shirts for the guys and Human League cloning for the girls.

Mixed with the £50-a-throw 45s on their obscure original Chicago, Detroit or Philly labels is a steady stream of little known brand new releases that never even find their way to import shops like Groove, Record Shack or Disc Empire.

As tonight's session finishes at one a.m. and there's no all-nighter for the crowd to travel on to, there's little sign of jaw-chomping amphetamine-popping apart from a few pairs of eyes with the kind of glare that no amount of Pils lager can produce. Nevertheless I soon stumble on to a couple of conversations about the respective merits of blues, green and clears, black and whites, sulphate and bombers.

The main fever, though, is not for "gear" – but for records. Dotted around the packed dance floor devotees are locked in deals over record boxes. A demo copy of Barbara Mills "Queens of Fools" on the original British Hickory label is produced and offered for sale at £50. Another collector flourishes a copy of the Del-Larks' "Job Opening" – an anthem for former Blackpool Mecca-ites – and demands £40 but the price is declared prohibitive as the disc is in less than average condition.

The bespectacled DJ drawing rounds of applause between each record for his selections is Soul Sam. Otherwise known as Martin Barnfather, he's a quietly spoken 40-year- old schoolteacher from North Wales who is earning just £20 for his spot.

A few years ago £20 wouldn't even have paid for the discs he played with their esoteric American labels – but Martin is now into "modern quality up tempo Soul" that takes a lot of tracking down but doesn't cost a king's ransom. His stance has put him on the blacklist of many clubs – who demand a diet of clip-clop popular oldies – and it is supremely ironical as five years ago he led a virtual civil war against new releases being played on the Northern circuit. The result was that the Northern world split into two with the "newies" crowd sticking to Doctor Buzzard, jiving, and leather trousers, and forming the truly great North West Jazz-Funk scene of '78/'79.

The remaining Northern Soul scene found itself isolated and almost killed off by the trend towards inane stomping British records, instead of the creative sweet soul of Van McCoy, Bert DeCoteaux et al. It did not die though – instead, encouraged by the booming 6T's scene in London, it regrouped itself around small local clubs, started playing great music again and rediscovered a sense of vitality and a real identity. As a result, the closure last year of Wigan Casino proved to be little more than a hiccup instead of a terminal disease.

"The scene is smaller now but it's very, very healthy," Soul Sam insists. He's taken aback that my photographer is painstakingly trying to set up a pic of him (page 23) looking through a record centre – the picture coverage for Northern jocks in the Soul mags usually consists of a Polaroid, a smile and a prayer. "I was opposed to what was happening in 1978, because it had nothing to do with the traditional values of what the Northern scene is about. It wasn't Soul music, it was just jumping on the disco bandwagon.

"I'm not being hypocritical at all; the quality of traditional Sixties style sounds deteriorated and DJs were playing garbage which so happened to be obscure and rare. So I started playing new releases. There are hundreds of records being made in the States now that are full of Soul appeal which don't make it to the main import shops and which the Funk clubs don't want to feature because they think they are old fashioned. So the Northern scene is promoting good quality American Soul music which would otherwise be lost and ignored. And that's always been what the Northern world is all about."

While we've been talking the music has changed to a series of well-received, dance-floor-filling "oldies" – 45s from Gwen Owens, Stanley Mitchell, Kenny Smith, The Van Dykes and The Salvadores – which mean nothing to the great British pop public but to Northern devotees are memorable yardsticks of good times in the past. The DJ is Chris Plant, a trainee cost accountant in his early twenties who earns £200 in a good week and spends as much of it as possible on his beloved record collection. His discs are inside two massive wooden boxes festooned with huge record label reproductions of Lynne Randell's "Stranger In My Arms" and Eddie Parker's "I Love You Baby". Chris happily pays £60 for an addition to his collection of Detroit label originals – not so much Motown as the "real" Motor City sound of Revilot, Ric-Tic, Golden World, Wheelsville, Tay-Ster, Groovesville, Velgo and D-Town – even though a DJ trip to Sheffield or East Anglia from his parents' Walsall-home will only net him £25.

"Financially it doesn't make sense. You could say the records are an investment like gold coins or stamps but there's always a chance that someone will find 500 copies of something you've just paid £50 for and so you only have a £5 record in your box. But the money is not my reason for getting involved. I just love the Northern scene. I used to go to the local clubs when I was young then later went to the all-nighters and all-day-ers all round the country.

"I'll travel 60 miles to a club but I don't go to clubs a mile from where I live because I'm not interested in other types of music. The Northern scene is great and in the last few years it's got really interesting again after going through a bad patch. Everyone travels from different parts of the country and meets up at the venues, dropping gear if they can get it to stay awake through the night. I makes you different from everybody else and the music is fantastic, different class to anything else."

Leafing through the assorted record boxes is Dave Krynski, aged 28, an office worker from Tipton: "Tonight's the first Northern gig I've been to for a while but it's the same as ever with people here from Manchester and North Wales, not just the Midlands. That's what has always made it so special, the fact that people come from all over and talk about the same things. Most people think you're mad, but here you're with your own kind.

"I've always been into Soul music. I grew up in the late Sixties listening to Motown and drifted into the rare soul scene which later became Northern Soul. I've had some great times and met some fantastic people. There's always been a drug scene involved but I've never been interested, I'm just into the music, that's enough for me. I love all kinds of Soul and I buy stacks of new releases, Jazz, Funk, Disco whatever, but I don't like the Jazz-Funk scene much, as it's now into elitist records. I went to the Rum Runner in Birmingham the other Monday and it was all obscure jazz.

"Four years ago the Jazz-Funk scene in the North was full of characters who had been involved in Northern Soul and there was a lot of energy; we had some brilliant laughs." Dave's fondest memories are of the Highland Room at Blackpool Tiffany's – known to everyone as simply "The Mecca" – where the Northern stomping sound widened to incorporate mid-tempo "floaters" and later, early August Darnell and disco. "In fact I was going to see Kid Creole tonight at Birmingham but I decided to come here instead to see what the Northern scene's like now," he explains.

"I'm amazed. It was virtually dead a few years ago but now the feeling of energy and something happening is back. The kids are into rare records just like I used to be and I've met people I haven't seen for five years. They have just been coming up to me, grabbing me by the shoulders and starting talking. Everyone is so friendly and together."

"That's why there was a Northern Soul scene originally. And that's why it will never die out" •

09 "HEAVEN IS A PIT COMPARED WITH THIS" JANUARY 1983

The Haçienda by David Johnson (excerpt)

"THIS IS A PRETTY desperate city as far as money goes, and silly reports which moan that we get only 200 people in here some nights forget that that's 200 more than anywhere else."

Paula Yates would give her right arm to sound as plausible as Howard Jones, manager of Factory Records' seven-month-old contribution to the new generation of megadiscos, the Haçienda. The discomfiting way he anticipated criticisms before they were raised suggested that those seven months have been spent polishing his answers. "We've had a lot laid on us because people tend to think we're in it solely for the money. Well, kids aren't exactly great drinkers. There are easier ways of making money than opening a club in a recession."

And easier places. Manchester is ruled by a regime which doesn't encourage use of its city centre: "If you're a Christian and out after 10pm, you must be up to something." Only recently clubs had to join the art galleries by closing their doors on Sundays. No clubs, no culture.

Killjoys apart, the Haçienda represents a brave experiment, like Nottingham's Rock City and Camden's Palace, in navigating the emergent mainstream coalition of all the cults. It meant the marriage of a venue for rockists of the raincoat tradition with a club for stylists weaned on dance and stance, and it wears its decor with northern determination.

A former warehouse, it's been prettied up with paint on its bricks, zebra-stripes on its pillars and traffic bollards lining the dancefloor, presumably because bollards is exactly where they're targeted when you miss the treacherous step down. Since this all amounts to Kerbside Tech, those can't be speakers and video-screens strung from the rafters – they have to be AA patrolmen parachuting in through the glass roof.

The place breaks every convention of disco design as self-consciously as the Pompidou Centre in Paris, and though the Haçienda photographs beautifully by day, on a Saturday night it has as much ambience as Central Station. As one member, Paul Smith, waggishly remarked: "Can you imagine Samuel Crompton riding through here on his mule?" (which for Southern readers is a nifty joke about a Bolton hero who invented a machine called the mule).

It's been said before that Lancastrians have a sense of humour "armour-plated against despair", and only the people who could call a record label Factory could give a pleasuredrome the same armour-plated name: Haçienda is Spanish for factory.

"This place is so bleak, it's Brontë-esque," Smith added in a poetic confusion of counties. Smith, at 18, seemed as typical as any. His friends dress in the futuro-punk mould; his musical tastes are a fragile coupling of Bauhaus and Glenn Miller. To him clubbing in Manchester means Legends on Thursday because "it has more class", and here on Saturday. But his "Brontë-esque" description instantly identified the Haçienda's dominant feature: space. Even on this body-slamming Saturday night space becomes the great divider, so visibly that you can read each square foot like a living roadmap of nightclub types.

Along a blue neon tube, sweat rises from a grim brick bunker wistfully called a cocktail bar: here stars on Factory hold court to an admiring youth club. Back at the entrance stands Kubrick's arch, a monolith by which wait the apes, pillocks and punks who daren't venture further on to the Haçienda's yawning shopfloor. Beneath a balcony along one side sit the off-the-peg trendies keeping an eye out for the next dance-step. Above them, the voyeurs bask in the lights like bullfrogs before mating – a distinctly older crowd, as you can tell from their tour jackets.

A short hike gets you to the bar with its promenade just big enough, in the words of John Andrews, "to hold all the trendy people in Manchester who by hook or by crook or by prostitution found the £2.50 to be here tonight" – another club within a club with video, drinks and cigs machines.

Here's Gerry, down specially from Glasgow, and Wendy from Liverpool and Melanie from Blackpool who's earned £10 today in a café to make it for her regular date with funkateer Greg. "Exciting" is Melanie's verdict. "Saturday is the only decent night," says Adrian Luck. "There's a terrible echo bouncing at you other nights. And Haçienda music is too funk-based."

Flat-top Johnny Marr disagrees: "I schlepp to funk." Caz and Mike like the warm people and cheap drink "but what they need is a talented DJ," while Wade, one of the few blacks in sight, says, "Heaven is a pit compared with the Haçienda."

What hits the eyes hardest is the dancefloor, a patchwork of *ra-ras*, ripped jeans, rat-plaits and creepers... your complete *i-D* line-up minus the World's End spendthrifts. "London wears clothes for effect but we wear them for comfort," observes Rosie, a make-up artist, nailing the North-South divide exactly. Come the Thunderbirds finale, all the cults join forces in one giant conga – another sight that you'll not catch south of Watford... •

10 69 DEAN STREET

FEBRUARY 1983

The making of modern club culture by David Johnson

----

69 DEAN STREET is an address implanted somewhere in the folk memory of every FACE reader. During the four years when the launchpad for musical experiment shifted from traditional rock gigs to the dancefloor, 69 Dean Street became a factory farm that has fattened each passing cult en route for today's richly-flavoured mainstream.

This is an upstairs-downstairs tale of two separate nightspots which share the same building and the same pioneering policy of fostering a different theme each night of the week. At Christmas the upstairs club, The Gargoyle, passed into history with the expiry of its lease, though the one-nighters it hosted are all now resurfacing elsewhere. Downstairs a lavish sign in the street proclaims the proud history of the second club: "Gossips, formerly Billy's".

Here is the home of the one-nighter through which the Trans-Europe Express once roared towards the Blitz and beyond. It was here that ritualised the weekly party. It is here that the nightclub has identified yet another role for itself in 1983...

The stripper retrieves her scattered tassels to a smattering of applause from the idlers in Burton suits. Pinki Pirelli scurries naked from the fifth-floor bar that was Soho's idea of plush when it opened in the Fifties, into the ladies to dress for her next appointment. She leaves by the lift and in the street pushes past a youthful queue waiting to take the same lift skyward for a night billed as "thoroughly nasty". Participants include the ubiquitous Siouxsie, music bizzybodies, a BBC producer who says he doesn't mind being two years late on the scene ("that's television") and a dazzling kaleidoscope of current cults you could describe extremely inadequately as Dracula meets the Muppets.

It is 11pm, and since this is Wednesday the rooftop Gargoyle club is undergoing its weekly transformation into The Batcave, the most unsubtle of London's one-night stands, fronted by a Jaggeresque youth in mascara and black lace and without doubt the runaway success of the year.

The rest of the week The Gargoyle becomes in turn a moviemakers' showcase, a Sixties soul night, a gay club which welcomes straights, and The Comedy Store, which, back in 1979, threw up the Alexei Sayle school of "alternative" comics who seem now to have colonised half our TV.

A few paces along the pavement a second door leads down to the cellars of the same building and the sinewy and refreshingly unfamiliar rhythms of Afrobeat. A white youth in a sabbath hat is greeting the kind of mix-it membership that's becoming a regular feature of nightlife: a gracious black beauty just in from Nigeria, a Camden Town trendy, Sixties art dealer Kasmin ("Is that his first name or his last?" asks a junior clubber called Lloyd) and in separate company, Kasmin's son Paul.

Since this is Wednesday this is The Gold Coast club, but other nights in the Gossips week are devoted to straight jazz, rapping, rocking blues, jazz-funk and roots rockers with Capital Radio DJ David Rodigan. By the time you read this any of these could have dropped out: in the world of one-nighters, two weeks means make or break.

Since 1978, when Rusty Egan's Bowie Night at Billy's ritualised the private party which enjoyed full disco facilities, Gossips astutely wised to filling the slack nights in its week. In came Pink Monday, Pistols, The Clinic, Jive Dive, Vidzine and five different Tuesday-night tenants in the past year alone. The nature of the one-nighter is its transience – that now-legendary Bowie Night ran only three months. Certainly fast bucks have encouraged exploitation of passing fads, but club-owners have had to depend entirely on streetwise young frontmen to bring them each craze. Central to the Billy's-into-Blitz axis of Egan as DJ, Strange as greeter, was the innovation that youth assumed the initiative. "These were the first clubs run for kids by kids without feeling we were being ripped off," it was said at the time.

Perry Haines with his *i-D* night was next off the grid with his "100mph dance music". He succeeded at Gossips. Stevo and Jock McDonald tried and flopped. Gaz Mayall's Rockin' Blues is now in its third year, and one reason why he's enjoying London's longest run is inevitably the universal appeal of the blues he plays. Another is Gaz's membership list. It reads like a hip Who's Who, without regard for age.

"A promoter's social register must be strong, and if it's not he won't keep a following," says Reid Anderson, co-licensee of the Gargoyle upstairs. With a former page-boy to the queen, the 24-year-old heir to a thirteenth earl hosting Tuesdays (called Soul Furnace, he says, because "it's hot"), this not surprisingly is the strongest night of the week.

Steve Strange and Perry Haines carefully constructed their own social registers, but most aspiring promoters who walk in mean a gamble for the club. "Gossips has always had the bottle to take chances," says Mick Collins, manager downstairs. "You need courage to let anyone who impresses you have a go. And you need courage to cut it if it fails on its first night. I've lost fortunes in the past advertising people's second nights." What happens of course is that some kid on an ego trip fails to realise that it's his job to promote the event.

With dwindling cash closing clubs two or three nights a week, last winter saw the West End stiff with handbills for Mod revivals, paisleyed psychedelia and mime-faced futurism. Some club-owners got stung. The Gargoyle scored a first for rapping, but when the air got a little too heavy The Language Lab had to go. Gossips, in line with a solid black-music reputation, gave reggae a home last winter, but now has to display signs requesting "Gentlemen: No hats on Fridays and Saturdays", which is a euphemism to blacks like "No jeans' is to whites. "

"That's our only restriction," says Collins, "and because of it the club feels safe. People can get away with a lot here, and that matters. Some kids can only afford one night out and they'll spend all that week's dole here. There's no longer the money to go out every night, so we've learned to vary our clientele through the week."

Upstairs, owner Don Ward has also made a strip club which had outlived its purpose viable. "As long as people leave here with money in their pocket, they'll come back next week. Yes, I'm taking a little off a lot of people. Each night's promoter works hard too. And the profits go to him."

69 Dean Street can trace its ancestry back to the dawn of clubmanship. It stands on the corner of a film-set, Soho's oldest intact terrace, and though a spraycan has dubbed this Rapping Yard, a tablet on the same wall dates it: "Meard Street 1732". The original Jethro Tull, wouldn't you like to know, was writing his revolutionary theories about English farming then, and in the building boom which followed the Great Fire, speculators spread mansions over Soho Fields. Artists quickly adopted the new suburb as London's fashionable quarter.

As recently as its 1930s incarnation, The Gargoyle boasted a theatrical-artistic membership which included Noël Coward and Tallulah Bankhead – for whom it daringly relaxed the evening-dress requirement. Up to the Fifties, as the haunt of Francis Bacon's Soho group, the club had Matisse's Red Studio hanging on its wall, arguably his most important painting, declined by the Tate and lost to America amid scandal when the Tennant family sold up.

Vestiges of lost splendour still shine, like an Art Deco staircase in steel and brass that links the Gargoyle dancefloor with the rooftop theatre and bar. As the Nell Gwynne revue staging three lavish stripshows a night, this was where businessmen came to clinch their deals over dinner and a hostess and whatever – until the last Labour government said sorry, but hostesses are no longer tax-deductible. The Astor closed, The Churchill closed, but in May 1979 The Gargoyle did some speculating of its own.

Don Ward, himself a one-time comic, imported the American Comedy Store format: an evening of stand-up comics plus an achingly trendy audience who gonged off the most hopeless performers. "I feel as welcome here as Hitler at a bar mitzvah," said one joker last month to a Saturday crowd that's still in its twenties but after three years rates only a Springsteen in trendiness.

The Comedy Store did prove to be a crucial staging-post in weaning young comics off left-wing benefits and onto the music circuits. Then last year along came the *éminence grise* who'd been trying to make Pythons out of the breakaway Comic Strip team, Simon Oakes, who also in the words of a friend "knows absolutely everybody" and those of a rival "has more fingers than there are pies to put them in".

What he injected with The Language Lab and Lord Ogilvy's Soul Furnace by putting music first was a social mix you seldom find elsewhere. So though you really can hear some Henry say "They let you in for half price after 1am – like a half-day ski pass," once inside you nevertheless find underage Wembley mods Doing The Dog beside young Lady Cosima Fry. "This club has been a great leveller," says Oakes, "because it's based on people, not style."

Likewise at The Lift on Thursdays. "Straights have such misconceptions about gays: people still ask me if I play the male or female role," says co-host Steve Swindells, who encourages gays to bring straight friends of all sexes. The bait is the hardest music in town, not the usual wimpy American gay disco, but rebel funk, BLT, Man Parrish. The DJ has scrawled across the wall "Boogie leads to integration".

If The Gargoyle has cast itself as an equal-opportunities crusader, Gossips pads the musical waterfront with just as much zeal. Vince, who has owned Gossips since the days when gay clubs like Billy's led musical taste, is a Soho legend himself, straight out of Shaft – huge hats, fistfuls of rings. His jeweller along Meard Street once showed me a mock-up for a mountainous ring he was making: "Eighteen-carat gold, 16 diamonds – it shone like a torch. I showed it to Vince and he said, 'I want more diamonds on it'."

One DJ said: "When Vince calls by even the manager stands to attention, so it makes sense that I should too." Gossips is the kind of place where nobody admits a surname until they know you. Yet everyone working there, staff and one-nighters, uses the same fond word about the few square feet of stonechip floor and mirror: atmosphere. Collins says: "It's not posh here. What we have, though, is heritage."

It's no accident that the nights which have survived the carnival of cults here say much about the dominant musical forces at work in 1983. Amazingly for a jazz-funk night Steve Walsh on Fridays pulls an almost exclusively black crowd: "Very upfront, advanced in their tastes – it doesn't appeal to the white party-crowd." Equally unusually for an essentially reggae night, Rodigan and his ace toaster Papa Face pull a healthy black-white mix. "It is rare," he admits. "We emphasise the rootsy, sweeter end of reggae – Rudi Thomas, Carroll Thompson, and that attracts a lot of women." With the lights out, the dancefloor throbs like a Ladbroke Grove blues. "Everyone dances to reggae: you have to get closer," says Dave Gordon, aged 18.

Gossips stands alone in championing reggae in the West End, and it is perhaps significant that it occupies the week's prime slot, Saturday.

Both of Gossips' other hit nights fall happily into play-school roles. Ghanaian Jo Hagan likes educating people and says the highlife he plays at The Gold Coast is a lot less aggressive than people expect, "but it can be intimidating not to hear an English word sung all night." His partner, Christian Cotterill, who owns half the records, says: "The press made African music flavour of the month, but in fact it's all so danceable. When Gasper Lawall played here Gossips had its most profitable night for a year."

If you want to see a genuine Stetson, check Thursdays and you'll find 24-year-old Gaz beneath one. When he began playing bluesmasters BB King and John Lee Hooker back in 1980, Gaz said, "People didn't know how to dance to this stuff, but they've been practising." For nearly three years Gaz, himself a vinyl junkie, has devotedly been handing down history – by numbers.

The impact of nightlife on the style of the past five years is not to be underestimated. However much Futurist-Romantic labels make the skin crawl, their legacy is evident in the vitality of today's streets and charts, obvious though the ingredients may have been in Britain's post-punk vacuum: SF movies, a Dada retrospective, headline-making performance art, a revival of intimate cabaret. Yet the positive accelerators of change were a handful of nightclubs. Photographer Derek Ridgers recalls that Tuesdays at Billy's were "like walking into a Hieronymus Bosch painting: furtive but lively and with a dedication that's never been equalled since."

Those formative Bowie Nights and Electro Diskows were parties with a vengeance, glorifying the individual, wresting power and profits from the elders. In particular the imaginative DJ became lionised for engineering new sounds, resplicing Kraftwerk, say, and eliminating the mid-range in playback.

As those events of '78 were a reaction to the music of *Fever* and Boney M, to dance-halls turning into discos, so the circle has turned again. What Moroder said then is as true today of the Palaces and Haçiendas: "Most disco-goers are not dancers." Nor are they convincing posers. Conceits which were once daring, the megadisco has now sanctioned. The mainstream giants have sanitised the cults, standardised the music and dwarfed the individual with pyrotechnics.

But what Billy's developed, the factory farm at 69 Dean Street went on refining. The small-scale nightclub has emerged as the customised club-night. It reasserts the supremacy of bedrock music and consequently attracts a strong social mix. And because allegiance owes less to age-group or to dress, it activates more socially rewarding reflexes.

What the one-night clubgoer has discarded is the disposable identity in favour of a confident expression of taste. The Pose Age appears to be buried. Here at last is the party which requires you to come as yourself •

11   THE GOOD MIXER

JUNE 1983

Steve Swindells and The Lift by David Johnson

IN A GAY PUB-DISCO the very week Culture Club first hit Number One, I watched Boy George take a real tongue-lashing. A lumberjack clone (check shirt, dormouse on upper lip) accused George of betraying gays by using the word "poof" in a newspaper interview. "In your position you should be defending poofs," the clone raged. George unleashed his own tongue: "I'm not exactly the most normal person in the world, right, but to me a poof is a mincing queen and I'm definitely not a poof. If people choose to flaunt their sexual identity that's their own look-out."

George said he dressed the way he wanted and fought his own battles, thanks. The clone was incensed. Gays should stand together, he said. Why, he'd been beaten up just for wearing a Gay Pride badge. So what, quipped George – he'd been beaten up for wearing a Mother's Pride badge.

"He didn't like that," George said later. "Those people have no sense of humour."

Anyone who knows George knows he's always been so cavalier – he didn't mind my reporting all this, he said, because he'd be telling the tale on radio next day anyway. And it could be argued that by disarming mums and dads with laughter, George encourages a certain tolerance towards an image they might otherwise call queer.

Humour, however, was no deterrent when that same pub erupted minutes after George had departed. Skinheads wrecked the next-door bar and clubbed the barman because "queers are trying to take the place over". Movements, the one-nighter in question, has since transferred to another pub in north London.

This episode makes two points that the straight world may overlook. First, it's a reminder of the divergence of opinion among gay people themselves and of the fragility of any potential gay community. And second, for all the sexual emancipation that fashionable London circles are said to enjoy, it illustrates the ugly realities which deter the majority of gay people from associating openly at all.

Many wholly or experimentally gay night-owls are limited to seeking relaxation among sympathetic straights, since the exclusively gay scene wears some intimidating guises. The writer who tries to observe this sensitive world is traditionally accused of partiality; so varied are the shades of sexual taste (seven according to Kinsey) from hetero to homosexuality that one wing or another always seems to take offence.

Enter Steve Swindells, on the clear understanding that he is already one of a minority who are prepared to be vocal. Swindells believes that the mystique the gay life holds for straight people is based on "amazing ignorance", so for nearly a year he has fronted The Lift, an itinerant gay club-night which flouts convention by welcoming straights. The bait is the kind of hard rebel funk that's alien to most gay discos. Its success is impressive.

The Lift occupies 28 Leicester Square on Thursdays and 5 Falconberg Court on Fridays, and apologies to readers of the April FACE who went to the Whisky-A-Go-Go looking for Lift Three there.

While the heterosexual empire of the Wag has just expanded to three nights a week there, The Lift was cancelled after two goes. "Too many smokes," say the management, though Swindells blames a reception committee of heavies making anti-gay jokes as members arrived. "Tom the boss asked, 'How do you know the women are women?'" says Swindells.

Such stone-age attitudes convince him that the so-called sexual revolution did little to advance understanding. Gay people might help, he says, if they were more honest with their families – his own mum can often be seen on The Lift's dancefloor – and as a songwriter he did his bit in 1980 by recording a gay album.

Swindells is a witty talker, and the dialogue that follows is necessarily more abrupt than our full conversation. He says he has no mission to convert anyone, but he is glad to destroy what mystique he can.

Why do you think so many people pose as gay these days?
Straights have a fascination with gay culture based on what they imagine goes on. Yet so many straight people, even in the fashionable demi-monde, would never go to a gay club and have never met a gay person in their lives. I can't understand why when places like the Palace and the Batcave are so ambiguous. It's partly because that Seventies move to admitting you're gay has halted. There's a new breed of closetry emerging. The fake decadence of Steve Strange and Marc Almond disturbs me because it encourages an image of the gay scene as dark, mysterious and perverse.

You mean it's not?
It may be true of the gay scene but let's distinguish the scene from the majority of people who happen to be gay. The habitués of London's pubs and clubs are a nucleus of only 500 people in a city of eight million.

Why is The Lift so popular?
We provide body music for people with minds of their own. The best thing is the lack of sexual pressure from any quarter, and our open-door policy works. We get a really nice mixture of the curious, the shy, the trendy young things, glamorous women I won't name, normal gays disillusioned by the die-hard gay scene and of course the A-team of funk freaks who are never off the dancefloor... Black Jack and Maurice who are unofficial bouncers; Fay, a beautiful black lady who gets everyone screaming and goes off to work at Harvey Nichols next day; Steve the Hat and sidekick Andy, Big Frederick and Angus and Merran – superb dancers who have evolved a Lift dance you might find in a black club but not a gay one. It's all legwork; the body might as well not exist.

People let their hair down?
Fridays have always had that black party feeling. Quite a few do come to get wrecked... and to pull of course. The Lift is a sexual place, but I hope on a more human level than most gay clubs which revolve entirely round sex. Instead of exchanging five words before sleeping together, we go for the whole sentence. One of the reasons I started The Lift was because I'd got pissed off with the general lack of communication – apart from sexual – between gay people. Sex is much easier to get than on the straight scene, but it can get like buying a drink because there's no social pressure to form relationships.

What's unusual about your music?
No other gay club plays music like The Lift. Period. Black clubs yes, but no way will you hear the Kashif LP or Lorita Grahame's "Young Free And Single" in a gay club, so we get

lots of whites who'd like to go to black straight clubs but are discouraged by bad vibes. The Lift is close in spirit to Manhattan's Paradise Garage who play amazing New York funk, but they don't have the benefit of British funk and reggae. In New York, gay clubs are still regarded musically as leaders, but here it's embarrassing trying out new dance records. It's taken so long for gay clubs to pick up on electronics because gay disco has such a hold. That's another bone of contention. You might as well call it Gay-Oriented Disco, it's so bland and monotonous and yet suddenly straight clubs are getting into it. Sure, classics like "Rock The Boat" and "Law Of The Land" are great, and in 1974 it felt good to be gay because our music was so far ahead. But not any more •

12   GET THAT PERFECT BEAT

OCTOBER 1983

New York disco and the men who made it by Steven Harvey

"Lord knows Where my body goes
Every night"
Nile Rodgers: "The Land Of The Good Groove"

IT IS POSSIBLE (and tempting) to perceive the recent ascent of new dance music as an isolated pop/style phenomenon – something like punk or new wave – that has emerged over the last few years and snowballed into an international fad. Yet to understand the new mood in NYC dance music, you must go back into its history. Back into the disco...

Escape into the disco: an underground pressure-valve from the work week. The names of some of the underground dance clubs in NYC in the early Seventies expressed this function – The Haven and The Sanctuary. Places where those relegated to the margins of society – blacks, latins, gays and kids – could affirm their own existence through the shared abandon of the dance. And central to the dance was the DJ.

At both The Haven in '69 and The Sanctuary in the early Seventies the DJ was Francis Grasso. Albert Goldman in *Disco* describes how, without a cueing system, Grasso would overlay two different tracks, superimposing "I'm A Man" by Chicago over the bass and drums from "Whole Lotta Love"; mixing soul like Bobby Byrd and The Stovell Sisters into rock'n'roll and ethno-beat like olatunji.

His audience soon spilled through the doors of the huge former church into the streets, where the kids would hang out practising steps and doing drugs. Regularly the police would arrive to close it down, but attempting to clear the 1,000 or so people inside and the same number in the street would take hours.

Francis Grasso was one of the first in a line that runs through David Mancuso of The Loft to Larry Levan of The Paradise Garage, John "Jellybean" Benitez at The Funhouse and others. Mancuso's first space opened in 1970, and he has been playing records at his once-a-week parties ever since.

But the tradition of the 12-inch single as the vehicle for disco only goes back to 1976, when Walter Gibbons remixed a three-minute album track, "10 Percent" by Double Exposure, for Salsoul, extending it into nine minutes of percussion landscape. Gibbons was the first to really transform the material specifically for the NYC dancefloor. He brought the mixing techniques that he had developed in live spinning into the recording studio.

Those early sexy swinging tracks like "10 Percent" or "Hit & Run" by Loleatta Holloway were the heirs to the Philly disco crown of the early Seventies. Anthems of the early dawn, they layered shimmering vibes, congas and electric piano into swirling, rapturous dance music.

Gibbons played live at Galaxy 21 in 1976 and was influential with a number of the new mixers. François Kervorkian, DJ and studio mixer (who is now producing Hubert

Eaves of D-Train for Island) had just arrived from France when he was hired to play drums along to Gibbons' live mixing. As he didn't know any of the tunes that Gibbons was playing, this was perhaps a less than successful experiment in mixing live and pre-recorded sound. Nowadays it is common for a DJ to have a synthesizer player accompany him, as Michael de Benedictus of the Peech Boys does with Larry Levan at the Garage.

Jellybean of The Funhouse was 18 and already playing at a club called Experiment 4, run by the owners of Galaxy 21. "I used to jump in a cab after work, just to sit and watch Walter for three or four hours. Everything he was doing back then people are doing now."

"Everything" included the various turntable manipulations like phasing (two copies of a record played slightly off sync to produce a flange effect) and Gibbons' extremely fast cuts between percussion breaks. Like the scratch-mix DJs, Gibbons played records that people wouldn't think of as danceable: "Flight" by David Sanborn, "What's The Story?" by Patrice Rushen (when she was still just a jazz keyboardist), "Changes Make You Want To Hustle" by Donald Byrd.

Nowadays, with some 50 new 12-inchers coming out each week, classic tracks are the connecting thread, a continuity of quality and feeling. A current trend is re-production. Taking re-mixing to the next phase: everything old is new again. When Dinosaur L's "Go Bang" was remixed from an album for the 12-inch by François Kervorkian, *Dance Music Report* (the trade paper associated with Tommy Boy Records) noted its similarity to the Gibbons sound of Galaxy 21 in 1976. Shep Pettibone's re-production of old Salsoul tracks peel off their period veneer. "Let No Man Put Asunder" by First Choice updates the setting for Rochelle Fleming's cry for marital stability, yet holds on to the pathos and humour of Fleming's ferocious vocals.

Pettibone, who has resumed the KISS radio mastermixes that initially brought him recognition, also remade an old Salsoul Orchestra track (the same players as MFSB) "Chicago Bus Stop" into "Love Break". Both were inspired by perhaps the penultimate underground anthem, the fast instrumental section of MFSB's "Love Is The Message".

The best example of a cult classic achieving new commercial success is "Weekend" by Phreek. Leroy Burgess and Patrick Addams concocted this perfect dream-fulfilment of finding a friend for the weekend, which came out on Atlantic in 1978... sort of. There was never a proper commercial version of the final long mix of the song, and import and promo copies continued to command collector's prices. Observing the song's continuous cult status, particularly at Paradise Garage, Sleeping Bag Records released a modern cover of it by Class Action, but with the brilliant stroke of having the original singer, Christine Wiltshire, update her vocals. "You're staying home with the kids tonight, honey," she tells her man.

As critic Carol Cooper once said, it is easy for writers to forget that dancing is a metaphor for sex, and in disco the lyrics have been traditionally regarded as a throwaway element because their primary subject is love and sex. In the Eighties, as the clamps come down on all kinds of freedoms, dealing with sexuality, particularly since disco has always had more room for women's views than rock, is a progressive stance.

The infatuation with sonic experimentation, the dub factor that has taken over the B-sides of most 12-inch releases, started with DJs moving from mixing live to the studio. Records like Bo Kool & The Funkmaster's "Money (No Love)" explored the possibilities of a hybrid West Indian/dub/disco, and NYC DJs were quick to learn. Larry Levan produced "Don't Make Me Wait", a landmark to equal his dense druggy mix of Taana Gardner's "Heartbeat". Pettibone slowed down "Thanks To You" by Sinnamon from its

"Call Me" clone sound to an ocean of synth and guitar waves and echoing vocals, and François Kervorkian (perhaps the most open in his acknowledgement of Jamaican music) executed his perfect gleaming mixes for D-Train's "Keep On" and "D Train Theme (dub)".

"Nowadays," says Shep Pettibone, "it is the dub factor that creates excitement in 'Planet Rock' type music." And as Jellybean points out: "It's only because DJs have been in the studio. I think producers are looking for a more polished sound and DJs are looking for the effects that are going to get the audience off."

Along with the pure pleasure-play of aural re-doctoring, the salient characteristic of new disco is the total electronification of the music. While many longtime music fans despair of microchip music, the mass audience of modern dancers respond to it like automata. The nexus of this beat-box sensibility is The Funhouse, where Jellybean, who mixed many of the Tommy Boy/Streetwise records, spins every weekend.

Three thousand kids are out on the floor. The rhythms of the Roland and Linn drum computers build songs weekend after weekend, programming them into memory/response, creating a kind of cumulative choreography. There is a constant shifting of bodies throughout the huge space: girls with bleached blonde patches and "tails" (little ponytails hanging from otherwise short haircuts) wearing black leather, studs and spray-on pants; the men in cut-off shirts and baggy drawstring trousers.

The kind of cool macho look of the Funhouse kids reflects the demographic of this once mainly Italian disco. Nowadays the clientele is drawn from a network of kids principally from New York's boroughs who are serious about dancing. Men dance alone in an acrobatic mating of slamming and breakdancing. The women crowd the ladies room to change into fresh outfits and make-up, applying coat after coat of hairspray until the "tail" is perfect.

In the DJ booth – a clown's open mouth overlooking the dancefloor – Jellybean is seaming tracks together into a hard endless rhythm. His studio work with the principal electro-beat composers like John Robie, Arthur Baker, Lottie Golden and Richard Scher of Warp 9, with rappers like Sweet G and Kurtis Blow, and with Madonna (for whom he has done his first solo production, "Holiday", on her new album) make The Funhouse a testing-ground for artists who bring in tapes-in-progress to check out on the audience.

The new intercourse of English groups availing themselves of NYC producer/mixer acumen is centered around The Funhouse. Robie's reworking of Cabaret Voltaire's "Yashaar" into arabic modern with metal edges, and Baker's grafting of perfect beats on to New Order angst in "Confusion" are Funhouse hybrids. New takes on a formula is what the audience there has come to expect. Herbie Hancock's "Rockit", produced by Material, with its metal machine sound and nervous vinyl scratching, is a record that sounds as if it was made for The Funhouse and underlines Jellybean's boast of the increasing influences of DJs on mainstream production.

The Paradise Garden when first experienced is likely to seem like the long-sought-after Perfect Club. The courteous staff, clear (members only) door policy, awesome sound system and the audience of serious dancers to Larry Levan's highly individual musical narrative combine to create an ideal disco.

A vast ramp rises in blackness towards the club's interior in what was once a parking garage. Pinpoint lights guide you towards the neon sign, emblazoned with the club's logo. Inside it is like carnival in Bahia, with black and latin figures stripped down for the lack of air-conditioning. The main floor begins to crowd after 2am and stays that way through into the morning.

On the balcony above the floor, Levan alternates Garage classics (Bo Kool, Eddy Grant, ESG, "Evolution" by Giorgio Moroder) on three Thorens turntables (much lighter and harder to manipulate than Technics). In between, he dubs a bass-line here, a sound-effects record there. The Richard Long custom-designed sound system sends bass waves flying across the wide floor until the sound literally collides with you. When the maximum temperature in the room begins to takes its toll, you retire to the rooftop garden, or nap in one of the adjoining chambers, before returning to the lift-off point on the dancefloor.

The inspiration for The Garage is located not very far away in SoHo, in David Mancuso's home, The Loft. As far removed from the commercial concept of a club as possible, The Loft represents another seminal definition of the perfect dance space – a house party. For 13 years every Saturday, Mancuso has opened up his place (which was originally several blocks away on Broadway near Bleeker Street) to his guests who come to dance to one of the world's great sound systems. Every element – the Paul Klipsch speakers, the Mark Levinson amplification, the Mitchell Cotter turntable bases and line amplifiers, and the hand-crafted Koetsu cartridges – is custom designed to provide the clearest audio rendition of what's in the groove. Sound as science. Mancuso is a magnetic personality, whose devotion to serving music has led him away from the mixing of records, which he used to do in the old Loft.

"David would make the most serious music," recalls Larry Levan. "He would make a mix and people would cry because it was so tender!"

He now uses neither headphones nor mixer, connecting the songs through narrative and rhythmic continuity or, as he says, by following a "sonic trail".

The Loft is like a children's party. Balloons cover every inch of the ceiling. The guests are open and warm as in no other club, and smiles adorn faces that know they have found some place special as they dance surrounded by the perfectionist Ouevo twirlers who spin around and drop with uncanny musical timing.

Mancuso has a host of songs that are Loft classics, like Fred Wesley's "House Party" (defining the Loft concept) or Third World's "Now That We've Found Love", and he has consistently fostered new music. In the early Seventies he brought the Barrabas album back from Spain; he has played Eddy Grant for years and his attitude of serving and supporting the music has influenced a generation of music people like Levan who came up going to The Loft every weekend.

A funky alternative to the membership dancehalls like The Garage and The Loft is Better Days, a black gay bar in Manhattan's Times Square district. For ten years a spectrum of black gay people have come to Better Days and the activity in the club's circular back room for dancing is a peak definition of nightdancing.

Originally the turntables were worked by Tee Scott,who has now moved over to Zanzibar in New Jersey. He was replaced by Bruce Forest, who plays a post R&B-style of disco highlighting great singers like Loleatta Holloway, Chaka Khan, and Rochelle Fleming.

When Shep Pettibone took a break from his KISS radio master-mixing, he would play at Better Days on Thursday nights. His extraordinarily active hands-on mixing style was amazing to witness. On the radio when he takes three different pieces of music and makes them fit together it seems comprehensible, because of the possibilities of tape editing. Live, however, it is different. He puts together three different versions of Diana Ross's "Love Hangover" or juxtaposes two different songs to create a third that

remains impossibly in sync.

He is always slowing down and bringing records up to speed, or dropping-in parts from other discs. Pettibone is the perfect example of the DJ as remaker; a Dr Frankenstein for the modules of music within each record. His two-record set for Prelude of KISS Master Mixes (volume two is in the works) remains one of the best recorded examples of what creative club DJs are doing.

The NYC clubs come and go, disappear and reappear, yet the ones mentioned here have set the standards. They define a new/old music that has been shaped more by the audiences and the DJs than by corporate boardrooms. Even now, when there is the danger of a repeat of 1978's "death of disco" with the arrival of dance oriented rock and flashdancing gentrification of a black/latin/gay medium, the physical energy and tangible love of the music among the underground culture provides new disco with its continued impact. Disco, for a long time the sound that dared not speak its name, has now become the single largest influence in popular music •

13   BENT FOR LEATHER

OCTOBER 1983

Skin 2 by Fiona Russell Powell

I AM CROUCHED on all fours on the tiny square dancefloor of Skin 2. The opening strains of a Walter Carlos synth dirge announce the beginning of my humiliation. My bare arse is on full view to the people who have crowded round to watch. The first Mistress approaches, holding aloft the instrument of exquisite torture, an ivory-handled multi-thonged whip. She teases me at first, stroking my cheeks with the leather thongs then, growing impatient, she begins to circle me, digging her stilettos into my ribs occasionally. All eyes are on my naked and vulnerable backside trembling beneath the spotlight. She stops behind me and rests one of her black patent stiletto heels in between my cheeks. Teasing, she then withdraws it and lightly stabs the fleshy parts with her six-inch heel. Soon she has had enough of humouring me and raises her arm high above her head, pauses long enough to watch me quiver with fear and excitement, then rapidly brings the whip down hard across my bottom. She sits astride my back and repeats this many times, often altering the amount of force to heighten the enjoyment. As the music gets louder, my cheeks get redder. Eventually the fine lines of blood appear. My Mistress relents for a while and kneads the glowing buttocks with her leather-gloved hands, but sometimes a sharp smack reminds me that my punishment is not over yet...

Orlando is a slave. He is also a 26-year-old South African, a sort of mutant transvestite (50 per cent Rocky Horror, 50 per cent Coco The Clown) and 100 per cent masochist. What you have just read is part of his Skin 2 fantasy, and one which he was lucky enough to have realised later. You will all have heard of Skin 2 by now – principally it's a rubber/leather fetishists evening held on Monday nights within a club dubiously named Stallions situated in a suitably seedy alleyway just off Tottenham Court Road.

Since it started at the beginning of the year voyeurs, trendies and would-be decadents have flocked to have a look at the "freaks" and "perverts" who patronise the premises. A cover story in *Time Out* really set the ball rolling and the *Standard*, the *Daily Mirror* and *Fiesta* rapidly followed suit, but they're always photographing the wrong people, always talking to the wrong people – Great Gear Market trendies who've nipped up to She'n'Me for a little latex something – and totally ignoring the real clientele which is mainly comprised of middle-class professionals.

However, by the time you read this, Skin 2 will be no more; a nine-month legend that has had to move to a secret address and change its name. Because, despite the fact that Skin 2 has attracted more press coverage and media interest than any club since Blitz three years ago, ultimately it has failed.

Maybe there just aren't enough rubber/leather/SM enthusiasts to go round. Or maybe it's because of the attitude adopted when writing about the club and its clientele. The general approach has been: "Great copy! We must do a feature on this club for PERVERTS. Get some SENSATIONAL pictures. EXPOSE these weirdos but pretend that we draw no conclusions. Leave that to the reader!" Of course this will be hotly denied, but it's not hard to see the angle behind those articles and it's made a lot of genuine people afraid to go.

The word "pervert" in this context is constantly misused, and invariably it implies a harmful sexual preference that is considered abusive, equated with violence and often thought of as something which neither party enjoys. The word is more accurately applied in the recent case of the six-year-old Brighton boy who was horribly abused.

Rubber/leather enthusiasts enjoy a fairly innocuous pastime. All it is basically is dressing up for sex, or, to quote Pat Califia's *The Sexual Fringe*, it is "high-technology sex". But the crux of the matter is that if you are not into a fetish then it's virtually impossible to understand.

Clubs like Skin 2 are a dime a dozen in some parts of America, although they tend to be much heavier and gayer. Ironically, SM is said to be the English perversion – Angela Carter recently drew an amusing parallel with our eagerness for punishment from the Iron Lady – but no eyebrows are raised in the USA either. In fact it's all rather a yawn, what with the *The Fetish Times* being an established publication available from regular newsagents. Certainly, a bevy of reporters haven't been sent down to California to investigate the Tickling Society. So why has Skin 2 generated so much interest and disapproval?

The answer is partly provided by the man who conceived Skin 2. David Claridge, a well-known entrepreneur in the music business (he was also responsible for the success of the Blitz) ran the club with his girlfriend, fashion designer Leslie Herbert, until the media discovered to their horror that he was also the man with his hand up TV-am's Roland The Rat.

"We wanted to take rubber out of the bedroom and put it in an acceptable environment," says Claridge. "There are a lot of people who enjoy experimenting sexually, but because of society being the way that it is they're always frowned upon. The club isn't there to be outrageous: it's there to reflect sexual tastes. Also, we wanted kids to be aware of the possibilities of dressing up for sex and not just finding it something to laugh at. It wasn't done to attract trendy Camden Palacers – we're not interested in those people; quite honestly they're outdated."

However, it did attract some unexpected customers. For instance, one of Skin 2's early pop-star patrons (of which there were many) was Kim Wilde. You may have noticed the discreet yet distinctly kinky leather number Kim constantly wore when promoting her last hit single, "Love Blonde". When I spoke to Kim recently I asked her about Skin 2 and that dress…

"I thought Skin 2 was a great club. We had a really good time… I bought the dress from Joseph at Sloane Street for £500. I had it altered though; originally it had a little cape over one shoulder but I had that taken off and an extra strap added…

"I love black leather. I particularly like the texture, and I find the rough feel very attractive and sexy. I also think that black leather is timeless and it looks quite sleazy, which I like."

Skin 2 was the first club of its sort for over 15 years, and it was obviously much needed as its membership has swelled to over 1,200 – four of whom I'm going to introduce to you. You won't have read about them before so be careful because they're real, as real as this magazine in your hands.

"First and foremost is the cool, smooth, stretchy feel and the texture; second is the pleasure of putting on a clinging and mildly restrictive material, and third the inexplicable ecstasy of the skin being lubricated with its own juices."

David is a 25-year-old nurse from a small town in Scotland. We're standing at the main bar of Skin 2 on a suffocatingly hot night and he's telling me why he loves rubber.

He's wearing a black all-in-one rubber suit (feet and helmet included) which he'd bought only that day in a Soho sex shop for £75. It was hard to get into at first, partly because he was so excited but also because it was one of the hottest days of the year. Two tins of Johnson's Baby Powder later and eager to try out his new purchase, he phoned one of the many Miss Bonds who advertise in sweet shop windows and went to see her. Hardly the "half-an-hour of hell" that he'd been anticipating: rather a fat middle-aged pro who weighed a ton, rode around on his back and spanked him every now and then. Still, to quote David: "It was only a tenner and you can't grumble at that."

After reading about Skin 2 in *Fiesta*, David hopped on to an Edinburgh-to-London shuttle, blowing his holiday time and money on a week of sexual humiliation and punishment. He thinks Skin 2 is a marvellous and absolutely necessary meeting-place for frustrated rubberists and he maintains that "the Scots still have a puritanical attitude to sex; anything but the missionary position is frowned upon". Apparently, the police in Edinburgh are currently exercising a massive "clean-up" operation, so David's only source of relief (from prostitutes) is fast drying up. The suit that he's wearing tonight is his first complete rubber outfit; before he's had to make do with leather, mainly because it raises fewer eyebrows but also because rubberwear outlets in Scotland are non-existent.

While we've been chatting, the legs of David's suit have billowed out slightly up to the knee. I thought it was trapped air at first but soon found out I was wrong. "I must be squelching around in about two pints of sweat," he laughs, extricating some sodden pound notes to buy another drink. He doesn't know why he's so attracted to rubber, but he certainly doesn't blame it on the nanny. What's David's rubber fantasy?

"It may sound a bid morbid but I'd like to be encased in rubber from head to foot with no eyeslits or mouthslits, just a nose-hole to let me breathe. Then I would lie down in a rubber-lined coffin, have the lid closed and padlocked over me and be left for two or three days." He breaks into a broad grin: "I think I'd just go crazy!"

Hmmmmm... All this is going in one ear while Mott The Hoople is blasting into the other. "Hello, I'm your friendly neighbourhood sadist..." DJ Chris has made a witty choice. The dancefloor is getting pretty outrageous now – a crippled dwarf in a wheel-chair is leering at a young latex-clad girl wriggling around watching her silhouette loom large on a screen on which chic-ified Helmut Newtonesque SM stills are flickering. The girl then picks up the dwarf and swings him around in her arms as she dances, while he uses the opportunity to feel her up.

All this is observed with a dispassionate eye by the hostess, Leslie Herbert. She really looks the part, very Bulle Ogier/Allen Jones, and very cruel. A black Cleopatra wig frames the "fixed severe expression for the night". Leslie wears a skin-tight latex dress, black of course, over smooth black rubber stockings rising from wicked skyscraper patents, and she carries the ubiquitous accessory, a riding crop. An evil outfit which means business.

Every week on the Skin 2 dancefloor, there occurs what could only be politely described as a "performance". It's usually a standard and spontaneous act of punish-ment and domination, with Leslie holding court over the proceedings.

"I don't whip people to hurt them. I always talk to them first and build them up for a few weeks before I do anything; then I know what they're into. They don't often want to be hurt; it's purely psychological power-games. One American man asked me to marry him the other day. He was following me around the club on his hands and knees, but I just ignored him. He'd do anything for me. He believes that I'm totally inaccessible. He said to me: 'All the others will hit me and beat me but you won't therefore you're the cruelest.' So you see, it's just mind-games."

Following the demise of Roland The Rat, caused – though no one has admitted as much – by the pathetic 'exposés' of Skin 2 ("a kinky sex club for perverts in Soho" according to the broad-minded *Sun*) in nearly every national newspaper, Leslie and her partner David Claridge have had to disassociate themselves from the club even to the point of denouncing it, which is a great shame because this will only serve to alienate rubber and leather enthusiasts further.

At the end of the night, after all the Monday evenings I spent at Skin 2 and after talking to and becoming involved with the totally normal and rather lonely people – even to the point of participating on one occasion – I would argue that a club like Skin 2 is a social necessity.

British society continues to hypocritically moralise over and ostracise this small percentage of people who find harmless pleasure in wearing certain materials for sex, while, operating on a system of double standards, we see the crime of rape reduced to a less than newsworthy two-line newspaper report. That, if anything, is the English perversion •

14   HIP HOP WON'T STOP

JUNE 1984

Electro by Paul Rambali and David Toop

PART ONE: DANCING IN THE STREETS by Paul Rambali

Trevor Birch is a B-boy. That's "B" for Bad, Beautiful, Black, Breaking, the Bronx. But in Trevor's case, "B" is for British. He couldn't tell you which subway line leads to the New York borough north of the Harlem river that has given him, at 18 in East London, an activity, and identity. But he has heard the records, seen the look, knows the moves.

He practises them up to four hours a day, during lunch breaks at the Community Project where he works with his old school-friend Gengiz Ozkadi painting murals, and later in the evening in the bedroom at Ozkadi's council home. To records like Newcleus' "Jam On It" and "One For The Treble" by Davy DMX, taped from Radio Invicta on Sunday nights because they can't afford to buy the records – thus pirating the pirates – they rehearse the flamboyant culture, dancing a zany improvisation on the micro-electronic pulse of the age.

And every Friday night they travel six miles to the Electric Ballroom in Camden Town. Both wear yellow peak caps and identical red and blue Adidas jogging suits over; it's impossible to say over what because they never take them off, never even unzip their anoraks. Oblivious to the writhing bodies around them, they stand facing each other on the crowded dancefloor, waiting for the mutant crack of the Linn Drum, the signal that galvanises them into tense, jerky spasms, swapped back and forth like a ball of invisible voltage.

"We like doing it," says Trevor. "We don't do it for money. It keeps us from doing something stupid." He picked it up three years ago from his elder brother, when it was called Robot Dancing. At the Tidal Basin club near his home, he kept abreast of the dance style that evolved into Body-Popping and Break-Dancing. He has never been to Covent Garden, where at times late last summer it seemed there were more Break-Dance crews than tourists to fund them. He and Ozkadi call their crew Technical Poppers, and they like to keep their moves up their sleeves. Once, at the Kensington club in East Ham, Trevor made the error of showing off his best style. "So many people took my moves that I had to go home and start all over again."

Competition is fierce, reputations are waiting to be made and lost. The threat of "Pirates" or "Biters" – people stealing your moves – is always present. The Technical Poppers, who never make their best moves at the Ballroom, have eight or so friends locally with other crews. "They're looking for a challenge, but I don't think we'll oblige them."

Right now, their main concern is tracksuits: Hummel red and blue tracksuits with diagonal white stripes that they've seen in a local sports shop. Trevor asks if I know of any clubs that want to promote a crew in return for the price of two Hummel tracksuits. They've got to have those suits. In two weeks' time there is the third heat of the All-London Independent And Team Body-Popping, Cracking And Break-Dancing Championship. The Technical Poppers reckon they have a good chance: "We've seen everybody else's moves, but they ain't seen ours!" But first they need those suits.

"You ought to have a flick book to explain it," says Robert Henry, a 22-year-old DJ and promoter who has been involved in organising the championship. "Popping by pros is a violent manoeuvre of the muscles. What they say is: You get tight, and you pop!" He clenches the muscles on his arm and releases them suddenly. "Cracking – that's a manoeuvre of the joints, like when your elbow or shoulder cracks." This time his arm snaps at the joints, as though a knot were passing along from one to the next and across the chest. "And Breaking is where you are more likely to be horizontal than verti-cal!" But there is no room to demonstrate the startling acrobatics that arose in the eight-bar rhythm breaks characteristic of late Seventies soul and funk discs.

No doubt about it though, this is the biggest dance craze to hit the UK since Robotics. "So many teams have come out of the woodwork," enthuses Robert. "We always knew the UK had the same creative power as the Americans." The first heats were held at a club near Brick Lane in east London. "We wanted to put the show on where Body-Popping came from. It's like a concrete jungle around there; it's the nearest thing to the ghetto." Teams and individuals came from all over: Battersea, Catford, Dagenham, Balham, Leyton, Tottenham – "Any run-down area in London."

Robert has a theory: It's caught on because it's such a radical form. It's expressive. All you need is the music and a street-corner, and you can get away from the pres-sures."His theory isn't new but it fits. And it goes further. Young Blacks in Britain who might five years ago have looked to reggae, with its potent figurehead of the late Bob Marley, for the trappings of cultural identity, now turn to the Bronx, to the Beat-Box and the Ghetto-Blaster. A style imported in the grooves of "Planet Rock" by the Soul Sonic Force in 1982 glimpsed on the faddish videos or mainstream pop and soul acts, a tough city-spawned seed, has taken root on England's pavements.

It has been nourished by the burgeoning electronic beat, rapid and solid, fast and frantic like the Swarmers on the third wave of "Defender".It finds its spirit in raps like "Gettin' Money" by Dr Jekyll and Mr Hyde.

"Everything is funny when you're gettin' money," they chant, adding a sardonic "Ha-Ha Ha!"

It has its fast-moving entrepreneurs in people like Morgan Kahn of Streetwave Records who, like Chris Blackwell with Island Records' ska and soul releases in the Sixties, is making this new sound accessible with his best-selling "Electro" compilation albums. It is sustained by DJs like Herbie of the Mastermind roadshow, who mixes the "Electro" albums for Streetwave and who, along with Paul Anderson of Trouble Funk, can be guaranteed to draw the crews.

It has even had its popular successes, if sometimes fake (Break Machine's recent "Street Dance") or trite (the Rock Steady Crew's hit last year). And it has an audience hungry for information. Trevor Birch missed the New York rap movie Wild Style when it came out, but when the Rock Steady Crew performed at an electronics fair in Olympia last year, the Technical Poppers were there. They weren't the only ones. The hall was full of Biters, who must have been disappointed. "Their Breakin' was all right but their Poppin' was dry."

In a suburban semi in Wood Green belonging to their manager's parents, the Soul Sonic Rockers are gathered watching a video of their heroes, an American crew named Dynamic Rockers.

"That's wicked, man!"

"His body's like rubber."

"Murder!"

On the video, a frazzled, black-and-white copy of a copy, one of the Dynamic

Rockers is doing a Helicopter – called a Windmill in the US – followed by a Headspin.

"That's my move," says Eddie. "That's one of the hardest moves!"

The Dynamic Rocker comes out of the Headspin, flipping upright into a pose, legs and arms intertwined.

"All Breakers gotta have a pose," laughs Eddie.

And all Breakers must have a nickname too.

The nicknames of the Soul Sonic Rockers are Virgo (Eddie, aged 19), Cream Cracker (Bec, 18), Sleepy Legs (Mussy, 18), Back Flip (Sonay, 16), Crazy Kid (Ozzie, 18) and Exterminator (Mus, 16). Nineteen-year-old Andrew's nickname is Chisel, because he sculpts the Soul Sonic Mixes they dance to, buying two or three US import singles a week with his dole money, and taking eight hours to mix a 45-minute tape with techniques culled from seeing scratching on TV and watching Herbie mix with the Mastermind roadshow.

Eddie and Bec, the two leaders of the crew, met at work in 1982 and formed what was then called the Breakers Crew. Outfitted in Tiger anoraks – "because," says Bec, "all the other crews were wearing Adidas and we wanted something unusual" – the Breakers Crew, which soon grew to comprise several of Bec's Turkish friends, began going to discos like Bananas, Buzby's, the Pink Elephant and the local Nightingale. By last summer, they were Breaking every weekend in Wood Green shopping mall or the West End.

"First time we went out, we got challenged," Bec recalls. A challenge works like this: "If we do 15 Headspins and they do ten, they gotta walk away!" Simple.

They quickly absorbed the language of Hip-Hop: Back Spin, Head Spin, Helicopter (spinning on the shoulders), One-Hand Glider (spinning on one hand), Body Slam (falling on the back), Scorpion (walking on the hands), Crab (it helps if you're double-jointed), Waving, Cracking, Popping. Jeffrey Daniel is the first person they can recall doing Robotics with a hint of Popping when Shalamar appeared on *Top Of The Pops* in 1980 and '81. And they admire the Dynamic Rockers because "they don't Pop, they Smurf and Break". There's an English way of spinning that used to get laughed at in America, they explain, because it was slower. American Poppers use their hands and feet simultaneously so it's harder to copy.

Towards the end of last year, their parents started telling them off for dancing in the streets. Just then, as luck would have it, Ozzie's elder brother saw them and offered to be their manager. They changed their name to Soul Sonic Rockers, after Soul Sonic Force and Dynamic Rockers. Now they have bookings at Hombres and Studio Valbonne, a Thursday-night residency coming up at the Royal Rooms in Edmonton, and their parents are happy. What about their girlfriends?

"They like it man. They like the funny moves!" Mus gets up to demonstrate, Popping his hips in a curious square motion. "But they can't do it. Good thing. Guys hurt themselves enough!"

Nowadays, when people ask them to demonstrate a move, they decline. There are too many Biters around. "We learnt rough, really," muses Eddie, "off the streets. That's where it comes from. The best place for anyone to learn is on the streets. You gotta have all the people around you. Not at home by yourself."

As befits their emerging status, they all now have new red and yellow tracksuits but, since that status is not yet assured, the same old Hi-Tec and Mitre trainers. "It doesn't matter what trainers you use," says Mus. "But you gotta have them. It shows you're a Breaker, you got the style."

Like their Puerto Rican counterparts in New York, Algerians and Africans in Paris, the sons of Germany's "Guest Workers" in Berlin, they have the style. An international style that suits any urban backdrop, fast and madcap like a video game, loose and light like the clothes, portable as a ghetto-blaster, plugged in to the digital rhythm. They are the technological primitives, the Future Tribe. And, as Man Parrish predicted in 1982, they don't stop.

Along with crews like Klymax, Phase 2, The Kleer Crew and Phinx, the Soul Sonic Rockers have come through to the semi-final of the All London Body-Popping, Cracking And Break-Dancing Championship. In the individual stakes, Horace Mills, Ricky Facey from Plaistow, a white teenager named Brian Webster who impressed everybody, and the well-known Soul Boy are all in the contest – which, incidentally, has as its mascot the "1994 Breaking Champ", a seven-year-old called Luke Skywalker.

At the finals in August at the Lyceum Ballroom, they will be competing for prize money of £2,500 – and the chance to emulate the professional success of crews like Zulu Rockers and Sidewalk, the first team to come out of the UK.

If the Technical Poppers win, Trevor Birch wants to use the money to go to New York, where it all started.

"I know they're not all that good but I wanna find out," he says generously. "If I go somewhere where the action is good – clubs open all night – I know I'll get better quicker."

In the window of a sportswear shop in Canning Town is a red, blue and white Hummel tracksuit, the only thing standing between him and the biggest break of all.

PART TWO: THE BEATBOX BITES BACK by David Toop

1984: Two am at The Funhouse and the giant video screen fills with the image of the Master OC's hands scratching an Enjoy 12-inch. OC and Krazy Eddie are vibrating the sound system for the Fearless Four, onstage (and ever-so-human) performing the robot raps of "Problem Of The World", "F-4000" and the one that made their name, "Rockin' It".

Twenty-four years earlier, one night in 1960, Bobby Robinson left his retail store – Bobby's Happy House Records on Harlem's 125th Street – got into his car and drove 60 miles to hear a tune called "Wiggle Wobble".

Robinson, a black record producer who released material by many R&B artists, had heard about the song and the dance craze that went with it. He remembers it clearly: "It was a thing called the Wobble. It was a kind of dance like a wobbling duck and everybody was doing it." The song was a dance instruction novelty performed by Les Cooper, a piano-playing ex-doo-wop singer. Bobby recalls the mayhem it was creating with the crowds and the trimming he felt was in order: "It was a song where people listen – 'You put your right foot forward and then you wiggle to the left' – and all this and that. So I said, 'The very first thing I wanna do is take all the words and throw 'em in the garbage.' So he had a fit. 'No! No! This is the instructions telling them how to do the dance.' I said, 'They know how to do the dance!'"

With his mouth shut firm, Les Cooper took "Wiggle Wobble" to a million sales and beyond on Robinson's Everlast label. It was far from being Bobby's only dance fad success. For the first release on a new label, Enjoy, he launched "Soul Twist" by King Curtis and over two decades later – on the same label – jumped the bandwagon again with "I'm The Packman (Eat Everything I Can)" by The Packman. The Packman wack-awacked electronically rather than wiggle-wobbling acoustically, but dance craze records are consistent over the years. Duck mania or Pacmania – what's the difference?

Records like "I'm The Packman" (tagged electro funk in this country) have made the chips hit the fan. An already sharply divided soul scene in Britain has riven into war zones – discos with mutually hostile rooms for fissured sub-subcultures, guerrilla tactics from fanzines like *Blackbeat*, civil strife in *Echoes* magazine, enemy sympathisers in

Black Music and heavy artillery from radio jock Robbie Vincent (a pithy dismissal, "that electro shit", in The FACE). To the chagrin of white soul fans (traditionalists and jazz funkers) many electro-consumers are young blacks: despite its European Asian influences it is still a major representation of black and Hispanic teen lifestyle in today's urban America.

1982 was the year when the funk warped out into hyperspace. An all-electronic black music had been a long time coming: Sly Stone was using drum machines in the early Seventies (check out "Time" on "There's A Riot Goin' On"); Stevie Wonder's "Music Of My Mind" and "Talking Book" albums established him as a synth innovator; and Sylvia and Joe Robinson's All Platinum set-up in New Jersey used frosty electronic backdrops for the pop disco of The Moments and Sylvia herself.

It was All Platinum, reconstituted as Sugarhill, Bobby Robinson's Enjoy and individual records like Vaughan Mason's "Bounce, Rock, Skate, Roll" which helped establish a new ambience in East Coast post-disco. Slow and heavy, it reflected South and West Bronx break beats. Like an update of Mississippi fife and drum rhythms filtered through the Isley Brothers it led to electronic pulse music only barely clinging to disco conventions. Free Expression's "Chill Out" in 1981 was a crucial record as was "Jazzy Sensation" on Tommy Boy. "Jazzy Sensation" convened hip hop DJ Afrika Bambaataa and various of his MCs with disco DJ Shep Pettibone and producer Arthur Baker. The record had contrasting rap versions of Gwen McCrae's "Funky Sensation" – both used electronic percussion but one featured bass guitar and the other substituted synth bass. You could almost smell the smoke from burning bass guitars and drum kits.

Bambaataa's follow-up, "Planet Rock", was again a collaboration with Baker plus MC group Soul Sonic Force and keyboardist John Robie. Bam wanted to recreate the melodrama of B-boy favourites like Kraftwerk's "Trans Europe Express" or Babe Ruth's "For A Few Dollars More" Morricone cover as well as using rhythmic ideas from Captain Sky's "Super Sperm" and Kraftwerk's "Numbers". A big fan of Yellow Magic Orchestra (you can hear Bam and Jazzy Jay cutting up YMO's "Firecracker" on the notorious "Death Mix" on Winley), he was deeply impressed by Kraftwerk's music and image. "Kraftwerk – I don't think they even know how big they were among the black masses back in '77 when they came out with 'Trans Europe Express'. When that came out I thought that was one of the best and weirdest damn records I ever heard in my life... That's an amazing group to see – just to see what computers and all that can do."

Being a B-boy or B-girl was about being cool. Kraftwerk's four besuited Aryan showroom dummies were passion from the deep freeze. Like a massive joke at the other extreme from George Clinton's theatre of excess, they were fascinating to kids who had grown up parallel with the microchip revolution.

The music tracks for both "Planet Rock" and "Play At Your Own Risk" (a record by Planet Patrol) were recorded in one night. Baker remembers that the sound was partly defined by the lack of technology at that time: "There was no secret to that sound – it was just that we didn't have racks of shit. We had this one PCM (a digital delay unit). In the last year-and-a-half technology has gone haywire. When we did "Planet Rock" that was one of the first records to use a Roland... now everyone has a drum machine."

Funk used to need human metronomes like Hamilton Bohannon, Fatback's Bill Curtis and The JBs' John "Jabo" Starks. Now it has the Roland, an analog drum machine with a microprocessor memory which, along with more sophisticated digital machines like the Linn Drum and the Oberheim DMX, has come to dominate dance music.

The usual whine about robotic machines (they are – that's why kids like them) is to a certain extent irrelevant.

Even if drum machines hadn't existed, disco mixes would have forced somebody to invent them. Bass drums were being pushed further and further to the front of the mix and by 1979 (the last year of classic disco) a record like Walter Gibson's mix of Colleen Heather's "On The Run" (West End) comes across like a four-on-the-floor bass drum solo with vocal accompaniment. The inevitable tiny inconsistencies become terrifying chasms in the pulse. Though drummers like Keith LeBlanc (producer of Malcolm X's "No Sell Out") at Sugarhill and Pumpkin at Enjoy reintroduced bass drum syncopations it was only a matter of time before the new drum machines were following, then outdoing, their patterns. Sharon Redd's "Beat The Street" from 1982 (a record not generally considered electro-funk) has a bass drum playing 16 notes – impossible even for Kung Fu masters or Bionic Women.

One of the first Beat Box records – Grandmaster Flash And The Furious Five's "Flash To The Beat" (Sugarhill) – was an official remake of a bootleg released on Bozzo Meko Records, a live recording from Bronx River Community Centre. "Flash To The Beat" showcased Flash throwing down vicious fills on his ancient Vox percussion box – on the illegal version putting Einsturzende Neubauten to shame.

"Flash To The Beat" and "Planet Rock" grew out of hip hop and were parallel to the late Patrick Cowley's Hi-NRG productions for Sylvester (derived from Giorgio Moroder's sequencer disco) and the electronic soul of D Train, Kashif, The Peech Boys and The System. Most of the latter type of records have proved acceptable to the "serious" soul fraternity in Britain – luckily so, since an enormous amount of black music is now being almost exclusively made with analog and digital equipment. It was the juvenility of electro, though, that stuck in people's throats.

Strange as it may seem, it's hard for some people to see pop culture as inspirational. Electro is craze music, a soundtrack for vidkids to live out fantasies born of a science fiction revival (courtesy of *Star Wars* and *Close Encounters*) and the video games onslaught.

Nobody can play Defender or Galaxian for long without being affected by those sounds – sickening rumbles and throbs, fuzzy explosions and maddening tunes – and when Gorf and Gorgar began to talk the whole interactive games phenomenon took on a menacing aspect. Do they know you've just spent all your mother's money? Do they care that your fantasies are saturated with deep blue space wars and glowing violet electronic insects? All the electro boogie records that flew in the "Planet Rock" slipstream used a variant on imagery drawn from computer games, video, cartoons, sci-fi and hip hop slanguage. Just as The Cuff Links defined relationships through nuclear war images in their song "Guided Missiles" (recorded in the A-Bomb-conscious Fifties), so, on "Nunk" in 1982, Warp 9 sang: "Girl, you're looking good on my video..."

Space breaking releases included Planet Patrol's "Play At Your Own Risk", Tyrone Brunson's "The Smurf", The Fearless Four's "Rockin' It" (with its spooky "they're here" intro taken from *Poltergeist*). "Hip Hop Be Bop (Don't Stop)" by Man Parrish, George Clinton's "Computer Games" album, "Scorpio" by Flash And The Furious Five and The Jonzun Crew's "Pack Jam".

Planet Patrol are a vocal quintet from Boston (a breeding station for asteroid funkers) originally called The Energetics, who applied their skills to a classic Baker/Robie rhythm. The record mixed acoustic piano with synthesizers and dub delay effects – tagged onto the end of the instrumental is a brilliant a cappella section which speeds and slows the hip hop version of applause (a sort of macho dog bark).

The dog bark turned up again on Man Parrish's record – produced by Parrish (a white Brooklyn-born synth-freak whose previous experience included porno soundtrack writing) and Raul A Rodriguez, a disco jock currently producing The Two Sisters on "B Boys Beware" and "High Noon".

"The Smurf" by Washington DC-born bass player Tyrone Brunson was pure dance craze instrumental. Smurfing was a New York dance inspired by one of the Saturday morning TV cartoon shows, a fertile source of imagery for graffiti artists and catch-phrases for rappers. Smurfs, like all great historical figures, have a complex back-ground. Originally based on characters from Spiro, a French comic of the Sixties, they became an international promo tool, a Dutch hit record (thanks to the genius of Father Abraham) and a series of dance discs. The latter included "Letzmeurph Acrossdasurf" by The Micronawts (actually a *Village Voice* critic, Barry Michael Cooper, with a dub mix by Bambaataa) on Aaron Fuchs' Tuff City label; "Salsa Smurf" by Special Request (a Tommy Boy collaboration between two contributors to NYC radio station 92KTU – Carlos DeJesus and Jose "Animal" Daiaz, who also mixed Rhetta Hughes' electro Hi-NRG "Angel Man") and "Smerphies Dance" on Telstar by Spyder D, a young man named Duane Hughes who, to my knowledge, is the only hip hopper to carry a business card.

Another dance craze of the period was the Webo or Huevo (Spanish for egg). The Webo had its very own audiotrack, typical of '82/'83 madhouse club mixes, called "Huevo Dancing" by Fresh Face. "Huevo Dancing" was a creation of veteran soul singer/producer George Kerr and keyboardist/guitarist Reggie Griffin. Its violent elec-tric drums and seemingly random attacks on the mixing desk faders give it a special place in my heart. Both Kerr and Griffin were associated with the Sylvia and Joe Robinson empire and Reggie Griffin went on to make his own electro boogie record "Mirada Rock" for Sweet Mountain Records, a Sugarhill subsidiary.

Also doing time at Sugarhill with some uncredited session work was Michael Jonzun, of the despised, yet totally brilliant, Jonzun Crew. "Pack Jam" on Tommy Boy is one of the toughest records of the last few years (I say that as a person old enough to have seen The Ronettes and Otis Redding live on stage). Like "Mirada Rock" ("I am a com-puter") or Tilt's "Arkade Funk" ("I am an arkade funk machine") there was no beating about the bush. "Pack Jam" was a video game record and if adults wanted to run scared that was their business.

Many of the electro musicians and producers recognise their music as the fusion that it is – street funk and hip hop mixed with influences from British synthesizer groups, Latin music and jazz fusion – all thrown into the robot dancing, breaking and moonwalk-ing meltdown. Lotti Golden and Richard Scher, producers/writers for Warp 9, Chilltown and Ladies' Choice, called their first Casio-powered Warp 9 release "Nunk", a hybrid of N-ew wave and f-UNK.

Electro is closer to past African-American fusions than a lot of the Seventies disco pro-moted by British disc jockeys currently running anti-electro campaigns ("Magic Fly" by Space, for example, a regular on early editions of Robbie Vincent's Radio London show) and it is arguable that it shows stronger black music roots than certain popular jazz funk or soft soul records of recent years. Everybody acknowledges the pioneering of Miles Davis and Herbie Hancock in combining electronics with funk, Afro, Latin and jazz (check out "On The Corner" and "Headhunters") and Material's production on Hancock's "Future Shock" was obliquely inspired by Hancock's own mid-Seventies albums.

The current phase of electro, particularly electro rap and scratch mixes, is like a black metal music for the Eighties, a hard edged, ugly, beautiful trance as desperate and stimulating as New York itself. Run DMC's records on Profile are direct-to-disc wall poems; The B Boys, The Boogie Boys, The Beat Box Boys, Davy DMX, Pumpkin and DJ Divine – all physical graffiti on music history books. For the Cold Crush Brothers, the Mad Max warriors of rap, their "Punk Rock Rap" is a reflection of the exotica of white rock uptown in Washington Heights.

Nothing is sacred in the computer age. As computer programmers, copyright lawyers and corporations struggle to protect themselves against micro raiders and mashers, the vidkids swarm down from the top of the screen, hungry for the cosmic crash.

Wackawackawackawackawackawacka •

15   SPEED!

MAY 1984

Thursday-night skating at The Ace, Brixton by Lesley White

THURSDAY NIGHTS AT The Ace in Brixton are deafeningly loud, impossibly hot and, if you stray on to the dancefloor as a novice roller-skater, very dangerous. Through his huge PA, DJ Tim Westwood halts the resounding electro beat for a moment to announce: "The BBC are looking for a black female skater under 16 for a ten-week TV series." A few hopeful glances are exchanged, the music cuts back to Divine Sounds' "Dollar Baby Dub", and with the first speed-session of the evening, the going gets tough. Ace skaters are 99.9 per cent black, mostly males in their late teens, and less concerned with artistry than simply being fastest. Local reputations are at stake; some-one estimates the top speed at 40mph but marshals slow things down when the pace gets too hot. The Ace reopened two months ago to cater for a skating/soul scene that had gone "underground and completely black" after the closure two years ago of the mixed and vastly popular Starlight in Hammersmith. "It is difficult to keep control," com-ments the exuberant Westwood, "but the crowd know me and I'm really strict with them. What's important about the place is the music; the kids come for that as much as to skate. For me it's the only place where I can play electro and soul music. It's not a purist crowd and that's refreshing with the soul scene being so split." For soul, the favourite tracks are: "She's Strange" by Cameo, Curtis Mayfield's "What's My Woman For" and the Fatback Band's "I Found Lovin'"; for electro the Ace movers are Newcleus' "Jam On It" and the Beat Box Boys' "Eat 'Em Up". "What we're trying to promote now is skate dancing," adds Westwood, pointing, though he hardly needs to, to a tall, track-suited young man dancing, aloof and alone in the centre of the floor. Ramsey Cain, a 26-year-old ex-carpenter with £100 worth of wheels on his heels, is out to make a living from all this. "I don't talk to anyone down here; they probably think I'm just showing off. I come to work out." Ramsey learned to skate dance four years ago at the Starlight – he's since danced at Gossips, the Embassy and the Hippodrome and has just obtained his Equity card. "I love it; it makes you feel special. I'm trying to become a cheerleader on *Top Of The Pops* – I've been there loads of times pretending I was one of the dancers. I got caught last time. I also auditioned for *Starlight Express*." And? "I didn't get it – they said because of my voice but I think I was probably too good!" •

16   BOYSTOWN NIGHTS

SEPTEMBER 1984

Hi-NRG by Dave Hill

ON DECEMBER 7, 1974, the second best-selling single in the UK was Gloria Gaynor's "Never Can Say Goodbye". The song had been a a hit three years earlier for The Jackson Five, but this was no pale cover imitation. The original mid-tempo tune now raced by in a sumptuous swirl of strings and sizzling hi-hat. Ms Gaynor's euphoric delivery transformed the lyric from one of despairing infatuation to one of delicious revelry. She sang with a new kind of ostentatious soul. The record oozed luxurious indulgence; a plush pursuit of the pleasurable. It was the first genuine, guaranteed-by-connoisseurs disco to go glistening overground.

As I write, another black American female singer has just made the chart. The FACE on the record's sleeve belongs to Evelyn Thomas. The voice, again is strong, ecstatic, delighted. It soars above an obtrusive, electronically-created pulse beat and a sequence of insistent ascendant chords. The song is all about being picked up on the street and falling directly in love. "Hi-NRG" is its title, and Hi-NRG is the label increasingly attached to the form. The significance of this record's success is that people are beginning to say that disco music has been born again. The philosophy remains the same, but the sound has moved into modern, silicon times. And this time it's in Britain that the pace is being set. The producer and co-composer of "Hi-NRG" is a white man from Blackpool called Ian Levine. He describes his music with almost evangelical zeal.

"What makes a good Hi-NRG record is very hard to define. As long as it has a fairly fast rhythm – something between 120 and 140 beats per minute – it has the potential. But it's also consistency of beat, and what I call the concept of light and shade. This is very important to me. Nobody else," he says, a little primly, "seems to have grasped it. To be exciting the record has to build up to peaks where everything is playing at once, and then drop down to areas where it's not, as if the floor had suddenly dropped away from under you. It's the concept of breaks. But more than that, it's realising what sets of chords cause the crowd to excite themselves as you approach the peaks; a set of chords that lift you up. That in itself is exciting and then the build-up is exciting again!"

Ian Levine's other career is the perfect partner to his work as a producer. He's been the resident DJ at Europe's largest gay-oriented disco, Heaven, since it adopted that name on December 6, 1979. Over the last year he has seen what he calls the most knowledgeable crowd in the country respond enthusiastically to a series of records with his name on the label: "Emergency" by Laura Pallas; "I'm Living My Own Life" by Earlene Bentley; "Primitive Desire" by Eastbound Expressway; and the market-tailored "So Many Men, So Little Time" by Miquel Brown. Scenting the prospect of crossover success, Levine and the Street Sounds label have put together a brace of compilations in which Levine mixes together his own work and hits by American artists like a rejuvenated Gloria Gaynor, Sharon Redd and (of course) Eartha Kitt with the contributions of British production contemporaries like Ian Stevens and Kevin Roberts. It was Stevens who produced Hi-NRG's second current Top 40 entry, Hazell Dean's "Searching". But it is Roberts' contributions to the second compilation that most strongly betray the heritage of disco's promised revival. Velvette's "Nothing's Worse Than Being Alone", Linda Lewis's "You Turned My Bitter Into Sweet" and Yvonne Gidden's "In Orbit" are all songs taken from the Hall of Fame Of... Northern Soul.

"Myself, Ian, Kev and Les McCutcheon – who put Shakatak together – all used to DJ on the Northern circuit. We all live in England, and between us we produce 90 per cent of the Hi-NRG stuff that comes from here. Somehow, between us, we've managed to bring those influences back into the music, rather than Seventies American disco. That, together with the new technology, has enabled us to somehow create a new sound that's been born from the old.

As a teen, Levine's mission in life was to own every Tamla Motown record there was. In the summer he'd holiday with his parents in Miami, and spend the time scouring America's Facelift City for the ones he couldn't get at home. He discovered other records which weren't on Motown but which had the Motown beat, and as the Northern scene grew at the turn of the Seventies at Manchester's Twisted Wheel, Levine's record collection was, he says, in demand. Still in his teens, he was too young to get in to all but the last three of the Wheel's all-nighters before it closed in 1971. But when the scene's focus shifted to Blackpool's Mecca Highland Room he got to spin the discs himself, alongside Tony Jebb and Wheel refugee Les Tickell.

Through the mid-Seventies, Levine found regular work during the constant turnover of venues, most notably at the Torch in Stoke-on-Trent and a revamped Highland Room from '73 to '75. After compiling a Northern Soul compilation for Pye, he got his break in record production, going to New York to work with a struggling band called The Exciters who'd found favour in the North with songs they'd recorded the previous decade. The resulting "Reaching For The Best" made number 31 in the UK; a Northern dancefloor crossover.

But in New York, something else was going on... "The disco scene was really building up in the gay clubs. It was parallel to the Northern scene, but nobody realised it. These were records with the same rhythm, but with the hi-hat sizzling. The Gloria Gaynor stuff was just updated Motown in essence. I discovered a fascination with the New York disco sound, as it was called then."

Back in 1969, a watershed in gay history had occurred. After years of harassment from police, the patrons of the Stonewall bar in Greenwich Village put up barricades to keep the cops at bay. The incident escalated into five days of rioting, and gave birth to the Gay Liberation Front.

"There was a new gay awakening after that, explains Levine. "There hadn't been any openly gay clubs before. Now people weren't afraid to go out and say that they were gay."

Along with a new rhetoric, the scene developed its own soundtrack. What would later become a seamless aural cocoon for a self-contained lifestyle began, at first, by accident. The DJ is playing current American pop records, but there's one song that he particularly likes which no one has ever heard of. He gives it the occasional spin, and sees the crowd respond.

"One of the first of these," Levine recalls, "was a B-side by The Four Tops called 'Don't Bring Back Memories', which had a different beat to the usual Motown stuff – more of a shuffle beat. The DJ, realising that people wanted more, would buy two copies of the record, work out how he could cue one into the other, making the record seem twice as long – which led to mixing. The DJ at a club called the Sanctuary was the first to actually mix rather than talk between records."

As artist and producers caught on to this new underground taste, the number of specifically disco records being made grew steadily from 1972 through to 1974. And then came Gloria, followed by a spate of hits by Crown Heights Affair, Silver Convention, and on and on. Few really matched the flair and strength of Gaynor, although the music's reputation for dumbness was not always justified. But the main reason for the transient impression given by this first overground burst was the anonymity of the artists. By 1976, what was needed was for the sound to become associated with a male het-hero to woo those clean US dollars. Either that or a milky-black Bad Girl with moist lips and a multi-orgasmic sigh. Both of them arrived. Hello John Travolta. Hello Donna Summer. "Love To Love You Baby"... OK!

"By 1979 every record company in America wanted to put out disco records. Andy Williams, Rod Stewart... they were all at it. And that beat goes right back to the days of Motown. It all started there with a Four Tops B-Side. 'Love Is Like An Itch In My Heart' by The Supremes is the ultimate Hi-NRG disco record, and the damn thing is 18 years old!"

Nine-thirty pm in Soho's Trident Studios. Ian Levine and his co-writer/arranger Fianchra Trench are squabbling. Trench is manning an electronic keyboard unit of some esoteric brand. Levine wants him to produce a noise like a horn section.

"Why not get a proper horn section to do it?" asks an irritated Trench.

"Because," replies pedantic Levine, "it isn't supposed to sound like a proper horn section, but it is supposed to have the same punch as one. What we're doing is using the influences of yesterday with the sound of today!"

They're going to be here all night, the two of them with their regular engineer. The team are working hard these days. Every Tuesday, Wednesday and Saturday night, Levine DJs at Heaven till 3am. The rest of the time he's in here making records for release on the label run by a Berwick Street shop, Record Shack. With the success of discs like The Weather Girls "It's Raining Men", plus those by Evelyn Thomas and Ms Dean, the boy from Blackpool has spied his ship on the horizon, and nothing will stop him from wooing it to the shore. His gift for self-promotion has already seen him lose a Hi-NRG music column for *City Limits*; Levine was caught giving rave reviews to 45s he'd mixed! But, remember, he missed out last time.

"We created a new scene at Heaven by playing purely American disco music, but it was at about the same time that the disco market slumped. It was just overkill. Donna Summer's album sales dropped, and suddenly there was a shortage of new records. We had to look to places like France, Italy... anywhere. Even Canada for a while. I explained to Howard and Geoff from Record Shack that I didn't want all the funk records they were selling to the straight DJs. I wanted much faster music, and they would have to get it."

Record Shack delivered, and within a few years became the nation's top supplier of Hi-NRG music. Levine persuaded them that with a couple of thousand pounds he could make the perfect 45 for the market, and with sales of ten or 15 thousand, they'd all make a decent profit. The record was "So Many Men, So Little Time". It did better than they hoped. It sold nearly three million copies worldwide.

"Now my name on a record in America means instant recognition," boasts Levine. "What goes at Heaven goes at the Saint; and the Saint I consider to be the top club in America."

For all that, though, Hi-NRG disco has its detractors. Levine complains that his music is often overlooked by Britain's black music press.

"*Blues & Soul, Black Music*, and *Echoes* dislike it because of its gay connotation," he says, "which is doubly ridiculous because it's not gay music. It's music that gays like. It is particularly hurtful too, because it is as much a form of soul music as

Jocelyn Brown or Tina Turner or anybody. The singing is incredibly soulful!"

And the arguments ramble on. Is Hi-NRG all body and no soul? Undeterred, Levine insists that he remains loyal to his roots in Northern Soul, and – for all his passion to win mainstream success – negates any suggestion that his original audience will be deserted for the sake of "respectable" pop acclaim.

"I'm gay," he asserts, "I'm a gay DJ in the largest gay club in Europe, and I'm making music which appeals to gays. But I go out of my way to make music which doesn't appeal only to gays. That's very important to me. Take Miquel's big hit. That's a woman singing that she'd like to sleep with a different man every night. The gays, of course, put themselves in her place, and plenty of them do sleep with a different man every night. Sure! But, at the same time, middle-aged housewives can very easily relate to the idea as well. The problem comes when you have a guy singing that kind of lyric, which narrows its appeal too much to one market. You see, we can't publicly acknowledge the gay aspect of it too much. Of course, it's not always true. We've seen Tom Robinson and Frankie Goes To Hollywood. Nonetheless, I don't think there's any harm in putting out gay scene records and not telling the public. It's when you deny it that I think it's wrong, like the Village People did. From Record Shack's point of view, it's better not to say anything, except to its gay audience. That way you're keeping faith with the people who've made you successful without alienating the larger public. I'm clever about it though… most of them are either universal love or hate songs, but you'll notice that they never actually include the word 'girl'."

Get Set For Sweat. The US-style dance-space buried behind Charing Cross station just has to be the most elaborately flashy club in the country. There are lasers, light shows and videos, there are hyperactive bars upstairs and down, and counters selling postcards of men with no shirts on. Out on the floor, bodies lurch, sway and glide. They are in Heaven. Upstairs in his control centre, Levine keeps a careful appraisal of the crowd.

"Gays like melodic, straightforward dance music that's not too funky. Like Motown it's zingy and pretty, but powerful. Blacks in the States are much more into electro and the street stuff. Gays are still into the simple 4/4 beat, but the vocals have to be soulful. The other thing with gays is that they love the glamorous female. Most gays like Barbra Streisand and Diana Ross. It's the outrageous, the over-the-top that appeals to them. My theory is that they prefer a raunchier type of female image, rather than the Page Three sort, because that's supposed to be the ultimate heterosexual idea, and they have no interest in that."

The term "gay" usually refers only to men – a single-gender appropriation which causes consternation in the politicised sectors of gay/lesbian communities. Scene insiders, though, rubbish Hip New Right accusations of rampant misogyny in the ranks, and folks of both sexes and every preference can sample Hi-NRG music at Heaven on Tuesday nights.

"Every gay person has to go through a period of soul-searching before coming out, and it takes great courage," says Levine, in defence of this particular men-only culture, "therefore we are entitled to a space where we can relax and socialise with our own kind." As someone recently said of Marilyn, Burns and George, everyone loves a Freak so long as it stays on the stage.

Meanwhile the beat booms on. At worst, Hi-NRG music can be monotonous, over-long and prone to self-indulgent producers. At best it is sexy, luxurious and scintillating… classically camp and funny. It urges independence, self-confidence, do-and-be-damned. Its dancers are far too involved to find time to pose, and conservative critics have been confounded by its broad-based consumer appeal.

"The Northern scene hates it," says Levine, none too stung. "They don't understand that all my stuff started from there. Ten years from now, of course, they'll discover it."

Right now, the new gay disco belongs to everyone •

17   DEATH BY DISCO

NOVEMBER 1984

Last orders for the English pub by Paul Rambali

WHEN CENTRAL GOVERNMENT served notice that, in the event of the Big Bang, town halls would be responsible for the safety of people, Hackney, London's poorest borough, gained national fame by simply shrugging off this great duty. We are too hard-pressed, claimed the Labour-led council. Surveying the debris of industrial decline, the crumbling warehouses, the empty factories, the boarded shop windows, you had to agree. Hackney turned the question on its head: will there be life before the bomb?

The district seems, in places, to have barely recovered from the last global flare-up. Acres of land lie idle from V2s that fell between the huge, sombre Victorian hospitals, no longer soot-blackened but still faintly satanic, one of which still guards the body of the Elephant Man. There are streets of prefabs with names like Peace Road, makeshift homes that somebody forgot to shift.

Given this setting, it's hard to believe what people say about the Hackney Road: that, at times, it looks more like Oxford Street. On Friday and Saturday nights, especially in summer, an area defined by the Commercial Road to the south, Hackney Road to the north, Old Street to the west and Bethnal Green to the east, becomes a bustling throng of Top Shop Girls and Youth At C&A.

Within this square mile-or-so, no less than 15 "pubs" have opened in the last few years to cater to young people's need for loud soul music, flashing lights, ritzy furnishings, plush carpets, mirrored walls and attractive, under-dressed bar staff.

You wonder why nobody thought of it before... The loud music fills those awkward gaps in the conversation, the flashing lights help disguise those awkward skin blemishes even as the mirrored walls provide for quick glances of reassurance. Heaven knows what plush carpets, wicker chairs and fake palms do, but attractive under-dressed female bar staff satisfy an obvious need – ie. they exchange cash for drinks. Only they do it more often than ugly male barstaff might.

Decorated in the international leisure style, these pubs are hybrids of the discotheque and the cocktail bar. They are hardly pubs at all in the traditional sense, though the patrons are evidently so accustomed to the type that they call them just that, as if a pub was never anything else but a little bit of the West End transplanted East. Perhaps the word is ineradicable from the British psyche. Discos and bars are things originally found abroad, and a pub by any other name...

The names are a study in themselves – Lipstick, Strawberrys, Tipples, Queens, 5th Avenue (who ever heard of a pub named 5th Avenue?). Like the stylistic cocktail of the decor, the names are straight out of a deluxe Freeman's dream catalogue. They denote: sex, luxury, travel. They sound like wine bars. But they are pubs. Look closely at the matt black exteriors, the darkened interiors, and you can see, painted over behind the neon lighting, mirrors and framed prints, the old wood beams and floral cornicing. Beneath the hot-pink and purple awnings that flash and beckon are the old frosted-glass windows covered as though with heavy mascara. Tarted up, so to speak.

All of them are tenanted – owned or run by landlords independently of the breweries. One such is a pub that used to be called The Beachcomber, and before that, The Arabian Arms, famed in the vicinity for being among the first to introduce strippers to the drinking public.

Run by the same landlord for 19 years, The Beachcomber, as it was then, would try anything – cabaret acts, drag artists, strippers, even a gay disco – to keep the tills ringing. Towards the end of the Seventies, though, the live entertainment had begun to pale, the strippers had nothing left to unpeel. Returning from a holiday in Miami, the landlord's son had an idea for turning The Beachcomber into a kind of bar similar to ones he had seen in the US.

At a cost of £50,000, they installed disco lights, a giant video, lasers, a thick dark-blue carpet, low-slung cane sofas and smoked-glass tables, mirrors on the walls, fake palms, even a small rock pool with a fountain and, yes, fish. Changing the name to Martin's, adding a cocktails-only bar and with the benefit of a late licence, they opened their doors to an approving new clientele.

Previously, you had to go to Stringfellows or pay a hefty door charge at local nightclubs to enjoy such an exclusive ambience. In the midst of the recession, Martin's was packed. Another pub along the road soon changed its name to Tipples, and yet more followed. Nowadays, the area draws people from as far as the coast, 50-odd miles away.

"It's all down to novelty," affirms Steve, who DJs while his father stands at the door, his jovial landlord's paunch covered by a fashionably coloured jumper. Novelty doesn't come cheap. "If you haven't got £10,000 worth of carpet you haven't got the customers. If you haven't got the decor they aren't interested. During the week they come in just to sit and look at the place." Steve spends £80 a week on records, mostly imports, and £200 a month on videos. "Staff and electricity bills are ridiculous – treble the cost of an ordinary pub."

All this is recouped, of course. Beer is £1 a pint, spirits with mixers £1.10, cocktails £2 each – average prices for the area. Pina Coladas are the favourite cocktail. "Otherwise, anything with a sparkler in it. We've run out of 'em at the moment, but if we're down on Tom Collinses, say, we stick a sparkler in it and sell plenty! Novelty – that's what they want."

Not least among the novelties are the barmaids, who sport a different risqué outfit each week. This week the theme, excitingly enough, is St Trinian's. "We've even tried roller skates once," adds Steve, gamely admitting it "didn't work too well..."

Leaving aside sparklers in cocktails and the latest videos, there really isn't that much to choose between Martin's and Tipples, or Good Sam's and The White Hart. Perhaps that's why most people don't choose between them, but progress from one to the next in a continual and steadily more drunken and raucous parade, finally settling in one or other of those with a late licence.

The proliferation of the disco pubs has been only slightly faster than the multiplication of customers, peaking this summer when swarms of people spilled through the streets, promenading back and forth during the warm evenings in a manner imported, like the ubiquitous Kappa tops, from the continent.

Examining these customers, one notes that the predominant male style is, well, casual. The brand names of Nike, Kappa and Gambicci are everywhere, and this season's new development seems to be the blouson-style overshirt with drawstring neck, stuffed into the usual Lois jeans with the usual frayed cuffs. Nothing heavier than a loafer treads upon the deep-pile carpets, lest it be the spike of a pair of high heels.

While the males are obsessively casual, the girls are ludicrously overdressed. That's not to say they are wearing a great many clothes exactly... just dressed up. Wandering into these pubs for the first time, suddenly surrounded by short sleeves and short skirts, there is the odd impression that everyone else has just changed from the beach. And maybe they have, because what is going on here is lifestyle, a state of mind as much as dress.

And the major breweries have not been slow to note it. They've taken just long enough to be convinced it's not a fad. Looking at Hackney's disco pubs, and at others like The Dun Cow, the Oasis and Gilley's south-east of the Thames, they have divined a trend. As enterprising landlords in other parts of London convert to this new formula, the breweries are busy conceiving their own fun pubs, theme pubs and – my favourite, since it's so garishly accurate – high-tech young-set pubs. Charringtons has its chain of Exchange bars, and Courage has opened Promises in Birmingham and Liverpool and The Boulevard in Bristol.

Pubs is not quite the word for them, cocktail bars is hardly adequate and even disco pubs is a misnomer. While they all feature loud music – always mainstream disco and soul – few have dancefloors or dance licences. Nobody appears to mind much, for this is disco as background, disco as lifestyle. Nobody even notices that it's disco at all.

But background to what? Not the sort of activity you'd expect in a disco. There is remarkably little pulling going on. Though the mating rituals provide an underlying current like the static from the carpet, it is energy that seems to go nowhere.

The girls giggle and disappear to the toilets in pairs. The boys booze in rowdy bunches. The cliques and groupings all seem familiar to each other, by sight at least. An easy, but oddly closed cordiality prevails. In this respect, if no other, you are back in the English pub. Back in Hackney, that little corner of England that will be forever Ibiza •

18   HOLIDAY BABYLON

SEPTEMBER 1985

Animal Nightlife in Ibiza by Don Macpherson

CHEAP AND OLD and exotic and beautiful was how the American novelist Clifford Irving described the island of Ibiza. When he settled there in the Fifties it was known as La Isla Blanca, the white island, a forgotten chunk of Mediterranean rock closer to North Africa than Barcelona. He and his bohemian friends savoured their paradise of "the simple life" where wine was drunk by the bottle, fish sold fresh from the harbour, and nobody bothered who you were or told you what to do. With its cheap property, all-year sun, lenient tax laws and absence of extradition treaties for foreign offenders, Ibiza became an attractive bolt-hole for expatriates like Irving and the Hungarian artist Elmyr de Hory. As long as the electricity worked for the fridge, and the telephone was connected to their agents in London, Paris, Rome or New York, Ibiza's legend as the playground of the artistic, rich and famous was made.

The island's cast list became strangely reminiscent of some low-budget Italian sex comedy featuring beach beauties like Ursula Andress, idling aristocracy like Baron Frederik von Palandt and a veritable colony of English cads and thespians such as Leslie Phillips, Terry Thomas, Denholm Elliot and Nigel Davenport.

By the time the package-holiday business discovered Ibiza it was already the home of an array of the rich and beautiful, con-men and fraudsters, would-be's and have-beens, models and movie stars, a variously posh and preposterous galaxy that included everyone from ex-MI6 drug smuggler Howard Marks to Lulu, Nikki Lauda and Jack Nicholson.

It was the democracy of the beach and the G-string, where millionaires rubbed shoulders and more with riff-raff and royalty from the corners of the free world, and the only class distinction was a sun-tan.

All those great artistic ideas and designs, however, just seemed to get half-baked in the sun. By the early Seventies, Ibiza's most famous expatriates, Irving and de Hory, were both in jail for fraud – Irving for faking the autobiography of Howard Hughes, de Hory for forging countless pictures by Matisse, Modigliani and Chagall. Nobody on Ibiza seemed to care, however. If anything, their misadventures actually made the island more attractive.

From Düsseldorf, Bilbao, Milan, Oslo, Zurich and Birmingham, people flooded in for fortnights in the sun, swelling the island's population of 65,000 to nearly a million in July and August. Maybe they didn't catch sight of Roman Polanski, Adnan Khashoggi, Harrison Ford or Goldie Hawn at the nearby discos or bars. But there was a good chance they might be at the next one, or the next one. Thus was born a unique form of nightlife, which involved a roving army of jeeps, sports cars and saloons obeying a strict schedule of pit-stop visits to a series of discotheques and restaurants that were haunted by the famous.

It only remained for British nobility to claim a foothold on the island, and Wham! were the first. Their "Club Tropicana" video was made in the remote and exclusive Ibiza hotel of Pike's, itself part of the island's mythology, establishing the icons of swimming pools, cocktails, pretty girls and handsome pop stars which anybody could imitate.

It was to have disastrous consequences.

Quisiera uno 'Coco Loco', por favor.
("A rum cocktail, please.")

If Ibiza hadn't existed, Island Records might have invented it as a backdrop for their new signing, Animal Nightlife. The five-piece London band, headed by singer Andy Polaris, were already local clubbing legends with songs such as "Native Boy", "Mr Solitaire" and "After Hours"; bittersweet descriptions of the delights of midnight commuting between the likes of Finsbury Park or Leyton and the bright lights of Soho.

But after spending last summer recording an album in Philadelphia, and preparing its launch in Britain and Europe, somewhere less... tacky was required: somewhere more exotic and beautiful than The Hammersmith Palais, more glittering than the Hackney Road, more swish than anywhere the 38 night-bus travelled, where the jaded palates of both the band and the likes of the *Mirror* pop column could be tempted. For that purpose there was only one answer: Ibiza's Ku Club.

The Ku is the sort of place that has anticipated some as-yet untapped part of Peter Stringfellow's imagination. It is a vast open-air fun palace of coloured lights, swimming pools, beautiful people, loud music and upmarket prices, situated just off the main road between the heavenly chic of Ibiza town and the packaged hell of San Antonio. Between the hours of 2.30 and 5.30 in the morning, this is the place to be.

But remember those hours. For you must obey the schedule. Before that time, you can eat, drink or attend clubs like the Pacha in the old town, Es Paradis in San An' or the new, classically-styled Summum discotheque, an event in itself. But attendance at the Ku before about 1.30am can be considered impossibly vulgar, especially if you want to extract maximum value from your £15 ticket.

It's this kind of unwritten rule, denoting exclusivity and flying in the face of all common sense, that attracted the attention of the *Mirror* pop correspondent, who revealed herself to be a Miss Marple-like sleuth of style and all matters trendy. Her beady eye missed nothing. Ha-ha! Some poor fool's wearing dayglo! Don't they know that was "in" last year? Some Spanish boutique assistant resembles Steve Strange! Hah!! At least two or three years out of date!! From the strict gaze of this Miss Style, no one escaped censure.

To this witheringly fashionable eye, Animal Nightlife's performance at the Ku must have yielded few clues. Clad in shorts and sandals whilst parading on the shell-like stage above a clear blue pool, the band resembled classic Englishers on holiday: they wore nothing more up-to-the-moment than a white T-shirt. As they progressed through their set of jazzy soul, Andy Polaris' voice accompanied by Billy Chapman's sax floated into the warm night breeze. In such an atmosphere, music and image seemed timeless, effortless, supremely relaxed.

The closest thing to a gimmick occurred when Andy Polaris appeared for a final encore clad in a towel, suddenly disrobed, and dived into the pool to great cheers. Hurriedly he dried himself and managed to return to the mike for the final chorus as the Ku's fountains were turned on to drench spectators crowded on to a catwalk. That was it. No fireworks, no heavy-metal-meets-hip hop, no costume changes, no last-minute filling the stage with transvestites... Miss Style looked sullenly over the crowd. There was not a *Mirror* headline in sight. What to do! What to say? Hah! Surely cool jazz was last year's thing? Yes!! Perhaps they're obsolete! But what if they're next year's craze? On the treadmill of style these days, nobody can be quite sure of the clues.

Luckily for the *Mirror*, the species of animal nightlife among the crowd was top Ibiza standard. On the dancefloor, quiffed male peacocks in turquoise and scarlet strutted in their own designs, while two or three bejewelled Madonna marmosets swirled deliriously in black chiffon. The parading population resembled a pride of baboons as they energetically displayed their technicolour rumps to one another in obscure mating rituals. A Deutsche fraülein, decked in leopardskin and thigh-length boots, valiantly roused her leathery mate to one more rock climax, while a balding man who looked very much like Charlie Drake – but with a G-string firmly pulled between his buttocks – boogied soulfully as his gut sagged in time to Tina Turner and The Eurythmics.

This was where the rich and the beautiful hang out, as well as just the would-be jet-set trash, their tanned features concealing the lines of age or class in their faces. Instead – in an anthropological reversal worthy of note by Levi-Strauss – tribal attention was focused on bottoms: bronzed by Hawaiian Tropic, giant wobbling orbs, or the aged DH Lawrence sun-worshipping variety revealing the truth of their owners. Among the club's animal nightlife were so many svelte cheetahs but not a few holiday chameleons, as well as less pleasant reptiles such as wrinkled lizards, hissing snakes, and the odd ageing vulture in varying states of undress. But in this menagerie, among all the extreme plumage, among the leather trousers, sombreros, Gaultier tops, one item of clothing stood out: a seemingly mild-mannered male, calmly sipping a cocktail by the bar, wore a T-shirt inscribed thus: "I FUCK LIKE A BEAST".

"Pillage and rape desolated Ibiza for centuries."
(*Berlitz Travel Guide*)

It was a slogan more in keeping with the bars of San Antonio, a few miles down the road, than with the Ku Club. For if the Ku is Ibiza's heaven, then San Antonio is hell. It's not really surprising, since the seaside resort is almost exclusively English – in Andy Polaris' description, "like Hackney transported to a tropical island, all Sharon and Debs and fish and chips".

In bars named The Londoner, The Irish Pub, The West End, The Village Tavern and Sergeant Pepper's, the videos of Max Headroom and the Whistle Test never stop and the cerveza flows until three in the morning. After this the alternatives consist of falling over, throwing up, punching someone, or jumping onto the bonnet of a passing car and seeing where you end up.

In the crowded streets, the San An' atmosphere is distinctly British: lads wearing shirts from Leeds Utd or Spurs, ladies in Top Shop or Chelsea Girl. Some risk ridicule and attempt to "go Ibizan", opting for dainty white suede boots and white flowing dresses. But it seems that nobody's heart is really in it. For this is Britain-on-the-Med, a tiny ghetto in which the pubs stay open past eleven and football-team fans can unite against a common enemy: Spanish police. At £157 for a fortnight, anyone can purchase the chance to visit Wham!'s mythical Club Tropicana.

In the end you have to hand it to them: everyone seemed so determined to have a damned good time, whether at The Playboy Club, the Miss Sexy competition or The OK Corrall bar, that onlookers seemed just to wish them well; sure, it was bad for Ibiza, and bad for tourism, but what the hell.

There seemed more potential *Mirror* headlines in San An' than at the Ku Club. For surely few stories are more appealing for homebound readers than the Hard-Luck-On-

Holiday-Island tale. It satisfies all: it leaves those back in Blighty soundly of the opinion that they were right not to cross the Channel, and it fuels the paranoia that the British holidaygoer's annual fortnight of debauchery might be spoiled by shifty foreigners.

The myths were plentiful this year, and the reality wasn't far behind: young Spanish thieves waiting outside apartment blocks at 3am to catch the drunks; gangs of thugs spoiling for fights; club rackets on air tickets, drinks and stolen property. The list was endless, but nothing seems to put the British off coming. Even if it isn't paradise, at £157 at least it's a bargain.

Of course, most of the members of Animal Nightlife had made it to Ibiza before. But it was to the San An' end rather than the Ku Club. As pop stars they got to make the transition from San An's West End video pub to the millionaires' bar at the Ku in one easy step.

For Andy Polaris the Ku was "like a Hollywood film set", but with the difference that they were the stars. For him it's a long way from slipping into the Lacey Lady club after school in Billericay, with his brother rubbing dirt on his face to make him look older. Andy had the sort of childhood where the long arm of the law extended to picking him up in Brentwood High Street on his way home wearing plastic trousers.

"As soon as I left the homes where I was brought up, I came to London and got a crappy job," he says. "When punk started I needed to get money to go to clubs like The Vortex. At that time it was real easy to make friends, and I used to hang around with X-Ray Spex, Siouxsie And The Banshees and The Slits, whom I used to love.

"But when punk started fizzling out, the whole Billy's scene started up, and then it was whoosh!" Recalling his squatting days with George and Marilyn, he feels it was only starting to sing with Animal Nightlife that took him out of the circuit of self-appointed beauties. "The band were all football boys," he says. "If I hadn't met them, I'd still be hanging around with the dressed-up crowd. The band have made me less pretentious. I don't bother to dress up any more, so when I look at photos of myself in George's books I just cringe. I laugh at it now. I was just very naive when I came to London. Everybody judged everybody on what they wore, and they were just as narrow-minded as the people they were slagging off. I got really bored with all that and just ligging at other people's parties. It was basically cretinous people anyway."

The group's ambience then occupied a slot since dominated by Sade, Matt Bianco and Everything But The Girl in the eyes of music journalists ever eager to lump anything without a yelled vocal or straight 4/4 rhythm into a fashionable catch-all category of "jazz" for readers' swift comprehension. But anything less trend-ridden than Animal Nightlife's music is hard to imagine, since it takes a traditional bitter-sweet soul approach to the hardy perennial themes of (a) dancing and (b) love.

"Our very first song was, 'Love Is The Great Pretender'", says Andy. "It was a backlash against all those lovey-dovey songs that were going around. The theme for most of our songs is rejection (laughter). You just learn from it because I'm used to being in that situation. Everyone's got their romantic ideal of affairs, but basically I'm quite realistic about it because of my own experience and that of people I know. That's why we have songs like 'Bittersweet', 'All Over Now' or 'Insomnijazz'. They're all about rejection – but some are more humorous than others."

All this, of course, was getting worse and worse for the *Mirror's* Miss Style. Traditional soul music? Bittersweet rejection? Bah! Still no clues to a new trend or celebrity in sight – and the standby snaps of nude beaches may be risky!

Even worse, Animal Nightlife actually appeared to be disdainful of the whole celebrity groove... Sacrilege!!

For the serious Ibiza hedonist, life is not complete without a major adjustment to the body clock. Pike's, for example, is one of the few hotels ever heard of that serves breakfast until four o'clock in the afternoon. It's a matter of Ibizan etiquette. For just as you're supposed to drink until you drop in San Antonio, or arrive at the Ku after 2.30am, the aptly-named Club Amnesia does not even open until 5.30 in the morning, and it would be impolite to depart before 8am. Thus, as dawn comes, the Club Amnesia's car park fills up with an eager congregation and the whole thing carries on till 11. As the sun gets hotter the wind billows through the sail-covers as about a thousand people regularly dance past breakfast, while the rest of Europe sleeps and unhappy labouring natives in cities prepare to reach for the snooze button on their alarms.

Here the crowd is mainly composed of Ibizan "regulars", the die-hards who return to the island season after season. From June until October they manage to survive on Ibiza, renting a villa, working in a boutique or shop, selling jewellery or clothes, dealing drugs, or just receiving commission on the tickets they hand out for different clubs. Like most tourist attractions, most of these beautiful people dressed in finery and sporting deep tans are veteran sponsored events, rented out by discotheques to create atmosphere every night for a few thousand pesetas. In the winter they vanish. They return to Milan or Düsseldorf, Oslo, Stockholm, Barcelona or Paris, leaving the island quiet until next season. But like the redcoats at any holiday camp, they're back again next year, encouraging people to enjoy themselves.

The scene is strictly international, and you overhear conversations taking place in smatterings of English and Spanish mixed with Italian or Franglais. But the core of regulars is mainly Spanish, coolly flamboyant, mostly gay, and quietly mocking of the tourist scene to which they are the unofficial jesters, and which labels them euphemistically as "non-conformist". They don't really seem to care as long as for four months of the year they get to live almost for free.

When the Club Amnesia shuts, you can sleep on the beach or back at the villa, wake up, bathe in the sea or the pool, then start the whole cycle all over again. It's all very pleasant, provided you can stand the strain. At the Amnesia there's one veteran campaigner who serves drinks with a huge grin and beaded hair. His conversation is really just a mumble and he's completely naked except for a different-coloured G-string each night. Some people laugh at him as he dances and waves his tambourine in the air at 7.30 in the morning, and he's known as the "Hamlet Of Ibiza", since nobody's quite sure if he's crazy or not. He obviously doesn't care. He probably doesn't even remember.

Next year on New Year's Day the old era will come to an end. Spain will then be operating a newly-signed extradition treaty with Britain and other European countries. In a nutshell, it means that like southern Spain's "Costa Crime", Ibiza will cease to be a safe bolt-hole. The effects will be only gradual. Over the next few years maybe some of the island's surplus cash will start to diminish, but like St Tropez and Marbella before it, its reputation as a playground for the rich and famous will stick. Of course, some of the regulars will move on, perhaps to a Greek island like Lindos or Ios. There may be a few more broken heads in San Antonio or a change of personnel at the Ku's millionaire's bar.

But as long as the sun continues to shine, the peseta remains low, the electricity and the phone work, there'll be raw material for *Mirror* headlines on the Island Of Stars for years to come. The cast list will grow, and a new generation of con-men and fraudsters, would-bes and have-beens, the posh and preposterous will dance like baboons to tunes by Wham!, Spandau Ballet and most likely Animal Nightlife as well.

Their next ambition is to play the real Club Tropicana in a place that's still "cheap and old and exotic and beautiful", where the wine is drunk by the bottle, and fish bought fresh from the harbour - Havana!

So the moral of this tale is really that some people are just never satisfied •

19   MDMA WE'RE ALL CRAZY NOW

OCTOBER 1985

Ecstasy's arrival in Britain by Peter Nasmyth

"I PUT THE WHITE capsule on my tongue and swallowed, hoping to God the source was reliable; that this really was it and not some new amalgamation of PCP or even LSD. My friend took her capsule and we stood looking at each other. What now? She told me it would take about half an hour to come on. With apprehension mounting, we decided to walk over to a nearby park; the trees and the sunshine might help me feel more at ease.

"Some time later I looked at my watch. Forty minutes had passed. I looked at my friend. Was she any different? Could I see into her soul as had been promised. Was I feeling great empathy and love?

"No, in fact we were having an argument. Tired of the park, she wanted us to go home, while I preferred to stay there with the hilltop view of London. There seemed to be no resolution. My heart was beating a little faster, but I put it down to anxiety.

"Another 20 minutes passed. Still nothing. Perhaps the drug was just too subtle for me. Disappointed, I gave in to her wish to go home. We started down the hill. But by the time we reached the bottom I'd forgotten how to be angry. We were having a new conversation, examining our goals in life. What had we done so far? Had we really followed those vows of adolescence? Did either of us know what is was like to be close to another human being? For the first time in years I confessed my childhood yearnings to become a marine; she told me she'd wanted to marry Woody Allen. Defences were dropping at a rate it normally took people months to achieve. Suddenly I knew I could trust her with my closest secrets... strange because not half an hour before I wouldn't have cared if I never saw her again in my life. I told her this and we both laughed.

"By the time we arrived back at the flat I noticed my heartbeat was stronger, but now I also seemed to possess an extraordinary mental calm, as if everything were on a very clean microscope slide. I viewed life out of a kind of benign fearlessness, but unlike the stronger sensations of heroin, I still wanted to talk, move around, be with people. Also it lacked the extroverted rush of cocaine. I was feeling good but without the superlatives, without the mystic euphoria. There was no distortion of the senses or hallucinatory tinge, as with, say, mushrooms. Rather a kind of winter's night, mugs-of-Horlicks feeling. It reminded me of someone's description of MDMA as 'the hug drug'."

MDMA, adam, essence, XTC or Ecstasy as it is also known, has been described in other ways. "A brief, fleeting moment of sanity," according to Dr Claude Naranjo. Dr Rick Ingrasci says it will "heal fear". More often it is claimed the drug will break down the barriers between therapist and patient, parent and child, lover and lover, stranger and stranger. But if it has inspired this kind of testimonial, it has also provoked equally strong warnings.

The unnamed Londoner's experience continued for another two or so hours before the symptoms faded. Afterwards he said he felt slightly fatigued, experienced minor difficulty in falling asleep, but otherwise had no untoward side-effects.

There can be little doubt this drug is now with us here in the UK; arriving from across the Atlantic every week via 747, turning up in flats and nightclubs and parties as the latest product of American drug mythology. Although it has created a real stir in the States, it is known here to only a few. To most its existence is largely rumour and misinformation. "X-ing" is a term that is yet to be heard around the majority of British coffee-tables.

But this is not the case down at The Ranch, a gay bar in Dallas, Texas. In June this year you could have walked in and bought Ecstasy, or "E" over the counter. It would have cost $20 plus the $1.23 sales tax. Nobody would have raised an eyebrow. You could charge it to all major credit cards. If you had a "coupon" you could even have got $5 off. It's also just possible that outside, someone would have approached you with a leaflet proclaiming "Ecstasy. Everything looks wonderful when you're young and on drugs". Or if you looked the popular type perhaps a different leaflet: "Flight Instructions for a friend using X-T-C." TV networks, magazines and newspapers are all running stories on "The new drug they call Ecstasy". "LSD without fireworks", "The choice of Yuppiedom". Soap operas like NBC's *Another World* were starting to include it in their scripts. T-shirts and bumper stickers began to appear with the warning: "Don't get married for six weeks after XTC!"

Why? Because it would appear America has discovered its "Drug of the Eighties", according to Timothy Leary, lapsed psychedelic prophet and Harvard doctor. His drug of the Sixties, LSD, is now receding into the twilight in America, back into the repertoire of psychotherapists, and this phrase coined by him in a recent article has been cropping up on television screens and street corners across the nation. It will be remembered that it was Timothy Leary who in 1965 put in motion a "new consciousness" saying "Acid is ecstasy, ecstasy is good for you". Now, over a generation and quite a few false chemical hopes later, one can almost hear the strains of longing for that innocent euphoria in the new name of MDMA.

Whatever it tells us of the times, its users generally agree that MDMA is not "ecstasy". It can make you feel very close and empathetic – you might feel like hugging your friends – but the affection it inspires is unlikely to send anyone into the frenzied raptures common in the Haight/Ashbury district in 1967. Ecstasy is a misleading name; the drug is so-called more for reasons of promotion than resolution. Yet unlike PCP's early tag as "the Peace Pill", it fortunately tends to overstate rather than understate. Like so many brand names, it represents what people want rather than what it is.

So what is it? Chemically speaking: 3, 4 Methylenedioxymethamphetamine. A synthetic compound modelled on a substance found in nutmeg and oil of sassafras, it is related to both MDA and mescalin but is not a psychedelic, and its effects, though similar to MDA, are shorter lasting and rely on a different activator.

Any description of these effects would be best prefaced with Aldous Huxley's comment: "We can pool information about experiences, but never the experiences themselves." With this in mind, it can be said that MDA is a mild mood-enhancing drug, seemingly not physically addictive. Excess dosage can bring on the symptoms of speed or LSD. At these levels it can also quickly become toxic; worth bearing in mind since tolerance develops rapidly to the desirable effects.

"Personally I find it boring," said an anonymous member of Soho's club-land. "I used to do it when it first came out a few years ago, but now I find cocaine a better buzz... and it's cheaper.

He didn't have more to add, except that at £20 a dose, Ecstasy must be making somebody a lot of money. For him it flopped as a party drug; the effect was weak by comparison with other drugs and the phase passed quite quickly.

But Ecstasy does have one remarkable feature, and this alone may have made it into the drug of the Eighties. Up until July 1 of this year it was completely legal in the United States. An emergency ruling from the Drug Enforcement Agency, alarmed at the escalating recreational use, placed in on Schedule 1, in the same category as heroin, pending hearings and a final decision next year. It turns out that in Britain, as an amphetamine type, MDMA is already illegal, though only a class B drug. The penalties are the same as those for speed. So far, according to the Metropolitan Police, there have been no prosecutions.

MDMA was first formulated in 1914 as an appetite suppressant by Merck & Co in Germany. It was left on the laboratory shelf until the Fifties when the US army began their search for chemical aids in the battle against Communism. Tested along with LSD, it was found to be more toxic but much less interesting. It failed to produce those memorable effects such as the weeping CIA agents running for the Washington monument, nor the GIs raving about "unspeakable beauty". Neither did it inspire such delirious plotting as the scheme to lace Fidel Castro's tea right before a 1960 television broadcast.

It seemed to have been forgotten, at least up to the mid-Seventies. By then, the hysteria over LSD had faded and new-age chemists were turning their attentions to more subtle variations, or "designs" of existing compounds. In a paper published in the Journal Of Psychedelic Drugs in 1976, Dr Alexander Shylgin, a Bay Area pharmacologist, described the properties of MDMA, an MDA analog. It was a rare mention outside of scientific circles. At around the same time it started to be used in psychotherapy, but again publicity was stunted.

Why? Because researchers and therapists like Dr Rick Ingrasci and Dr George Greer realised they were on to something. This drug was exceptional. It induced miraculous breakthroughs in therapy and could be relied on like no other to produce that vital and transforming factor in psychiatric sessions – honesty. And the insights would be remembered afterwards. Its proponents in the psychiatric field realised that if they played their cards right, they might not have their baby snatched away by the government, as happened before with LSD. But they also faced a problem: how to let word pass around to the right people?

It took until around 1981 for the word to reach the wrong people. The arrival of MDMA on the streets meant that someone had seen a way to make a financial killing. A new name was coined, Ecstasy. Distributor networks began to appear and soon catchphrases like "a safe psychedelic" began circulating around campuses, clubs and dinner parties. Demand grew, according to the DEA, from a nationwide usage of 1,000 doses a month in 1975, to 30,000 plus a month for one major city alone in 1985. Drug manufacturers began receiving huge orders. Its appeal, according to writer Joe Klein, was that it offered "adventure without weirdness, transcendence without alienation, a Yuppie way of knowledge". It was too good to be true.

"I've heard a report of someone locked in a foetal position for three days," said Dr Ronald Siegel of UCLA School of Medicine, "and regular accounts of poisoning symptoms, nausea, dizziness and jaw tension at the onset of MDMA experiences. I've also heard of people having loving, harmonious experiences. But so far all we have to go on with this drug is folklore: we don't have one published scientific study."

For Dr Siegel, a DEA witness and researcher into the street use of drugs, the word "scientific" is of great importance. He is adamant that this "potentially toxic" substance be kept out of the hands of unqualified users or non-medical therapists. He recalls the claims being made for cocaine as a nonaddictive panacea as late as 1970 and points out that there are now an estimated 10 million US coke users, four million psychologically addicted. PCP (Angel Dust) too was greeted with enthusiasm at first.

"To my knowledge the scheduling came about from reports of clinical problems resulting from widespread abuse... and so far I've already heard of two documented cases of PCP showing up as MDMA on the streets."

Attempting to counter this official pessimism is MDMA's most vocal and enthusiastic supporter, Rick Doblin. As a long-time seeker into the mystical placed reaches of truth he feels better to evaluate MDMA, or "Adam" as he prefers to call it. Why Adam? Because the myth of Adam's body being made up of all the races on earth recalls MDMA's sensations of universal warmth and communication.

As one might expect from such a campaigner, Doblin comes across as helpful and optimistic, if maybe just a shade too optimistic. He single-handedly revived alternative architect Buckminster Fuller's Earth Metabolic Design Foundation for the cause of MDMA. He also contacted the United Nations, the FDA and Nancy Reagan's organisation, the National Federation Of Parents For A Drug Free Youth, in the same open-handed spirit. They unfortunately didn't quite grasp his intent. The son of a physician who runs a drug clinic, he is trying to organise an entirely new pharmaceutical company. The aim is to fund the necessary testing to make MDMA a prescribable drug in the future.

"It's a false dichotomy the government is trying to make. Recreational use versus therapeutic. Actually neither are bad, although it should never be used casually. They're afraid of the whole concept that people can have a worthwhile drug experience and not become addicted. Thus they blew up these University of Chicago MDA (not MDMA) experiments way out of proportion. It's just like the LSD story really, when they talked about chromosome damage. It just hasn't happened. There aren't thousands of kids walking around warped just because their parents took LSD. There are dozens of people here with a ten-year history of using MDMA. We don't see any observable effects."

As ecstasy was hitting a peak earlier this year as the new party drug, the one everyone had to try, a group of clinicians and researchers gathered at the Esalen Institute in Big Sur, California. Among them were several veteran researchers into psychoactive drugs and a number of psychiatrists who had been using MDMA in their practices for many years. On the fourth day of the meeting, Dr George Greer directed a session in which 13 of those present took the drug, each monitored closely by another doctor.

Among those who read with interest the report of this meeting was the anthropologist Francis Huxley, nephew of Aldous, whose book *The Doors Of Perception* and many experiments with mescalin helped shape both the psychedelic era and the Esalen institute itself. Though he didn't see himself as a spokesman, Francis Huxley felt the meeting brought attention back to the essence of the drug.

"Adam... is like a slow influx of warm vigour; very subtle, but suddenly you discover you're feeling remarkably well and normal. You could say functioning as you should... If you look at the mind you could say you have a sphere with the outside being all one's faculties. Adam doesn't affect the inside, it affects the outside, it works on all the instrumentation of the mind and sort of networks it together.

"Therapy is one of those dirty words that seems to cover just about everything, but if it can be used to help people find each other in a social mode... then that's as good a use as I can think of. If it ends up going totally underground it will be rather sad, because it will breed a paranoia which one doesn't want in any form of social intercourse."

Yet this will probably be its fate. Legislation is unlikely to dent the existing demand for the drug. Furthermore, Schedule 1 declares it to be "of no accepted medical use", thus denying it even to the therapists who have been working conscientiously with it for over a decade, and are now lobbying for milder classification. By reacting so strongly the DEA have simply promoted MDMA's connections downward into the underworld, where it will be gladly made and heavily peddled.

"It's a shame that it's been criminalised, because it could have taken its place in the pharmacopoeia," says the psychologist RD Laing. "I'm sure it's here to stay," he adds. "It's easy to manufacture... "

Moreover it has now acquired taboo to add to its growing mystique. And there does seem to be something compelling about the idea of such a drug, if not the thing itself. In all the accounts of the Ecstasy experience, you can hear an unusual undertone of unselfconscious advocacy.

"It made me feel how all of us would like to think we are anyway," says Laing. "It's the very opposite of acid. Nothing like a transcendental experience."

It also appears to have some very cunning merchandisers behind it. Several years ago, the first of the so-called "designer drugs" appeared on the West Coast, a "synthetic heroin" analogous to the pain-killer Fentanyl but slightly altered through chemical engineering to avoid illegality. Sold openly to junkies, its high strength caused many deaths before the formula was made illegal. Immediately, the designers made a new, slightly altered analog. The same techniques have created a companion for Adam, with a few minor chemical adjustments. She's called MDE or Eve.

An so Ecstasy just won't go away. Curiosity has spread its name across America, and doubtless many more will be drawn to it. As the Londoner at the start said, it can act as a reminder of a kind of honesty rarely found in human relations. Certainly, nobody needs a drug to tell them of this, and it may be that the message Adam brings is the reminder that ecstasy has always existed without it •

20 SERIOUS DANCERS

APRIL 1986

The Great British Jazz Revival by Robert Elms

THERE ARE THOSE who say, but then there always were, that we are living in a Golden Age, a Jazz Age. The legend of the British jazz revival is one of the more abiding modern myths. Perhaps it's just a recurrent wish on the part of those who care, but we certainly had a bad case of it a couple of years back. In the autumn of 1983, Sade, Working Week, Everything But The Girl and The Style Council were all suddenly making carefully-crafted jazz pop. Julien Temple was talking about making a jazz musical of the Colin MacInnes novel *Absolute Beginners*. Paul Murphy was becoming famous as a latin/jazz DJ, and The FACE was writing for the first time about his sweaty Camden jazz room full of sharp young black kids dancing a remarkable fusion of 100mph Tap and Break to Art Blakey and Cecil McBee. They were Britain's – and the world's – first "jazz posse". Now, three years later, a sharp-shooter named Courtney Pine has formed The World's First Saxophone Posse and *Absolute Beginners* has just been released.

"We are finally seeing the results of all the spadework done over the last 'ew years," says Richard Cook, editor of Britain's jazz magazine *The Wire*.

It was bound to take time. You cannot simply pick up a horn, strike a pose, and play like the masters. In order to communicate through the medium of jazz you have to learn the language. Nearly three years after the "jazz revival" there are youngbloods speaking in fluent, distinctive voices.

The British jazz scene, one based on fine new players working within the tradition of Afro-American improvised music, is a reality. Live, improvised music must always be at the heart of jazz and London right now is throbbing with all manner of great jazz musics. But before we hear them, we should return for a while to the dance...

Paul Murphy first started spinning a mix of Fusion and Latin music for discerning soul boys as far back as 1980, but he wasn't the only one. The much-derided jazz-funk scene of the late Seventies wasn't all wedge-heads, wet T-shirts and weekends at Caister. There were DJs like Colin Curtess and Baz Fe Jazz who refused to toe the mafia line of limp funk and mindless chat, and instead were out on a jazz limb. At all-nighters and all-dayers around the country they had dim-lit side rooms set aside for the serious dancers.

Almost exclusively male, these were the boy buffs who bought expensive Airto and Flora Purim albums and wore their loafers wafer-thin. Those who "cut" and "killed" at the fastest Batucadas, those who could match their moves to the meanest souls went where Murphy went. Hailing from the Essex heartland of the Southern soul scene, Paul Murphy began DJing at the Horseshoe pub in Tottenham Court Road, soon gaining a reputation for playing the hardest.

His crowd consisted of the purists, the mainly black kids who specialised in the lightning footwork and spins of jazz dance, the kids who would search out obscure Afro-Cuban sides from his record shop and turn out in their hundreds when Murphy began promoting gigs by vibes player Joe Hoggard, The Heath Brothers and Tina Maria. These were the Ballroom Boys, the ones Simon Booth first saw flying to "Nights in Tunisia".

Booth, the founder, composer, guitarist and jazz evangelist of Working Week, plays a key part in this. As well as writing a handful of genuine British jazz tunes, he has been vital as a bridge-builder between the disparate elements of the scene.

When the one-time shop assistant from Mole Jazz walked into Murphy's sweatroom it seemed to him like a dream come true. His long-cherished vision of a young, radical jazz movement taken out of the libraries and into the nightclubs was literally spinning in front of his very eyes. Pretty soon his other dreams would be coming true too.

Within a few months, Simon Booth's new band Working Week were recording their first single with some of the finest young players in Britain. "Venceremos" featured Larry Stabbins, Annie Whitehead, Bosco, Kim Burton, Stuart Matthewman from Sade's band and Tracey Thorn from Everything But The Girl on vocals. IDJ (I Dance Jazz), a dance troupe formed in the Electric Ballroom, were featured on the sleeve and in a Julien Temple-directed video, and the whole thing appeared on the Paladin label started by Murphy and his irrepressible Millwall-supporting partner Dean Hulme.

On the day that veteran arranger Gil Evans flew in to work on "Killer Blow", a song Simon Booth and Sade co-wrote for *Absolute Beginners*, it actually seemed as though we were in the middle of British jazz revival.

Since then, of course, there have been fights and factions, splits and regroupings and times when it seemed more like a dark age than a renaissance, but there has also been consistent, gradual growth. The IDJ troupe has danced ever since, adding a vital visual element to live bands. The hardcore black jazz scene from which they emerged has been reluctant to leave its ghettos, preferring the muscular elitism of exhausting dance-offs in exclusive dance rooms. But IDJ have been joined on the circuit by Manchester's famed singing/dancing Jazz Defektors, who have recently signed a record deal with Epic-Sony Japan, and a new posse from Birmingham called the Jazz Five.

All three will be competing to cut the floor around the revered feet of Art Blakey, when they join his Jazz Messengers on stage at the Camden Jazz Festival mid-March. It should be borne in mind that nobody dances to that music anywhere else in the world.

The seemingly unique ability of Paul Murphy to get a response to jazz records in a disco has virtually taken him around the world. Japan is the latest country to benefit from Murphy's selections, but his biggest journey was from Camden Town to Soho.

Leaving the Ballroom for the Wag meant going public. Due partly to some less than wonderful records, Paladin has failed to live up to the excitement of "Venceremos". New signing Aldeoni, a young British-born Brazilian singer, may change that, but, whatever happens to Paladin, Murphy and Hulme have been vital catalysts for jazz music both live and on record in nightclubs.

There have been jazz rooms in Manchester, Brighton, Newcastle, Glasgow, Nottingham and Bournemouth, inspired by their lead. People who two years ago had never heard of Blue Note records have been dancing to music that veers from Mose Allison to John Coltrane, the pre-"modern" style of jazz. In London right now there is still the jazz room at the Wag club every Monday where Baz and his Team Ten crew have replaced Paul Murphy, Steve Holloway moving between the Wag and the Sol Y Sombra with a hot mix of Bossa and Bop, and Murphy and Hulme's new Room IV Jazz at the Comedy Store.

Between the regular rooms and the frequent one-offs, they provide not only jazz on disc but also venues for live music. The second wave of British jazz pop – Moontwist, Esposito and Seconds Of Pleasure – alternates with Georgie Fame and his rejuvenated

Blue Flames and the authentic bruising hard-bop of Tommy Chase's steam-roller quartet. A growing roster of London club bands owe their audience, if not their existence, to the scene Paul Murphy started. And that's only one scene...

"When you say jazz," reckons Simon Booth, "everybody gets offended because they all have their own definitions."

Trendy London jazz clubs where boys in oversized suits eye girls in overtight pants to the tune of "Mac The Knife", as foreign journalists look for witnesses to the now legendary Blue Rondo A La Turk, have become a capital institution. But out there in the soul suburbs, probably the largest single jazz audience, maybe the largest of all the jazz scenes, is the one ruled by pirates.

Because of its position atop the southern part of the city, Crystal Palace has long been a haven for the buccaneers of the airwaves. One street is known locally as Pirate Row because of the number of illicit stations pumping out perpetual black American music to the insatiable sons and daughters of the suburbs. Always the prime consumers of import dance music, a sizeable proportion of them have long danced to jazz.

Gilles Peterson is the Bluebeard of the blue notes. For much of his youth he resided on Pirate Row. A 20-year-old from deepest Surrey, Peterson began at 16 playing contraband Fusion from a tower block in Wandsworth for Radio Invicta before reaching the big league of Pirate Row with Horizon where his weekly jazz show attracted an audience of thousands. He could tell because that's how many turned out to the jazz gigs advertised only by piracy.

Leaning heavily towards Latin America, he is the main man for the Bossa posses and Samba crews who flock to jazz-only pirate, with the help of the ubiquitous Simon Booth. Peterson also compiled an album of club jazz cuts for Street Sounds aimed squarely at the white-sock section of the market. Sales in excess of 20,000 proved just how big that is, prompting Peterson to bid for one of the licenses currently being dangled at the pirates. In a bid for legality the station is currently off the air, but licensed or otherwise, he pledges, "K Jazz will return". In fact, the disco-pub jazz buffs have never gone away. But few of them go to see the real thing. The soul jazz scene is dominated by DJs rather than live bands. The Escort youth will drive up in force for Tania Maria or Gilberto Gil, but the thriving homegrown London Latin scene looks more to hippies than hipsters for its audience. Yet there is a remarkable pool of both imported and indigenous Latin players shared among bands like Sonida De Londres, the Robin Jones Band, Sambatucada and the masterful London Samba School.

Playing a seemingly endless round of benefits and festivals, the London latins are currently making some of the hottest, most joyous live music available. And when the resident Columbians and Brazilians turn out to dance their dignified, straight-backed shuffles to the Sambas and Merengues you hardly notice the social workers in the house.

"London today is an unfolding crucible of world sub-cultures," says David Defries, lead trumpeter with Loose Tubes.

There are 22 members of Loose Tubes with an average age of 24, among them some splendid jazz musicians. Big bands are a vogue at the moment; occasional conglomerations of like-minded sessioneers and regulars coming together to play a variety of jazzes. Loose Tubes were the first to play The Tube and release an album, which hints at the potential of such prominent bloods as soloist Iain Bellamy, percussionist Steve Arguellas and the much-touted Django Bates taking care of keyboards and composition.

The Loose Tubes album is bold, brassy and anarchic, if a trifle overburdened with the clumsy humour of street theatre. The more avant-garde swing of Trevor Watts' ten-piece Moire Music album shows another side of the current British jazz scene. An electric time-warp of funk and improvisation from some of the country's finest fringe players, it is a sign of how widespread that client is. Outside of Loose Tubes the likes of Bates and Bellamy are to be found deep in the mainstream of the London jazz world, which functions both in the newer, hipper venues like the Bass Clef and the Pizza Express, the wonderful atmospheric after-hours jam sessions at the 606, and land-that-time-forgot jazz joints like the Bull's Head and the 100 Club.

The transfusion of new blood into the main arteries of British jazz has livened it up, but done little for the prospects of the numerous superb instrumentalists whose talents are all too cheaply on offer every night of the week.

Don Weller, Stan Tracey, Pete King, Kenny Wheeler, Alan Skidmore, Tony Oxley, John Surman, Tony Kinsey... some of the finest and most respected jazz musicians in Europe – many argue, in the world – are queuing up to perform in the back bars of pubs. Britain has always produced great players, the late Sixties and early Seventies in particular pouring forth a generation of jazz talent which has since been dissipated. Some, like Evan Parker, Elton Dean and Derek Bailey, were forced to move to the continent. Others like Keith Tippett and John Stevens now work on the fringes; Larry Stabbins augments his pure jazz work with the pop jazz of Simon Booth's Working Week, while others like Kenny Wheeler struggle to work at all.

"You've got to be 12 to get a gig right now," says Alan Skidmore with a resigned grin. One of the finest tenormen currently working in the Coltrane mode, Skidmore is typical of the young turks thrown up by the great British jazz revival. Having played with everybody from Elvin Jones to Charlie Mingus, Weather Report to Airto Moreira, he topped jazz polls throughout the Seventies and headlined throughout Europe. Here in jazz-age Britain though, times are tight. "It's tough being a jazz musician full stop! You cannot make a living playing jazz in this country; I hope the new lot prove me wrong – that would be fantastic – but we'll see."

A lifelong friend of "Skid", Larry Stabbins is aware of some of the mistakes that were made last time round. "Jazz alienated people; it forgot that they do not only go to gigs and buy records for the music. It is a whole set of values, and if you ignore that you get into trouble."

For years now the promised land was due to arrive with the National Jazz Centre. Despite millions spent on a prime Covent Garden site, the great white hope of the old guard still lies unfinished and two years overdue. But there are always the great black hopes...

It is remarkable how quickly and how high hopes can be hoisted. The Jazz Warriors, a 17-piece, predominantly young, exclusively black, all-British band, have played only two gigs, in Brixton and Deptford. But most who saw them and plenty who didn't have been talking about little else since. "We knew it would create interest, that's precisely why we did it. When has there ever been a black big band in Britain? It had to be done," says Warrior Gayle Thompson.

The line-up of the Warriors is standard big band plus percussion and a trio of vocalists. The surprise came from splitting up into a series of small "posses": the sax posse, the vocal posse, the rhythm posse... before regrouping into the ragged, full-scale, full-frontal attach of the ensemble. The line-up included Gayle Thompson, Ray Carless of Light Of The World, Mike Rose from Aswad horns, Philip Bent (a remarkable 19-year-old flautist from the Royal College), percussionist Mamadi Kamara and vocalists Carol Thompson of Lovers Rock and Floy Joy fame, Juliet Roberts from Working Week and a terrific newcomer, scatman Cleveland Watkiss. Courtney Pine, 21, stood in the middle, overcoat, goatee and soprano.

Here were flat-tops, razor partings and rasta playing a ramshackle but razor-sharp blend of warped trad, big band, be bop, a cappella, solos, ballads and standards. It was dance- and awe-inspiring music. With the vocalists, the jackdaw approach to jazz history, and some blistering post-Trane soloing it brought to mind experiments like Archie Shepp's Attica Blues Big Band, Edie Gale's "Ghetto Music" and Lester Bowie's joyous "Trans Traditional Suite". But most of all it brought to mind the fact that this was something we have long been waiting for.

Gayle Thompson, a charming and forceful alumnus of Herne Hill and the Royal College, took the baritone seat in Charlie Watts' recent big band season at Ronnie Scott's. Just up the horn section sat Courtney Pine, fresh from playing reggae with General Saint, who blew them all away.

"Courtney is an excellent player, a marvellous player," said Alan Skidmore, who also played in the Watts band. From an acknowledged master, that is praise indeed, but Pine's playing, with echoes of Coltrane and Shorter, is also a precociously individual voice.

Gayle Thompson and Courtney Pine decided that they should form their own big band for all the other young black players who deserved attention. She set about organising, while he set about recruiting the Jazz Warriors.

Based around Community Music, a north-London jazz workshop project founded by drummer John Stevens where both Courtney and Gayle teach, they drew in young British blacks from reggae and funk, and more importantly, from the generation of trained players emerging in the music colleges. The idea was for an occasional band that would be a focus in itself but also a springboard for other projects. For Courtney, a quiet, rather serious young man, it has already meant more attention than may be healthy, and he is very aware of that. But it has also meant major record-company interest in recording not only the Warriors, but the sax and vocal posses and Courtney's own young black quartet.

The wealth of players emerging right now is such that Thompson is setting up yet another big band, The Blackjazz Orchestra.

But despite all the excitement, Gayle Thompson, who has been playing jazz professionally for ten years, still insists that "the British jazz scene is very unhealthy, don't doubt that, and it can never get better until people start paying, or all this talent will get lost."

There has never been an indigenous black jazz scene in Britain before, and the fact that one is emerging with such force and energy makes this, if not a Golden Age, at least a fine time •

21   SAMPLE AND HOLD

SEPTEMBER 1986

The House sound of Chicago by Sheryl Garratt

"Sue the bastards!"

WE'VE BEEN IN Chicago for two hours now, and for reasons too ridiculous to explain we are sitting in an Armenian restaurant talking to Jay B Ross, attorney at law for DJ International. Ross, a respectable if portly-looking citizen, suddenly reveals that he too has a deal with the label and launches into a performance as The Rapping Lawyer. Events have taken a distinctly surreal turn. Only in America could an attorney sell himself via "Sue The Bastards" T-shirts with his name and number on the back; only in Chicago would a label sign its own lawyer to work on a song with Farley Funk, Arthur Baker and two 15-year-old hip hop hardliners. Even more confusingly, the label has also signed William "Refrigerator" Perry of the Chicago Bears, Indiana soul lady Loleatta Holloway, a Greek pop group, several hip hop crews, NY punkette Screaming Rachel and other oddities too bewildering to mention. Which makes the question we're here to answer seem all the more difficult: what is this "House" music they're hyping so heavily back home?

A day later I'm in Paragon Studios to hear a re-recording of Marshall Jefferson's song "The House Music Anthem" for London Records' upcoming House compilation. Chicago studios, I've found, are unlike any other; when one person cuts a House track, everyone else comes down to watch. There's a party going on in the control room: Harri, vocalist on the classic House track "Donnie" by The It, is dancing with a dog's choke chain and lead around his neck '76 style, and Marshall is doubled up on the sofa in a fit of anguish, envy and admiration. "Aw God, I wish I could look weird like that!" he wails, fishing out a nappy pigtail from behind his standard Afro for my inspection. "My girlfriend made me grow this so I'd look more like a recording artist, but I wish I could deal with people staring at me like that."

Backing singers Rudie Forbes, Prof TC Roper and Curtis McClay are here, while Lewis Pitzele, DJ International's vice president in charge of promotion is – as always – on the phone. Chip E, the label's 20-year-old vice president in charge of A&R (living proof that in Chicago, every boy can grow up to be vice president) sits quietly in the corner; DJ Ron Hardy revolves on a chair and Frankie Knuckles is busy working on the mix. John Stoddart is taking photos, Marshall is videoing his first ever interview with a British journalist, and in the background the vocals float through the monitors: "This is House music." It seems as good a time as any to pop the question, so I do. What is House music? Suddenly, all hell breaks loose.

"House music? I couldn't even begin to tell you what House is. You have to go to the clubs and see how people react when they hear it. It's more like a feeling that runs through, like old-time religion in the way that people jus' get happy and screamin'. It's happening! It's... House!"

"Let me see if I can put it better. It's more like Eighties disco songs in Eighties style."

"It's Chicago's own sound."

" 'Cept it came from New York, and they don't know it."

"It's rock till you drop, that's what it is!"

"It's a status symbol to party all night at The Muzic Box. Everybody goes there – all the hippest kids in the city!"

"You'll leave there a changed person. You might go and seek religion afterwards! You'll love it. It's gonna be hot, it's gonna be sweaty, and it's gonna be great. What you'll experience is honest-to-goodness, get down, low down, gutsy, grabbin' type music. Boom boom boom!"

Long a centre for gospel, jazz blues and advertising jingles (really), the Windy City is revelling in its new-found status as a dance music centre. There's a new (and beautiful) city for the UK hacks to fly to en masse, and the man from *The Chicago Sun-Times* is calling my room to ask how seriously The FACE is taking all this. "It hasn't crossed over to the Yuppie crowd here," he tells me with satisfaction, citing a commission to write about Chicago rock bands for *Creem* as one of the best things to emerge from the affair.

Local radio, meanwhile, only started introducing House records to their regular playlist after DJ International took their crew to the New Music Seminar in July, held a party in NY's Better Days Club, and began attracting media interest. Larry Levan had been playing the music at The Paradise Garage for some time along with a few other NY clubs. Arthur Baker has recorded his own homage, "Chicago", but Lewis is adamant that "it took the English media to make the radio play its own local talent". Yet Farley "Jackmaster" Funk claims a crowd of 2,000 at La Mirage on Friday and Saturday nights, while Ron Hardy at The Muzic Box on Thursday and Saturday and Frankie Knuckles at COD's on Friday both attract capacity crowds. Maybe it's because the faces are mainly black that they don't count.

But let's begin at the beginning. In 1977, New York DJ Frankie Knuckles was asked to come to Chicago to establish a new gay club called The Warehouse. At the time, he recalls, DJs were a rarity in the city, and all except two bars – Le Pub and The Bistro – used jukeboxes instead. Things didn't look promising, but the club had the advantage of being the only after-hours venue, opening at midnight and closing when the last dancers left on Sunday afternoon. A small three-storey building with a seating area upstairs, free juice, water and munchies in the basement and a dimly-lit dancefloor in between, Frankie told the owners to give him five years to create an impact. It took him two.

"It was absolutely the only club in the city to go to," he recalls with little visible self-congratulation. "It wasn't a polished atmosphere – the lighting was real simplistic, but the sound system was intense and it was about what you heard as opposed to what you saw. Comfortably, the place held about 600, but coming and going all night I'd say we did about 2,000-2,500 people. The crowds came in shifts – those who were always outside at 11.45, they'd 'jack' until about 3-4am when the bar people would arrive. Then there'd be a whole different crowd that would come about 9am which is how the parties carried on until the afternoon.

"Most of the music I played was inspirational – all the dance things that were popular in '77/'78, but the voice had to have a nice sound and a message that was more than just 'I met this chick'. Most of the time it was either really heavy instrumentals or vocals talking about doing something for oneself. Like D-Train's 'Keep On': 'I can't let nobody keep me from reaching the top'. That type of stuff."

Frankie's seamless mixing and his combination of obscure US oldies with Euro imports meant that while hip hop swept across America, disco never died in the Windy City. It wasn't long before the straight kids too were crowding through the club's door, and when they began walking into record stores demanding Frankie Knuckles music or "that sound they play down the 'house," House music was born.

Some still maintain the name comes from the house parties held in the mainly black South Side of the city or in the Bronx-like projects called Cabrini Green, but most of those with suss say the term came from The Warehouse. Such was the infatuation with the club that younger artists such as Chip E and producer Jessie Saunders' brother Dr Derelict clearly remember a time in the early Eighties when all the youths were dressing gay, acting gay, trying their hardest to be gay. The scene is still a remarkably amiable mix of sexual tastes largely free of macho and misogyny, though mention should be made here of Farley Funk's mildly amusing nasty (as in rude) romp "SMMFD" ("Suck My Mother Fucking Dick"). It appears on the flip of "Jack The Bass" under the alias Jackmaster Dick and comes complete with Dickappella mix, fetish fans. Besides, when the radio stepped into the scene, most gave up the idea of being gay and decided to be a DJ instead.

The mix shows started on WGCI, but things really took off when rival R&B station WBMX responded by gathering together a group of street DJs under the title The Hot Mix Five. Led by Kenny Jason, the team also included a young DJ popular on the South Side: Farley Keith Williams, aka Farley Jackmaster Funk.

The Hot Mix Five have since defected to WGCI, leaving Frankie Knuckles to head the WBMX side, and the mixes are now an integral part of Chicago city life. Thirty-minute mixes are aired at regular intervals throughout the day – around 18 records per session, mixed together as one continuous medley without repeats. The serious event, though, is on Saturday night when the stations air five-hour shows with each DJ offering an hour-long mix. From 250,000 to a million of the city's inhabitants tune in at some point – about a fifth of the population.

"In my neighbourhood there seems like a million kids all on the streets with radios blasting," laughs Shawn Christopher, backing singer for Chaka Khan and the voice on the DJ International single "People Of All Nations".

Farley is reputedly the wealthiest and definitely the best-known of the House DJ/producers, and although he owes much of his success to the radio, he is as dismissive of it as the rest. The stations' alleged refusal to acknowledge their records outside of the mixes and to play anything more energetic than 117bpm has earned them almost universal contempt among the House fraternity, although Farley admits it was the Hot Mixes that spread the scene.

"Chicago is a DJ city," he insists. "If there's a hot record out, in Chicago they'll all go buy two copies so they can mix it. We have a talent for mixing. When we first started on the radio there weren't many, but then every kid wanted two turntables and a mixer for Christmas. We've been on air for six years now, so a kid who was 11 then is 17 and a DJ or at least a fan of the mixes. And if a DJ can't mix, they'll boo him in a minute because half of them probably know how to do it themselves."

The frequent exposure also meant that they soon ran out of what Farley calls "Bootsy Collins/SOS Band-type tracks" to mix, and so they turned to Paul Weisburg of Imports Etc for ideas. Now selling an odd mix of hot House tracks and dusty $13 LPs by the likes of Wire, even the mighty Farley bows in homage to the shop and to its owner's inventiveness. "He was the only person in the city selling those imports. Italian records like Trilogy's 'Not Love', 'I Need Love' by Capricorn, 'Brainwashed' by Telex. There was one called 'Don't Forget To Buy This Record' – a tripped-out name for a record! That was really big here, but we couldn't get no more imports so somebody bootlegged it – that happens a lot."

Another variation was digging out old Philly songs and adding a faster, boosted rhythm track. Farley started taking his drum machine to play along with records at his club The Playhouse, and there was a booming trade in records consisting solely of a bassline and drum patterns, often recorded by local DJs.

From this to complete records was a short step, and Farley finally made his debut with "Aw Shucks" on his own House label. Showcasing the distinctive thumping bass drum – "Farley's foot" – it was overlaid with computer samples of a dog barking, James Brown grunting and lots of silly voices. Like all House records, it comes in a choice of mixes, was made cheaply and somehow sounds even cheaper. But that, everyone tells me, is part of the appeal.

It's the reason why Frankie Knuckles hasn't yet indulged his fantasy of lush, layered productions à la Trevor Horn ("Frankie Goes To Hollywood were sooo big here!") and as Farley explains, "Our sound is so different because we can make just a bassline and a rhythm track and we can sell 10,000 copies of that just in the city. All you need is a feel for music. There are people who've been to college to study music and they can't make a simple rhythm track, let alone a hit record. It's weird. And it seems like a waste of time to learn all that because now a little kid can pick up a computer, get lucky with it, and write a hit. It's no use working with ancient sounds."

For aspiring artists, then, this is the House that Jackmaster built:

"Basically, it's a good vocalist with a nice bass drum pattern that really thumps. I love the foot, because that's what really gets people moving. The foot establishes the beat, the snare sustains it and from there the hi-hat picks it up and gives it energy. There's a lot of funk in House, which people don't realise – they say it's Hi-NRG but it's not because it has a lot of soul in it; it's real funky."

Now making his own records (14 at last count), producing other House artists, remixing outsiders such as The Dazz Band and branching out into rap, Farley finds less time for the clubs but still says they are central to his work. "I love playing for the crowd – it's unbelievable when 2,000 people really get going. I can make a record on my four-track recorder at home, take it into the club and play it on the reel-to-reel. If they like it I'll copyright it then play it in the Hot Mix about two weeks later, then I'll call round the record stores. If you play a record in the mix, kids will go into stores with the tape and ask for it, and if there's a demand, right away I'll try to get it out.

"I was looking for a deal with a major label, but it's kinda hard because I'm the type of person who would put out five records in two months and they'd make me wait."

Vince Lawrence of The Bang Orchestra has just released his debut LP and a single, "Sample This", on megabucks label Geffen, and Jessie Saunders of Jes Say Records is in the process of signing to the major too, but on the whole House still works on the level of ducking and diving. Chip Edhardt became DJ Chip E while still at high school, but in spite of guest spots at The Muzic Box, The Playground and The Candy Store, he didn't get big enough quick enough. A spell behind the counter at Imports Etc convinced him he could make records as good as some of the DJ product he was selling, so he sold his turntables and spent the money in the studio laying down some rhythm tracks. There was enough cash left to make a single test pressing: "I already knew the Hot Mix Five so I gave it to Kenny Jason and he played it immediately. Then Farley took it and it got passed around and gained a lot of popularity from that. So by the time I had my first 1,000 pressed – I borrowed my mother's income tax cheque – we sold 500 in the first day out of one store, and the rest within a week. I ordered another 3,000 and we sold them in about a week. That was the 'Jacktracks' EP."

Meanwhile, Rocky Jones of the record pool Audio Talent had decided to help one of his DJs, Steve "Silk" Hurley, release a track called "Music Is The Key" by JM Silk. When the first pressing sold out, he swapped his hot-rod Corvette in exchange for 10,000 more copies: DJ International was born. Chip was amongst the early signings, producing the stuttering, stripped-down dance track "Like This" and the upcoming "Godfather Of House" under his own name, working with Harri and friends on "Donnie" as The It, and producing/mixing other artists for the label and its subsidiaries.

For Chip, the formula is much the same as for Farley: "A lot of bottom, real heavy kick drum, snappy snare, bright hi-hat and a real driving bassline to keep the groove. Not a lot of lyrics – just a sample of some sort, a melody to remind you of the name of the record so you go out and buy it."

How long can you keep doing this, I ask, before people get bored? Chip looks thoughtful for a while, then turns back to face me with a grin.

"I'd say about the next 20 years" •

22   LOFT CAUSES

OCTOBER 1986

The end of the warehouse party by Sivan Lewin

ACROSS THE RIVER from St Paul's Cathedral, in a once-busy commercial district of London, lie acres of abandoned warehouses. In one of these, three storeys high and covering several thousand square feet, a party is going on. It's the biggest party in London that night; everyone wants to be there. They come and go throughout the night. At its height, around 3.30am, there are more than 1,500 people inside, crowded in the darkness, clutching cans of beer, dancing amid the dereliction to raw American funk.

There was nothing exceptional about this scene, taking place early in July of this year. It was one that could be witnessed, weekend after weekend for the past five or six years, in various dark and run-down corners of London inspired by New York loft parties and beginning with the infamous Dirtbox at London Bridge. Sometimes as many as three sound systems would set up, offering reggae, funk and pop-soul on different floors to thousands of people. Often known only by their location – places like Battle Bridge Road or Rosebery Avenue – they became a new social focus.

At the riverside party in July, though, there was a subtle shift in the atmosphere. One regular partygoer described it as "the worst-organised one I'd seen. There were 500 people outside fighting to get in". He also noticed "a definite commercial operation selling speed and dope". A journalist at the *South London Press*, he filed an item on this aspect, which over-eager subs assumed implied all manner of evil. The article associated the organisers, "Family Funktion", with crime, vice and drug peddling. Picked up later by the *Standard,* it presented a scandalised picture of so-called warehouse parties; hell-holes of "junk, funk and sex".

Late the following Saturday, six police Sherpas drew up in St Pancras Road, outside Soul-2-Soul's party in the warehouse district of King's Cross. Scores of police made their way into the building – a disincentive to any party. An hour earlier, Retro's party in nearby Old Street had been closed down too. Crowds hung around but soon drifted off. The organisers were left with caseloads of undrunk beer and, in King's Cross, there were arrests for threatening behaviour.

It wasn't the first time these parties had been visited by police, who would often make a discreet late-night inspection and, occasionally, arrive early to close the whole show down. The week before, "Arena", billed as the biggest ever, was thwarted when the joint-organisers arrived to find their disused plant boarded up and the police waiting. What had happened, though, was that warehouse parties had gone public. They had become the scandal-fodder of the tabloid press...

In Soho, central London, on a Saturday night, the word starts to spread. In the clubs, brasseries and bars of pubs like The Spice Of Life, invitations and street names are bandied about. On a good night, the determined Soho-boho might hear of as many as six parties, such as "Night Train" in Old Street or "Yo!" at a fire station in Camden Town. The derelict locations – warehouses, car parks, railway arches – with their dusty floors and industrial ambience, offer only crumbling walls, a loud sound system, and the potential for anything to happen; unpredictable and unrestrained, the parties are imbued with the thrill of their dubious legality.

This is a sub-culture away from the high prices of the West End and the restrictions of licensing laws and strict door policies. The excitement comes from the rich new mixture of people, a different and more diverse crowd than at the clubs, drawn by different crews and DJs.

Music is what makes a warehouse party. Heavier beats and harder tunes than most clubs would play: funk classics, hip hop and Go-Go, mixed down this summer with a House beat. Dancing was the best reason for being there, right through until dawn shows through the broken windows.

The rich mixture of people – DJs, rappers, dancers and artists – created hot-spots of new talent. Competition between the different crews, always striving to throw the best party, has bred sophistication; warehouses decorated with new artwork and videos. "Westworld" stole the show with their much-talked-about bumper cars, while Mutoid Waste Company filled a warehouse under the Westway with their eccentric industrial sculpture: cars appearing to crash through walls and hanging, suspended from the ceiling. At Family Funktion's King's Cross party, Robert Shepherd covered the railway arches with huge drawings, breaking away from the strong influence of New York styles.

The energy of the street fuelled the frenzied activity, but it seems the proliferation of these parties over the last year has ultimately brought their demise. With most organisers now competing for crowds, there have been muggings and threats. One crew was forcibly relieved of a night's take, which can run to thousands. Since the *Standard* story, the paper has had calls from crews trying to spoil rival parties by publicising them. Publicity, finally, may have forced the police to take more conspicuous action.

"Trespassing on private property is a civil matter," says Scotland Yard. "But we are trying hard to stop them because liquor is sold without a license, there are youngsters taking drugs and there is a health risk because the buildings are often unsafe."

Given the present attitude, it looks like the heady days of the warehouse party are over for the time being. What the press and the authorities never understood was that warehouse parties were about hedonism not vice; positive energy on the flipside of Thatcher's wastelands •

23   CUT AND TRUST

APRIL 1988

The Disco Mix Club by Sheryl Garratt

ONCE, DJS SIMPLY played records: now they tear them apart to make new ones. Once, not so long ago, DJs were reviled in the music press, symbols of the dreaded disco which threatened live music; now they're cover stars. As the marketing and launch of a new pop name becomes increasingly expensive (and so controlled), it is the DJs who are out playing every night, in touch with their audience's needs and leading new trends. Club play can now make or break records without reference to Radio One, and DJ remixes can save mediocre records, revive old ones or transform new ones.

DJs are the new underground stars, and, ironically, it is they who have been left to carry the slogans of punk: plunder and destroy, refuse to worship the past, and remember that anyone can do it.

But in the fuss over the sampling techniques favoured by the likes of Coldcut and Tim "Bomb The Bass" Simenon, live mixing skills that were considered radical (and writworthy) themselves five years ago have been overshadowed. Mantronik has been saying for some time now that the days of the turntable as an instrument are numbered, but though it's no longer enough just to add a few scratchy beats and throw in a Chic riff or "Another One Bites The Dust" to be hailed as the new Grandmaster Flash, names like Cash Money, Jazzy Jeff and Red Alert still show that there's mileage in the live mix yet.

The Disco Mix Club's prestigious World Mixing Championship proves the point. Held in discos across the country, this year's British heats featured entrants as diverse as Spanish resort DJs home for the contest to Paddington's 14-year-old Scratch Professor – ranked third in the UK as a mixer, and a strong contender for first prize in the sharp haircut stakes. Gimmickry ruled – mixing with feet, noses, dildoes, bikes, footballs, shoes, anything but a simple pair of hands – but it was timing as well as showmanship that won the aptly-named Cutmaster Swift his place in the world finals at the Royal Albert Hall.

A subscription organisation for DJs worldwide, DMC's general outlook can be seen from the contents of their monthly publication *Mixmag,* where wet T-shirt contests and Page Three PAs still get more than their fair share of picture space. Yet their structure has grown along with the status of their members: Jam and Lewis and Janet Jackson were amongst the guests who flew in for DMC's dance awards and mix finals in '87, while this year James Brown himself graced the stage.

Last year's UK champion, CJ Mackintosh, has since enjoyed a hit with M/A/R/R/S and signed to ZTT with Nasty Rox Inc, as well as cutting his own solo singles. But this year's contestants should perhaps note the huge success of London's Discoteque where DJs Ben & Andy are under strict orders to take requests, drink heavily on the job, and lay on the schmaltz with a towel for the hourly "erection section" smooch-time.

From the wheels of steel through to sample and steal, the role of the DJ has changed radically. At the moment, it seems, there's plenty of room for them all; even the old-fashioned disco wallies •

24   JAZZIE B GOOD

MAY 1988

The rise and rise of Soul II Soul by Lindsay Baker

EVER SINCE THE King's Cross warehouse parties back in '83, Soul and the Funki Dreds have been apparently unstoppable. Their Sweatdown parties on Sunday nights at The Africa Centre strengthened their already loyal following on the underground club scene, and allowed them to expand with their recording studio and clothes and record shop in the basement of The Great Company Store in Camden High Street. Jazzie B and H have just returned from their second tour of Japan with Norman Jay and Barry Sharpe (of Duffer Of Saint George/Diana Brown And The Brothers fame), this time concentrating on "the fashion side of things", as well as playing at a venue in Korea.

Despite their reputation as Rare Groove DJs, the music they play is mixed, as Jazzie B explains: "Soul II Soul cover the whole spectrum, from ballad music to the deepest hip hop to the hardest fat funk tunes around."

Not content, however, with mere DJing, the Soul II Soul crew have now made their own single, "Fair Play", produced by Jazzie and Nellee of The Wild Bunch and released this month on 10 Records. Like their music policy, the Funki Dreds' single avoids being pigeonholed. It's a slow funky tune, with plenty of percussion, an R&B bassline, a hip hop drum pattern and soulful vocals featuring Rose Windross, a former reggae singer. Jazzie sees the progression from playing music to making it as a natural one: "We've been cutting our own tunes for the set for a while and we've always used different MCs. So most of the people used on the record came through the sound system." "Fair Play" differs from the current spate of DJs' records in that sampling was kept to the absolute minimum: "Whilst musical instruments are still in existence we should make good use of them. One day they might be extinct."

Jazzie, the man with a finger in every pie imaginable, also DJs on Kiss FM every Friday between 10 and 12pm. And as if this wasn't enough, Soul II Soul are now designing their own clothes. You can catch Jazzie B and the Funki Dreds in full effect every Sunday night at 173 Old Street, London EC1, where they play the best dance tunes around, including their own. And why not? As Jazzie says: "I've been DJing for a hell of a long time. The end product is me playing my own material as a DJ. I think that's pretty hip, I'm bang into that" •

25 SEVENTH CITY TECHNO

MAY 1988

Dancing in Detroit by Stuart Cosgrove

"IT'S NIGHT-TIME in an obscure sidestreet somewhere in the seventh city. Far away, a banshee police siren wails. A falling body screams and the innocent suffer all the while. Unheard. This is Cabaret Seven."
Gambit And Associates , Detroit, 1987

The underground comic *Gambit And Associates* tells the story of a weird technocracy. It is set in Detroit, the seventh city, the murder capital of the USA, and the home of America's most progressive musical underground. The comic is drawn by a Detroit DJ and follows the exploits of a punk detective called Johnny Gambit, a fan of the Belgian group FRONT 242, and a dude who can draw a gun at 122 beats-per-minute. The streets are littered with bodies, the innocents go unheard, and the buildings crash against each other in disordered shapes. According to Detroit's premier producer Derrick May – the brains behind the mutant dance music of Rhythim Is Rhythim – the comic will be available as a companion piece to his next independent 12-inch dance record, and is the only accurate tourist guide to the city of Detroit.

Although the Detroit dance music has been casually lumped in with the jack-virus of Chicago House, the young Techno producers of the seventh city claim to have their own sound, music that "goes beyond the beat", creating a hybrid of post-punk, funkadelia and electro-disco.

The self-proclaimed captain of the new Detroit underground is Juan Atkins, a 26-year-old producer who releases records under the name Model 500. He originally rose to prominence in the early Eighties as a member of the electro band Cybotron, whose hit "Techno City" appeared on the old UK compilation LP "Electro 4". Juan operates a makeshift basement studio in his home in West Detroit and sees the city's new underground sound as an inevitable by-product of advanced technology.

"Within the last five years or so, the Detroit underground has been experimenting with technology, stretching it rather than simply using it. As the price of sequencers and synthesisers has dropped, so the experimentation has become more intense. Basically, we're tired of hearing about being in love or falling out, tired of the R&B system, so a new progressive sound has emerged. We call it Techno!"

The Detroit Techno scene is a mesmerising underground of new dance music which blends European industrial pop with black America's garage funk. Its main exponents are Model 500, Rhythim is Rhythim, Reese and Santonio, Triple X, Dynamix, Blake Baxter, The Flintstones and Eddie "Flashin'" Fowlkes. If the Techno scene worships any gods, they are a pretty deranged deity, according to Derrick May: "The music is just like Detroit, a complete mistake. It's like George Clinton and Kraftwerk stuck in an elevator."

Techno began in West Detroit, or to be more precise in the corridors of Belleville High School, where its three most ardent devotees, Juan Atkins, Derrick May and Kevin

Saunderson, were at school together. Although it can now be heard in most of Detroit's leading clubs, the local area has shown a marked reluctance to get behind the music. It has been in clubs like The Powerplant (Chicago), The World (New York), The Haçienda (Manchester), Rock City (Nottingham) and Downbeat (Leeds) where the Techno sound has found most support.

Ironically, the only Detroit club which really championed the sound was a peripatetic party night called Visage which unromantically shared its name with one of Britain's oldest New Romantic groups. And strange as it may seem, the Techno scene looked to Europe, to Heaven 17, Depeche Mode and the Human League, for its inspiration. Eventually support arrived in the form of a hip local DJ called the Electrifyin' Mojo, who plugged it on his nightly sessions on Radio Station WHYT.

Kevin Saunderson, one half of Reese and Santonio and a student at East Michigan University, claims the city has held the music back. He was once sacked from a local radio station for being "too ahead of his time". He returned to the station with evidence of Techno's growing popularity, only to be rebuked again.

"I took them a clipping from *Billboard* and they told me to come when we were on the front cover. That's Detroit. I've turned my back on this city. I don't care if they never buy one of my records – other people will."

Saunderson's confidence comes from success outside Detroit. Model 500's interstellar dance record "No UFOs" has been one of the underground club scene's biggest-selling records over the last three years; three releases by Rhythim Is Rhythim – "Nude Photo", "Strings" and "The Dance" – introduced the club scene to the buzz-term "acid house"; Techno labels like Transmit, Metroplex and Incognito are in permanent demand; and Kevin Saunderson's "The Sound" has been bootlegged in Berlin, London and New York.

Getting sacked for being too hip seems to be an occupational hazard in Detroit. Derrick May, now generally recognised as one of the club scene's most in-demand mixers, began his career on the wrong end of his boss's wrath.

"I used to DJ at a local club called the Liedernacht. The crowd were completely against dance music. They only wanted to hear The Smiths or Severed Heads. I was playing black underground sounds and they couldn't take it. They used to say, 'Get this nigger shit off!' They even went as far as having a sit-down strike on the dancefloor. All these dickheads in black shirts trying to be so English and so progressive and refusing to listen to underground music that was happening under their noses. We built up the crowd until it was racially mixed. The manager told me he didn't want a black club and I was fired. They play my records now, but I can't get in. I'm banned for life."

Members Of The House, three young Detroit Techno-freaks who recently recorded the excellent 12-inch "Share This House" for less than $2,000, have similar reservations: "This is an automobile city but some people's heads are drawn by horse and carriage." They favour a basement approach to music, working in restricted conditions. "Techno is all about simplicity. We don't want to compete with Jimmy Jam and Terry Lewis. Modern R&B has too many rules: big snare sounds, big bass and even bigger studio bills."

Techno is probably the first form of contemporary black music which categorically breaks with the old heritage of soul music. Unlike Chicago House, which has a lingering obsession with Seventies Philly, and unlike New York hip hop with its deconstructive attack on James Brown's back catalogue, Detroit Techno refutes the past. It may have a special place for Parliament and Pete Shelley, but it prefers tomorrow's technology to yesterday's heroes.

Techno is a post-soul sound. It says nothing to the Lord, but speaks volumes on the dancefloor. Whilst modern singers like Anita Baker, Whitney Houston and Alexander O'Neal still carry the traces of a gospel past, for the young black underground in Detroit emotion crumbles at the feet of technology.

Derrick May's revolutionary backtracking on the Technics decks and Santonio's Yamaha drums are stripped of any sense of authentic emotion: they just percuss you out. Even vocalist Blake Baxter sees his style as a distant voice at odds with the emotional power of soul. His techno hit "Ride 'Em Boys" is a promiscuous dance record featuring a sampled woman's voice and a barely audible vocalist. "I don't really sing," says Blake, "I speak in a soft voice almost hiding beneath the beat. I love records with whispering vocals – it's nothing like the gospel sound."

Significantly, the greatest British response to the new Detroit sound has been in the North. There is no obvious reason why. Soul sociology sees it as a musical re-working of the North-South divide, and cult theory sees it as an unconscious return to the values of the old Northern Soul scene, where uptempo dance music, obscure records and the city of Detroit held an unrivalled esteem. It sounds ridiculous. It is ridiculous. But there may just be a grain of truth in the rare soul theory.

When Virgin's 10 label releases a double album of Detroit Techno music this month, it will be the first time the music has had a substantial presence in Britain. The album will be issued in conjunction with Neil Rushton, a former Northern soul DJ who owns a West Midlands House label called Kool Kat. (For those of you who love the pursuit of trivia, Kool Kat's name is homage to an old Detroit label which Northern Soul collectors still pray to every night.) Some of the tracks on the album have been recorded at United Sound Studios, home of the legendary Detroit overlord Don Davis, who was responsible for countless soul classics including Johnnie Taylor's "Who's Makin' Love", The Dramatics' "In The Rain", and Parliament's "Mothership Connection".

But despite Detroit's rich musical history, the young Techno stars have little time for the golden era of Motown. Juan Atkins of Model 500 is convinced there is nothing to be gained from the motor-city legacy. "Berry Gordy built the Motown sound on the same principles as the conveyor belt system at Ford's. Today their plants don't work that way – they use robots and computers to make the cars. I'm probably more interested in Ford's robots than in Berry Gordy's music." The lack of interest in Motown sometimes spills over into resentment. Juan's protegé Eddie "Flashin'" Fowlkes feels Motown "left and took the whole structure of Detroit music with them. They left a vacuum that has taken over 15 years to fill."

Motown's departure in the early Seventies was a symbolic moment in Detroit's industrial fortunes. In the years since, factories have closed, car plants have contracted, and the city centre is now virtually bereft of any sense of community. More than any other place, Detroit has taken on a post-industrial identity.

It is 4am and Derrick May is on the 30th floor of a shaded glass hotel looking across the skyline of his home town. His friend Alan Oldham, the comic artist turned DJ, is somewhere else in the city about to play Rhythim to Rhythim's "Chaos" over the airwaves of Radio WDET. Played alongside the Skinny Puppys and New Order, the sparse and confrontational dance record gets a fittingly dramatic introduction. "Stand by for some post-industrial chaos. Techno from a long-lost world."

Derrick has quietened down now. After a night of running up hotel walls and arguing with bouncers at The Taboo Club, he is in a reflective, almost alienated mood. "This city is in total devastation. It is going through the biggest change in its history. Detroit is passing through its third wave, a social dynamic which nobody outside this city can understand. Factories are closing, people are moving away, and kids are killing each other for fun. The whole order has broken down. If our music is a soundtrack to all that, I hope it makes people understand what kind of disintegration we're dealing with."

Techno is light years away from the happy frivolity of The Supremes. "Say what you like about our music," says Blake Baxter, "but don't call us the new Motown... We're the second coming!" •

26   HERE IS THE NEWS

OCTOBER-DECEMBER 1988

Acid house: the sound and the fury. Extracts from FACE Club news

----

IT'S TAKEN 20 years, but the tabloids have finally found out – people take drugs in nightclubs! What next – an exposé of the sinister cult of dancing?... The sex'n'-drugs'n'acid house story has even spread abroad, with one FACE photographer reporting a call from Italy asking for "singers standing in their acid houses". (October 1988)... The acid hysteria continues apace: Radio One's new boy Philip Schofield apparently got "a good talking to" after his extraordinary on-air outburst on This Danger To Our Nation's Youth, but the misinformation persists. Contrary to front-page headlines in the *Sun*, London's members-only club Spectrum has not closed, but it has become careful. Even the tops of socks are checked at the entrance with a much-improved atmosphere inside as a result: no dealers, but plenty of dancing (November 1988)... An acid club at Birmingham's Powerhouse was closed after just one night, after a local promoter indulged in yet another acid = ecstasy "exposé"... Blackpool DJ Pete Haigh sees the music now as a gift to what he calls the "scally element" currently crowding into clubs. "The new Smiths haven't come along yet, Echo And The Bunnymen have all but split up, then this scene comes along and it's great because there's not too much black music involved, it doesn't have that worrying 'ethnic' element." This is probably also the reason why West End venue owners and police were initially tolerant of acid: it brought the white suburban crowd back into the clubs, and ended the racial mix of funk/rap venues like the old Delirium (December 1988) •

27

DID DEPECHE MODE DETONATE HOUSE?

FEBRUARY 1989

Why Detroit loves the boys from Basildon by John McCready

"I used to play Depeche Mode as a DJ, before I even knew the name of the group – their music was very hot at that time, records like 'Strangelove'. We were influenced a lot by their sound. It's real progressive dance, and had this feeling that was sooo European: it was clean and you could dance to it."
Kevin Saunderson, Inner City

"They've set the standard in what they do. In America they've been able to please almost everyone, from a guy like me who's a dance addict, to the stadium crowds. They're right on time, right in synch, and they can't even help it."
Derrick May

"I only really played one of their records, but a lot of people I've worked with were influenced by them, especially Jamie Principle. I know that Jesse Saunders was a big fan, and so was Farley [Jackmaster Funk]"
Frankie Knuckles

IT'S JUST AFTER 1am at the best club on the planet. This is Detroit's Music Institute, an all-night and most-of-the-next-day juice bar with a sound system designed so that recurring phrases like "feel the music" begin to make sense. House and techno trax weave in and out of the club classics like Dinosaur L's "Go Bang" to make up the Saturday-night soundtrack. The DJ could be Derrick May except for the fact that he's just led us through the queue at the door. Perhaps, then, it's Kevin Saunderson or Juan Atkins, both of whom regularly direct the mix at 1315 Broadway.
With Chicago's Warehouse, where house took shape, and Larry Levan's Paradise Garage having both passed into legend, the Music Institute is now the music's flagship. Depeche Mode head straight for the bar. Having spent the previous evening with them, I know they're fond of a drink or three. Obviously not aware of the dance-till-dawn concept of the juice bar, Andrew Fletcher turns to me and announces incredulously, "No alcohol". Beginning to get the hang of things, Martin Gore calls out, "Waters all round". The heads of the immaculately turned-out young blacks around us begin to turn.
Despite the fact that we are all beginning to look like death warmed up following last night's late late warehouse rap party in New York, Depeche Mode are very quickly "recognised". Within minutes, Martin Gore has a tape from local Techno group Separate Minds thrust into his hand. Had this been Shoom, The Kool Kat or the Haçienda, the group might have been blanked, laughed at, or even insulted. In Britain, Depeche Mode are a kids' group, a "pop" group: they're Bros, but older. In the gun capital of America, the reaction is inevitably different. Will they get shot? Only with a camera.

"Smile, please," says a beautiful young girl as her friends crowd around the group.

"Oh, God!" says another, "I can't believe it! This is great, Depeche Mode in Detroit... Why?"

Believe me, it's a long story.

With a career spanning seven albums, what seem like several hundred singles and over nine years, Depeche Mode, despite having most uniquely combined creative progress with ever-increasing record sales, are second only to the combined forces of Kylie, Cliff and PWL when it comes to being subjected to the acid wit of the pop media. Pieces about the group usually consist of two-parts jokes about leather skirts, one-part references to their New Romantic tea-towel-wearing period, and several gratuitous references to Basildon.

Yet in America they are spoken about in the same reverential tones as New Order and even Kraftwerk. Frankie Knuckles won't deny owning a well-worn copy of "Just Can't Get Enough", and Todd Terry will talk about them as his favourite dance group. In America, Depeche Mode are a phenomenon, a white English "pop" group respected on the black club scene in New York, Chicago and Detroit through records like their 1983 single "Get The Balance Right" – a $25 "disco classic" in Manhattan's hip Downstairs Records. And this is despite the fact that their knowledge of club culture is such that they haven't heard of most of the people who control your night-time soundtrack. Here, they remain a laughing-stock thanks to a received impression of them as fools lost in the pop machine.

"We accept that we are partly responsible in creating the problem in Britain," says Andy Fletcher, the group's diplomat and all-round diamond geezer. In the hotel bar in Detroit we begin the interview proper. Depeche Mode are in America viewing the final cut of *101*, their first concert movie, which was put together by legendary pop film-maker DA Pennebaker. A mixture of documentary and concert footage, it echoes the candid style of the director's *Don't Look Back*, made during Bob Dylan's early-Sixties tour of the UK.

It records Depeche Mode's 101st concert, held before a 60,000 crowd at the Rosebowl in Pasadena, and illustrates their obvious overground success in America. The film accompanies a new live LP set from the same concert. That job done in New York, here, in the interests of providing another view of a group whose name is always accompanied in British magazines by an italicised cynicism from an unidentified "Ed", Depeche Mode are taking a techno holiday, their curiosity stirred after hearing some of the city's innovative new dance music. The trip also provides a way of approaching a group who are now in a position to refuse the standard tape-recorder-on-the-table trial.

Having been introduced to the group the day before, I negotiated their guilty-until-proven-innocent reticence at an Indian restaurant, where the hapless Fletcher brought a glass-fronted picture crashing to the ground by leaning where he shouldn't have. Dave Gahan, pissed as a fart at 4.30 in the morning, pronounces me "All right", having decided before my arrival that I would be a bastard in designer shoes who wouldn't get his round in. The fact that most of the people who put The FACE together look like refuse collectors seems to come as a great surprise to most people. By the time the tape recorder does make its scheduled appearance, their inbuilt suspicion is at an all-time low. At this point it's decided that there is a difference between the great British music press and me. Stories of disreputable gentlemen of the press in berets begin to flow through, aided by the tongue-loosening properties of potent bottled beers.

"When we began, we couldn't believe that anyone was interested," says Fletch. And we did every TV show, every interview that came up. We were wrapped up as a pop group, nothing more and nothing less, and we have suffered from that image ever since." He takes time out to explain that there is nothing inherently wrong with pop music. We agree that it has become a simple term of abuse due to the critics' common viewpoint that what is popular is therefore crap: bad logic in anyone's philosophy book. Alan Wilder – who can look as sullen as a Spurs fan on any Saturday afternoon but instead turns out to be another diamond geezer who doesn't get enough sleep – adds that the power of the pop press is such that those who like the group find themselves having to explain why – something I'm used to. New Order, who began life as Joy Division, thereby giving music critics the opportunity to prattle on about cathedrals of sound, are seen in America as similar white dance practicians. In Britain, the respect they have overseas is more than equalled. It's an attitude which frustrates rather than puzzles the group.

The situation seems massively ironic where the full extent of Depeche Mode's American success becomes clear.

Derrick May, one of the originators of techno who records as Mayday, Rhythim Is Rhythim and R-Tyme, looks after us in Detroit. He's keen to talk to a group he sees as part of America's underground dance scene. "They have dance in their blood," he says. Aligning them with Nitzer Ebb, New Order, DAF, Yello and the rest of the European rhythm invaders, Derrick believes that Depeche Mode were an important part of the club collision that evolved as Chicago house. The Detroit techno sound was created on a musical diet of Clinton and European rhythm-based tracks like Depeche's classic "People Are People". This intercontinental collision at the heart of Chicago house, techno and Todd Terry's New York sample sound is the key to the future of contemporary American dance music.

When I mention Todd Terry to Andy Fletcher and he asks me who he is, it's clear that the group themselves are blissfully unaware of their influence. Perhaps the fact that they remain largely uninterested, preferring to concentrate on creating more of the same, is the key to their dance success. Dave Gahan relates that their much sought-after 12-inch mixes were created not for clubs, but for bedroom listening.

"We had to do these 12-inch records so we made sure they were interesting all the way through. We spent a lot of time putting them together so that people would want to listen to them from end to end."

The dub techniques and intuitively rhythm-conscious sound collages that resulted are landmarks in the development of the house sound. Whether you like it or not, "Just Can't Get Enough" is a dance masterpiece which, like "Disco Circus", "Love Is The Message" and Klien and MBO's "Dirty Talk", helped shape the most fêted club sound of the decade.

Most of the other British groups who emerged from the white dance boom of the early Eighties would have paid dearly to hear their records smoothed into a mastermix on New York's Kiss and WBLS radio stations, or even to share a minibus with Derrick May. Duran Duran courted the attentions of the Chick Organisation, yet they have so much to do with current club success, and are the only British group to come close to Depeche Mode's American standing in the clubs.

As musicians with a genuine love of black music, they tried to build on that success by attempting to mould their very European awkwardness into something more soulful. Millions of pounds were spent on the "Crash" album, produced by Minneapolis studio gods Jam and Lewis. The move did nothing but upset a black audience almost bored by a million and one immaculate arrangements and endlessly capable voices. They want to hear an English accent and a synthesiser and be persuaded by a different sound. They wanted Phil Oakey to be Phil Oakey singing "Being Boiled". When Phil Oakey nearly became Alexander O'Neal singing "Human" they lost interest. The Human League blew it by trying to assimilate a sound their American audience already knew by heart.

Depeche Mode, far from capitalising on their appeal, believe they, too, are about to upset their ironic alliance with US club culture. Alan Wilder tells me that the new material they are working on builds on the slower tempos of the "Music For The Masses" LP. Martin Gore, the group's only songwriter, who, curiously, listens to old rock'n'roll for inspiration, believes that Depeche Mode aren't capable of making dance music anyway.

"We can't create dance music, and I don't think we've ever really tried. We honestly wouldn't know where to start."

Two days later I'm in a car in Miami listening to a radio mix show. The DJ cuts from The Beat Club's "Security" to Front 242 to Black Riot and Depeche Mode's "Strangelove". I change stations and Noel's "Silent Morning", a hugely-influential Latin hip hop track, knocks me sideways. Suddenly, it is unmistakably Depeche Mode's "Leave In Silence". The full extent of the irony starts to hit home. I think of all the desperately crap UK acid records I get through the post and start laughing.

As usual, with the tape recorder switched off people start telling good stories. Our planned visit to Majestics, an Anglo-obsessed "English Beat" club which Derrick tells us is haunted by Numan clones and tea-towelled futurists, is the subject of comic anticipation. The group admit that they benefited from their association with the kilt and make-up scene of the early Eighties. But as the tag became a critical liability and Depeche Mode grew into the wilful pop stylists of "Leave In Silence" and the brilliant "Get The Balance Right", it proved hard to shake.

Dave Gahan recalls a concert in Paris about two years after the whole scene had died. Arriving at the hall, they couldn't help but notice huge posters announcing DEPECHE MODE: KINGS OF THE NEW ROMANTICS.

When we get to Majestics, Bauhaus's "Bela Lugosi" is stirring up the dancefloor. This is Retro Anglo or "Nu Musik", and these are the people who have helped create a market for groups like Information Society who try to recreate the awkwardness and the essential Englishness of the early Depeche Mode sound. As a man in a green fishtail parka and a flat cap passes me I am mysteriously reminded of Chicago's Bedrock Club, where one of the main attractions for the house nation seems to be the exotic charms of Watney's Red Barrel. A big man in mascara crushes past and I decide that Depeche Mode may not leave without giving the assembled crowd a quick blast of "Photographic", an early Basildon New Romantic classic. Here, as in the Music Institute, which we head for after a minute or so of "Just Can't Get Enough" signals we've been spotted, the autograph requests begin. We drive to the Institute with the group discussing their music and the Techno sound with Derrick May. They want to know why almost every house track utilises the very specific sound of the Roland 808 drum machine. Later, Dave Gahan tells me that they don't really feel part of what's happening.

"Still, I can feel the excitement of it. In a way it's confirmed that what we are doing has been right all along. House seems to me the most important musical development of the Eighties, in that it's combined dance and the electronic sound. What Derrick is doing looks to the future."

With a grin on his face, Fletch recalls a British interview where the opening question was, "What's it like to be playing old-fashioned music?"

"This was before house – a really dark time for electronic music. At the time electronic was a dirty word. People were talking about guitars a lot. It was like, 'How does it feel to be finished?' Dave nearly clobbered the guy!"

As we approach the club Dave is taking the piss out of Derrick's hyperactivity and Derrick is taking the piss out of Dave's accent. A mention of Kraftwerk changes the subject, and provides the best explanation for the phenomenon that is Depeche Mode's American club success. While most British groups dealing with America try to be American, Depeche Mode are, like Derrick May and Todd Terry, still listening intently to Kraftwerk and chasing the elusive European electro sound created and perfected by the masters of Düsseldorf. The admiration for Kling Klang techno ties them all together and makes sense of the line to be drawn between Depeche Mode's "New Life" and Derrick May's "Nude Photo".

Of course, there is another way of looking at it. "Some of our records have a good beat and that's about the end of it," says Dave Gahan •

28

GOING UNDERGROUND
FEBRUARY 1989

London's new generation of Tube parties by T-Cut-K

AROUND 9.30PM AT the Embankment tube station, Circle Line, 150-odd people glowing with an aura of "street cred" gather at the far end of the westbound platform, dancing to ghetto blasters with LED meters at peak before cramming into the last carriage of the 9.55pm train. Sporadic events since 1979, the new generation of Tube parties are organised by World Crime and The Bash St Kids and are set to a strictly alkaline, funky musical format. Since advertising is mainly by word of mouth, most tubers know or recognise each other and solidarity is strong. In general they feel dissatisfied with what's on offer elsewhere, as Drax of World Crime explains: "Clubs are rubbish – they're too financially organised." And who can disagree when a club in Brixton claiming to appeal to "lowlifes, celebrities, punks, dreads and other idealists for change" charges £15 at the door? Passengers have other carriages to move into if the rave is not to their liking, though most seemed more bewildered than intimidated. "We should have more of it!" said one, Gerry, while another said, "I'd do it myself, mate!" Ticket inspector Mr O'Connor reflected, "As an LRT employee I'd have to say no, but as a member of the public – as long as they don't hurt anyone, why not?" The parties are free, non-elitist (there's no VIP carriage) and reasons for attending are as varied as the ravers. Izzy, a student at Brighton Poly: "We're all taxpayers, and should be allowed to do what we like with public property." Michelle, another student: "Yeah, I'm a rebel!" And Drax on whether he's an anarchist: "No, just bored" •

29   NIGHTS IN WHITE SPANDEX

JUNE 1989

Hard rock at The Hippodrome by Sarah Kennedy

"WE DIDN'T THINK we'd last more than three weeks," says DJ Krusher of his Wednesday rock night, now into its third month at London's Hippodrome. Devoid of beer-sodden zombies straight off the Donnington bus, here we have the pristine version of rock'n'roll. Roland synthesiser reps in tight satin tights and white cowboy boots mingle with rock "legends" like Iron Maiden while the dancefloor pulsates with Led Zeppelin, Anthrax and the *Clockwork Orange* soundtrack. At midnight a band comes on to do the genuine thing, complete with guitar solos and mike stands, and the silver-studded audience lets its hair down, so to speak. With the rock beast's popularity currently returning to early Seventies-style proportions, Wednesdays are level with Saturdays as the chrome-plated hell-hole's busiest night. "It's the dry ice machines that pull them in," claims Krusher, though the chance to bang on down to classic tracks in public for the first time since the scout disco may add to the appeal. "They still love Motorhead's 'Ace Of Spades' and AC/DC's 'Back In Black', because they're fucking great tracks!" says Krusher. "This isn't your fickle pop crap, in one minute and out the next." Snigger not – the final word goes to an American tourist who had been enticed in by the Stringfellow hype (there are no signs outside warning that Wednesday is rock night) and found himself far from disco city. "I can't believe what rockers you Brits are! This is your biggest, best dancehall and you're all getting down to Whitesnake. Acid my ass!" •

30 THROWING SHADE

JULY 1989

Vogueing by Laurie Pike

THE FASHION EVENT of New York happened weeks after the shows: The Love Ball, an Aids benefit organised by bewigged nightclub hostess Suzanne Bartsch. Voguers, mainly from gay black and Hispanic "houses" in Harlem, had never before performed to an audience this straight (sexually or culturally). *Vogue* itself contributed substantial sums for its pissy editors to sip champagne and witness the acrobatic dance inspired by poses from its pages. In fact, many buyers of the $500 seats were media people, so rural American trendies will soon be using terms like "throwing shade" (putting another dancer to shame) and "realness" (convincing drag). A panel that included David Byrne, Iman and Thierry Mugler judged first a contest between the original houses of Pendavis, Magnifique, Elite, Extravaganza etc, then one between the "houses" of 14 corporations, designers and magazines. Williwear simulated a movie take, starring top model Cindy Crawford; Body Map dressed madly gyrating drag queens; but the ball gowns made out of magazine pages won first prize for the popular underdog, *Paper* magazine. The trophies were decorated by various NY artists, so that the works of Keith Haring, Francesco Clemente, Kenny Scharf and Julian Schnabel now sit proudly in Harlem tenements •

31   THE WE GENERATION

DECEMBER 1989

Clubland's new era by Sheryl Garratt and Lindsay Baker

BIOLOGY, OCTOBER 21. We finally get through on the phone at midnight, only to be told to go to the Byfleet services on the A31 for further instructions. An hour later, we arrive to find the service station under arrest. Police ring the Happy Eater to protect it from crazed clubbers demanding hamburgers, and a small group blocks the entrance, waving cars on.

Following processions of similarly packed cars, we drive on to Farnham, but there's nothing there: bemused, but generally friendly local bobbies; clusters of clubbers round payphones listening to the same recorded message we'd all heard two or three hours ago; cars parked in rows while people run anxiously from window to window asking for news. Some aren't even looking for the same party: they have tickets to a different rave, but just followed the crowd. Drive decisively in any direction, and you find yourself leader of a convoy; pull up and everyone assumes you're a guide waiting to give out instructions.

For hours we play the clubland version of treasure hunt, winding down country lanes, circling the same roundabouts again and again, then on to the Fleet services on the A3, which have also been swamped by police. By now it's 5am, and the car park is all but deserted. In the shop, a few would-be ravers queue quietly for Coke and crisps. No one seems angry – in fact, for people who've spent £25 each on a futile drive around the countryside, they seem positively benevolent. The search is part of the pleasure; as police actions and rip-offs by cowboy organisers increase, the search often *is* the pleasure.

Back in London, we tune into a pirate in time to hear that the party has been cancelled. On the TV news the next day, the only raised voice belongs to a motorist trapped in the services by a police roadblock. This is ridiculous, he screams, all these kids want to do is enjoy themselves. Why is the law trying to stop them?

All this is a long way away from the warehouses of the early and mid-Eighties. Even last year, the huge parties for up to 15,000 people at the Hordern Pavilion in Sydney, Australia, seemed awesome to clubbers in London, where an event for 3,000 at the Brixton Academy was deemed feature material for listings magazines like *Time Out*. Now such mass events are almost commonplace: promoters judge their success on the numbers they attract, not the names in the VIP room, and the clubbers come not to be seen but to hide in the crowd. The Me Generation has been replaced by the We Generation: in clubland as elsewhere, a new attitude is taking over. Soul II Soul call it "a happy face, a thumping bass for a loving race". De La Soul call it The Daisy Age. Magazines talk of Cabbage Patch Kids, New Age Clubbers and Nouveau Hippies, while the tabloids, somewhat tragically, still insist on calling it acid. Names, though, are irrelevant. The flyers for these events give an idea of the attitudes behind them: elaborate, full-colour leaflets now show cosmic, quasi-hippy mystical images to advertise raves like Infinity, The Meaning Of Life, Humanity, Phantasy and Live The Dream.

But this is more than just the old hippies with a new soundtrack. Nicky Holloway used to end nights at The Trip with The Rolling Stones' "Sympathy For The Devil", and there have been reworkings of Fleetwood Mac's "Oh Well" and Led Zeppelin's "Whole Lotta Love", but if clubbers are looking back at Sixties values, what they see is filtered through an awareness of what's happened since. In the Aids era, free love is replaced by expensive raving, the crowd is more likely to chant "Mental, mental" than "No rain", while girls don't buy the Earth Mother routine – faces scrubbed clean of make-up, they wear much the same as the boys. New York DJ Frankie Bones was astounded by the different approach. "Where we come from, girls sit behind the mirror for eight hours before they go out, they're into glamour. The field and the girls just wouldn't mix. In England, it's more of a comfort thing."

But are these happy happy attitudes drug-induced, or signs of a more fundamental change? Is the We Generation also the E Generation? It's impossible to have a reasonable debate on drugs in the current climate of tabloid hysteria, but the drinks companies probably have more to worry about than do parents. Partly due to licensing laws that mean all-night parties can't legally sell booze, and partly because alcohol and all-night dancing don't mix too well, drink plays very little part in the new raves. And although Ecstasy helped shape the early scene, by no means all the dancers in those sweaty, euphoric early nights were on unnatural highs.

Nor does it totally explain the new, more positive feel: Ecstasy is not a new phenomenon in London. At least one mid-Eighties warehouse featured a backroom with rugs and furry cushions where clubland personalities got off their famous faces while stroking the soft furnishings; more My Little Pony than summer of love, it hardly provoked a mass wave of peace and happiness.

The clothes, too, are about as far from the monochrome set as possible. The old uniform of Levi's and MA-1 jackets, black with perhaps a touch of white, is now almost as dated as stripy tank-tops and long-collared shirts. It is possible to spend serious money on raving gear (footwear especially – neither trainers nor Timberland boots come cheap), but designer labels are all but irrelevant.

Instead, there's a new sense of fun in fashion. People wear their lilac romper suits and Osh-Gosh dungarees with pride. It's a swift and street-level reaction against the self-consciousness of the "cool" designer Eighties. Wallabees, Kickers, trainers and Timberland boots have replaced DMs and brogues, and clothes tend to be practical and layered: an eclectic mix of ethnic prints, ornate waistcoats, oversized Peruvian jumpers, ponchos, African hats and pendants, tracksuit bottoms and dungarees. In the crowd you may also spot the odd man in navy Top Man tracksuit, immaculate new trainers and strange accessories such as bandannas or Smiley badges – these are plain-clothes policemen or tabloid journalists. Otherwise, the colours are garishly bright or soft pastels.

It's a style that has spread rapidly: a year ago, four people in dungarees standing round a phone box constituted a meeting-point. Now it's just as likely to be a bunch of Brosettes dialling the *Smash Hits* phone-lines. Follow a gang of kids clad in pastels and you're as likely to end up in a school disco as an all-night party.

No one seems to resent this. On the whole, the We Generation don't dress to stand out. They don't want to be Chosen Ones, ushered in through the doors of small West End clubs because their clothes are sharper than the poor plebs in the queue. The We Generation like nothing better than dressing up like their mates in comfortable, baggy clothes, piling into a car together, then dancing all night with a few thousand like-minded souls. Like their older brothers and sisters, who travelled miles armed with whistles, foghorns and water pistols to the soul weekenders and all-dayers, they like the power felt in numbers: the point is not to be noticed, not to be more knowledgeable or stylish than anyone else. The point is just to be there, to share that euphoria. "It appeals to people who were scared of clubs before," says promoter Tony Colston-Hayter.

A look at Colston-Hayter's computerised membership list reveals a surprising cross-section of people: bankers and barrow-boys, Sharons and Selinas can all put on the uniform and blend in as long as they have the admission price and the transport to get there. You don't even have to be able to dance: cool has been replaced by sweaty, and you just wave your arms in the air, smile and jump around. The addresses are equally revealing: there are members from Scotland, Devon, and significant numbers in all the big club cities. London membership is spread across the capital, from suburbs to inner city, whereas a similar survey of, say, the Wag's core clientele would reveal few from those districts that languish at the end of tube lines.

The current rave culture is, in many ways, the revenge of the suburbs; ousted for much of the decade, they've suddenly come back into their own. In the suburbs, the car is all: you get driving lessons for your 17th birthday, you save up for a wreck bound up with gaffer tape from the start of your first Saturday job. In a club culture where mobility is essential, the suburbs rule.

Eighties club culture divided paying customers into two categories: the Chosen Ones, those with the right looks/clothes/connections to be admitted into the inner sanctums of cool; and the Terminally Naff, the Kevins and Sharons who took their shiny suits and white stilettos to The Hippodrome and all its smaller suburban disco equivalents. The Chosen Ones aspired to access to every VIP room, to be on first-name terms with the doorman, to be one of the few. The Naffs wanted a good time, a pick-up, a laugh with their mates. If they aspired to anything clubwise, it was Stringfellows.

From The Cult With No Name through all the various subgroups and movements catalogued first in magazines like this one then later by the mainstream media, the Eighties has rejoiced in diversity. When acid first arrived, it seemed to be just another passing phase – the south of England finally discovering the house music the rest of the country had known about for some time.

Some grumbled that it excluded the majority of the black clubbers who had finally been integrated into the West End (the early scene was very white), others rejoiced in the diversity that meant that indie bands, European disco and US imports could mix on dancefloors previously dominated by snobbery or kitsch. As the scene continued and expanded, the complaints got louder: this was a suburban crowd, not real clubbers, sneered the old guard. They weren't there for the music, they just wanted the high. They couldn't even dance. As it turned out, these were the grumblings of a generation who were being replaced: those who didn't want to go with the flow were, in the end, run over by it. There are still plenty of London clubs where such DJs play and such clubbers gather – many of them still the liveliest in the capital – but even they would concede that the main action is now elsewhere.

here will always be those who do not wish to be part of the main action anyway. For many of those, usually older clubbers who have stuck to the smaller raves, the thrill of subcultural creativity outweighs what they would see as the conformism of the big raves. Boy's Own fanzine, a pioneering force on the early house scene, is a case in point. The four-strong Boy's Own crew, DJs as well as writers, have held several successful but deliberately small-scale parties and are staunch defenders of the "underground". "It was supposed to have broken all the rules," they say, "but it's just changed them. When it started it was 'listen to what you want, doowatchalike', as the record goes; now it's 'you must wear this, you must listen to this, or you're not in the gang'."

The fragmentation of the Eighties has been largely replaced by a new homogeneity, a music that knits the various strands together as one. This music can encompass African chants, flamenco guitar, indie thrash, Eurodisco, Chicago house, hip house, Detroit techno, New York garage, rap, skacid, acid jazz, and almost anything else you want it to. And so now the Sloane girls from Crazy Larry's dance next to posse boys from the North Peckham Estate, while suburbanites have traded cowboy boots for baseball boots and rub shoulders with deliberately dressed-down West-Enders.

"It's not segregated here," notes Frankie Bones. "Music has one face, one colour. This kind of thing could never happen back home. It's a territorial thing. New Yorkers are much more aggressive and egotistical."

Indie bands have slowly, grudgingly conceded that the old punk adage "disco sucks" isn't always true, but records like New Order's "Blue Monday", accepted by both camps, have been rare up to now. But suddenly, we have the Happy Mondays, Stone Roses, The Beloved, KLF, The Shamen; the grey macs came to the club, decided they liked the strobes and the attitude, and have settled down to stay. "The indie scene's catching up," says Jon Marsh of The Beloved. "It's been absurdly élitist in the past. It's good that dance ideas are beginning to get absorbed." For their part, the clubbers have dropped the snobbery, and after an initial period of passing off indie bands as "Balearic", they now accept them for what they are: good dance records.

The effects have been felt in the music industry too. It's no longer Radio One playlisting or clever marketing that sells records, it's the raves, and, in London at least, the new breed of pirate radio stations. Centreforce is back on the air after a recent, heavily publicised bust, along with Obsession, Sunrise, Fantasy and newcomers Freedom and Dance. Records like Quartz's "Meltdown" and 808 State's "Pacific State" were brought out almost anonymously on small independent labels and with no promotion. The route to chart success has been revolutionised.

"People don't realise how huge it is," says Frankie Bones, who has taken to exporting British music to the States, launching it onto an unsuspecting latin hip hop crowd in Brooklyn. "I've witnessed them dancing to 808 State for the first time in a frenzy. The buzz is out there too now. There's gonna be a lot of innovators coming out of London in the Nineties. Paul Anderson, Trevor Fung, these guys are gonna make good records. This is the new school."

Live music, too, is seeing a resurgence, with keyboard, percussion and trumpet players performing over records as well as alone. "Technology has progressed substantially, which makes it easier to play live," says Simon Monday. "It's become a lot more self-contained – all you need is a sequencer, keyboards and a digital mixer."

So what will the future bring? A quieter winter, for sure, as the large scale events wind down with the colder weather (though watch out for some spectacular New Year raves). With recent police clampdowns the scene will have to change to survive. We may even see the return of the smaller, more intimate rave. The next plan for Boy's Own is an all-night cinema club for around 100 people: "We're a minority, but a minority that's growing."

There is talk, among the more civilised elements in Whitehall, of registering the more competent party organisers and letting them run properly policed events in venues checked by safety officers. But there is also talk, from an increasingly desperate Tory government, of adjusting existing laws to make prosecution of ravers easier. Huge fines, imprisonment, confiscation of profits and equipment have been suggested, and it is becoming increasingly hard for promoters to hire sound systems, marquees, or even venues: £20,000 is the going rate for a field at the moment.

"Winter will kill off the cowboys," says Colston-Hayter. "I welcome it getting smaller, a bit more personal again. Last winter was brilliant – the best Sunrises were then, with crowds of 2,000 people in equestrian centres. The illicit parties have finally come to an end because the police really mean business, but it'll explode again next summer." He is now paying policing bills of around £5,000 an event, and fighting to have his M-rated phone lines (0836 numbers) reconnected. Though porn lines are OK, it seems party details "bring the system into disrepute".

For their part, clubbers have been more irritated by these particular infringements of their civil rights than other, perhaps rather more important government measures, such as the poll tax or privatisation. The same methods that send thousands of people to obscure country locations could, some have been heard to say, send them into the centre of London at a few hours' notice for a mass demonstration.

Others argue that the whole phenomenon is a product of Thatcherism. "Thatcher might hate them but they're her creation," says Terry Farley of Boy's Own. "Ten years of Thatcher's government has created Energy, Biology, Sunrise. It's the sort of Yuppie, city whizzkid, 'I've got a Vodaphone and a Porsche, let's have a party' mentality."

On his side, Colston-Hayter blames the press for attracting the cowboys: "They want to make a million pounds, as seen in the *Sun*: 'Tony Colston-Hayter made £1 million last night!' They've attracted a lot of people into the business."

And if they are a product of greed, the parties are at the same time a strangely egalitarian, collective reaction against the them-and-us, divided nation, "me" mentality. Huge, peaceful gatherings of young people is hardly a situation conducive to divide and rule.

It remains to be seen which attitudes will win through. Will, as Boy's Own fear, the new generation take club cowboys as their role models? Or will the strength, unity and fighting spirit of the We Generation prove stronger?

Meanwhile, sports and casualwear may continue to threaten those designer labels that rely on a younger clientele. What you are will become more important than what you own, and it will become more difficult to sell consumer durables to the young in the name of style (though pseudo-green products will thrive). Maybe, just maybe, some of these New Age values will filter down and people will be a little more open, a little less selfish in the next decade. Whatever happens, it seems likely that youth culture won't be as fragmented as it has been in the Eighties; teenagers are a threatened demographic group. There just won't be as many of them, and if they don't want to disappear altogether under a rising tide of CDs and copies of *Q* magazine, they'll have to stick together.

"As long as the licensing laws mean that no one can dance after 3.30am in this country, there'll always be a place for these parties," says Colston-Hayter. "I had the best time of my life in Shoom and Future, and people still enjoy it now for those same reasons; they don't get drunk, and they want to dance all night"•

FIGHTING FOR THE RIGHT TO PARTY

FEBRUARY 1990

HM Government vs Acid House by Sheryl Garratt and Chris Taggart

----

ON DECEMBER 31, 1989, World Wide Promotions, the company behind Sunrise and Back To The Future, had planned to welcome in the new decade in style. On that Sunday afternoon, three big tops and some smaller marquees stood on private land, interconnected by tunnels and furnished with matting or specially built wooden dancefloors. Lasers, sound systems, screens and special effects were in place. DJs and PAs had been booked. Fire exits and extinguishers had been checked, the sound system – from a company that has supplied both Wembley and the London Arena – was fitted with decibel monitors, and some of the guests were already en route. It should have been one hell of a party. But it never happened.

The story behind the eleventh-hour cancellation of what may be the last attempt to hold a large-scale, legal rave for some time in this country is an instructive one, showing just how far the authorities are willing to go to stop all-night clubbing. When they begin to take holidays here over the next few years, Eastern European visitors may find some of Britain's restrictions on personal freedom strangely familiar.

Contrary to popular opinion, the Sunrise/Back To The Future parties are not illegal. They don't need a drinks licence because alcohol is not on sale. Nor do they need to be licensed under the 1982 Public Entertainment Act, since they are a private member's club – only members can buy tickets, and to join, you have to apply, in advance, with an existing member as a proposer. In 1989, two court cases established without doubt that Sunrise was a members club, most notably a full magistrate's hearing in Maidenhead last November, when the prosecution was unable to prove that any member of the general public had ever been able to buy admission to a World Wide event on the night.

To ensure that everyone arrived at the venue before midnight, the original party location – Harlow, in Essex – was printed on the ticket, avoiding the usual runaround of phonecalls and motorway service stations. But the week before, World Wide's lawyers did a search on the land and discovered that it wasn't owned by the person who had hired it to them. As a consequence, the party moved to the back-up location in Norfolk, and organiser Tony Colston-Hayter called Essex police to tell them Harlow was off. On Tuesday, December 26, he faxed details to the Norfolk police, and meetings were held with senior officers regarding routes, safety and parking arrangements. (Interestingly, when we contacted Norfolk Police, their press officer said they had heard about the party not from the promoters but "on the grapevine".)

On Saturday lunchtime, the Sunrise team were surprised to see police arriving at the farmhouse they were using as a base. They waited four hours to see the site owner, who declined to interrupt his Christmas holiday. Finally, they presented Colston-Hayter with an injunction. The party, they said, was off.

The rest of Saturday and Sunday morning were spent frantically preparing to appeal. World Wide's lawyers saw no problem. An injunction under the Public Entertainment Act wouldn't hold up, as Sunrise had already been legally proved a private club. "We stayed up all night writing statements about safety, noise levels and parking," says Colston-Hayter. "We were 100 per cent confident, lulled into a false sense of security because we were within the law. But they just twisted it – it was unbelievable. I didn't realise they were so determined."

At a special hearing on Sunday afternoon, Mr Justice Potter ruled against World Wide. If North Norfolk District Council were subsequently proved wrong, he argued, then they could afford to compensate World Wide for their losses.

As a result, World Wide are planning to sue the council for £200,000, and the New Year's revellers who had paid from £18 to £25 a ticket were guided instead to a free party in Slough. At the same time, central London was packed with revellers all hyped up by the start of a decade, but with nowhere to go. Only one club in the capital – the Brixton Academy – was granted an all-night licence, and as New Year's Eve fell on a Sunday, many had to close at 2am and a few didn't open at all. In Manchester, the Haçienda was given a choice between opening late on either Christmas Eve or New Year's Eve.

"The annoying thing is that there have been no fights at our events, no injuries or public order offences," says Colston-Hayter. "They're banking on the fact that people like us will be ruined by legal bills, and they're pushing it back towards the people who break into warehouses without permission and just hold parties outside the law."

Meanwhile, the Government continues to act against the scene. In a statement on December 5, the Home Office announced plans for changes in the law to enable summary fines of up to £20,000 and prison terms of up to six months for party organisers breaking the Public Entertainments Act, along with confiscation of profits in excess of £10,000 for landowners and promoters and confiscation of equipment (this would make it almost impossible for party promoters to hire equipment from established companies). Graham Bright MP has agreed to steer these measures through parliament as a Private Member's Bill, which stands a good chance of becoming law before the summer recess.

In the interim, the Home Office recommends that the 333 local authorities adopt the Private Places of Entertainment (Licensing) Act 1967, a law requiring private events to be licensed in the same way as public events "enabled" by councils. Few councils have this law on their books (Norfolk did not at the time of the Sunrise party), but most are expected to pass it by the end of February, effectively closing the loophole that has allowed members-only parties to remain legal.

This is fully supported by the Association Of District Councils, which issued a press release late last year outlining "the acid house party problem". At the Department of Environment's invitation, the ADC suggested 21 changes to the law, some of which are now included in Graham Bright's bill.

Like the "acid packs" apparently sent to police forces around the country, briefing them on pay parties and explaining what measures can be taken to stop them, the ADC's reaction immediately assumes that a gathering of young people for the purpose of all-night dancing is "a problem". A special intelligence unit, led by Chief Supt Ken Tappenden, has been set up in Gravesend. Like all the police representatives we tried to contact for this piece, they were remarkably taciturn when we called them ("We make no press comment whatscever"), but according to a *Sunday Telegraph* report, the incident room has around 20 detectives from a dozen counties tracking down parties on a full-time basis. A special "acid house rapid deployment task force" of 250 officers costs £20,000 every Saturday night – money and time that could surely be better used elsewhere if the parties were legalised and controlled.

The authorities' determination to clamp down on the scene also showed in the sentencing of the organisers of a Greenwich boat party late last year. On November 4, 1988, the police raided two boat parties in "Operation Seagull", eventually making 18 arrests. Nine of these have so far been fined or convicted, including Clive Reynolds, who was found in possession of 58 tabs of Ecstasy. He was sentenced to four years, but the party organisers fared worse; Robert Darby and Leslie Thomas were sentenced to ten and six years respectively after being found guilty of "conspiring to manage premises where drugs were supplied". The tabloid press rejoiced, and on the January 9 edition of the TV news programme *Thames Reports*, Det Chief Inspector Albert Patrick said, "It was an excellent result. The first conviction of its kind in the country."

It also sets dangerous precedents. If, in a raid on a club, drugs are found, will the organisers get longer sentences than the dealers? Was Robert Darby's crime really greater than those of the rapists, muggers, child molesters and thugs who rarely get such stiff sentences? The fight is becoming about more than the right to party; civil rights are being abused with alarming regularity.

The National Council For Civil Liberties (Liberty) has repeatedly pointed out that the police have no general power to set up roadblocks, even though they are now doing so on a scale unprecedented since the miners' strike. Since parties don't necessarily constitute a breach of the peace, this "appears to be an unjustified infringement of the right to freedom of movement".

Mass invasions of police to break up parties are also illegal, unless they have been specifically invited to enter by the landowner, they have a warrant, or they wish to arrest a specific person for a specific offence. Nor, under current law, are police entitled to confiscate equipment, even though they have done so.

According to Liberty's Madeleine Colvin, the only way to stop this would be by test cases in the courts, and "we would certainly consider taking a case to court if one came to us".

As for the new proposals, Keir Starmer, Legal Officer at Liberty – and also one of the lawyers who has been representing Sunrise in recent cases – says, "Further police powers are unnecessary and set a dangerous precedent whereby ordinary citizens would be prohibited from assembling together for whatever purpose without informing the police beforehand and without being subjected to police restrictions. Such measures pose a serious threat to democracy."

Graham Bright MP is not impressed, dismissing Liberty's claims as "the sort of loony comment I'd expect to come out of that organisation. I don't take them seriously at all, I'm afraid."

Bright, the Tory MP for Luton South, is described as "a self-made businessman" in *Roth's Parliamentary Profiles*. He is for hanging, against pornography and pollution, and has campaigned vigorously against the expansion of Luton airport. He sees parallels with his current bill and the legislation against video nasties that he helped to pass in 1983. "I'm always interested in protecting young people. That was my main motive with that one, and my main motive again is the same.

"I've gone to pains to point out that I'm after illegal acid house parties, and the fact that the majority of them are illegal is neither here nor there. This doesn't affect things like the tennis club barbeque, or the boy scouts. We're after those making personal profits, the Mr Bigs who are getting thousands out of this, and in some cases endangering people's lives. The fines are now totally inadequate (up to £1,000). They make a mockery of it."

When announcing his bill, Bright claimed all-party support for the measures: "I have not found anyone who is in any way opposed to what I am trying to do, such has been the impact of news stories relating to illegal acid house parties." Indeed, for a party keen to court the youth vote, Labour has been remarkably quiet on this issue. Though the party organisers have reported that, on the whole, Labour-led councils have been far more open to the idea of giving out licences to well-organised events, the Parliamentary party seems both indifferent and ill-informed.

There will, says Labour's Home Office spokesman Barry Sheerman, be no instructions to Labour MPs to oppose the bill: "We don't normally officially oppose that kind of bill, or propose them. It'll be a free vote, I should imagine."

After much fudging (including the rather strange idea that the young are "forced" into clubs for entertainment due to lack of alternatives), he eventually agreed that Liberty were "on the right track", and that Government measures did appear to be "quite Draconian". Sensibly condemning parties used to distribute dangerous drugs and those that cause nuisance to local people, he said (and this, like Graham Bright's quote, is an edited version):

"The Labour Party does not want unnecessary legislation that basically acts as a killjoy for young people enjoying themselves legitimately and pursuing their interests in music and dancing. It's bad to introduce laws in an atmosphere of hysteria whipped up by the popular press which gets the perception of the problem totally distorted. It is a problem – it does cause real nuisance to some people – but it's a small problem, and some of the Government's reaction is a total overreaction to something that can be controlled by existing legislation. This kind of reaction is not good for democracy. This is a very authoritarian government of Mrs Thatcher's. Their liberalism is only an economic liberalism – and even that's a bit fuzzy in this case. The atmosphere is restrictive on a lot of young people trying to enjoy themselves, and, with reasonable safeguards, I think we should liberalise things."

Most of the promoters spoken to for this article would more than welcome "reasonable safeguards". Many complain that attempts to bring in police and safety officers beforehand merely lead to banning orders, and party organisers must be the only people ever to receive a bill for police services with joy; like organisers of football matches, concerts, regattas and airshows, they would prefer to pay for the extra policing they create the need for, and co-operate fully with the authorities.

Whatever the rights and wrongs, it is too late to clamp down on clubbing by attacking organisers and suppliers. By the time the media picked up on acid in a big way in September that year, the Summer of Love '88 was already over, and a lifestyle, a music and an attitude were firmly established. In a recent poll of record buyers, over a third of 15- to 19-year-olds claimed their favourite music was "acid house", and it was revealed that that age group spends around £3 million a month on house albums alone. Uniting almost all the youth sub-cults of the past ten years, the scene has created a demand that cannot be killed by merely banning T-shirts from Top Shop, records from Radio One, or persecuting party organisers.

More people visit Europe than ever before, and see clubs open in Spain, Italy, and just across the channel in France and Belgium and don't see why they can't have the same. Even in Glasgow, Europe's 1990 City Of Culture, clubs can open till 5am and pubs till 2am.

Meanwhile, many of the straighter party organisers are giving up. Some are applying for licences everywhere in the hope that some come through. Others, like the Freedom Fighters, are organising admission-free parties totally outside the law. Sunrise are trying to organise a licensed summer festival and perhaps even a weekly London night closing at 3.30am, but in the meantime they aim to organise weekend raves outside Britain, starting in Amsterdam. Energy are running monthly events at Brixton Academy, but no outdoor raves.

"It's not worth putting money into illegal parties any more," says their spokesman Jeremy. "It doesn't make sense when they're likely to be stopped. It's more like gambling than business."

There have been stories of armed police arresting security men travelling to sites or even in their homes; of organisers dragged from cars by over-eager policemen who then discover they can't actually arrest them for anything (yet); of illegal searches at roadblocks; and of lists of party organisers being circulated to licensed club venues with the implication that, should these people be allowed to run club nights at the venue, their licences may be in jeopardy. Some of these stories are apocryphal, or just plain untrue, and there is much wrong on both sides.

No one is denying that drugs are sometimes taken at these parties. Drugs have always been taken in clubs. It is nowhere near on the scale the tabloids seem to believe, and is only encouraged by their lurid reports. But by forcing the promoters outside the law, police make it almost impossible for them to turn in dealers, or call for help when things get out of hand, and – as in any area where there's money to be made – organised crime is starting to move in.

Frightening tales are emerging of parties being violently broken up when protection money is refused, and of gangsters taking over on the night, controlling the door, taking the money, and selling drugs (a little smack with your E, anyone?) while the organisers look on helplessly.

Almost all the party organisers we spoke to for this piece said they would readily accept regulation of their parties on grounds of safety, noise and nuisance in exchange for the same legal status accorded to club organisers elsewhere in Europe or in Glasgow.

Everyone would win: it would mean revenue for the Government and local councils; it would mean safe venues, profits for promoters, DJs, hire companies, and everyone else involved (isn't that what enterprise culture is all about?); it would leave the police free to do more important work. Most of all, it would mean pleasure for thousands who often end the weekend with an unused £20 ticket and massive phone and petrol bills.

The door of the Pay Party Incident Room in Gravesend apparently has a crossed-out Smiley logo with the slogan, "Don't worry. Be happy." In the end, that's all any of us want •

33 WEIRD SCENES IN THE WEST COUNTRY
GOLDMINE MAY 1990

Smith and Mighty and the Bristol sound by John McCready

IT'S BEEN A MAD day, one of those days when you know you're speed-walking through something special. A blur of faces, names, handshakes and information make it hard to focus. With the amiable Charlie as our guide and go-between, we've been to back bedrooms, front rooms, and flats full of records and recording equipment. My ribcage still rattling from bassic vibration, I ask the question: "What's it all about, Charlie?"

Charlie, a member of Bristol's Three Stripe posse, puts his key in the front door and we head back to the living-room studio where producers Rob Smith and Ray Mighty cook up inspired combinations of the old and the new. But Charlie doesn't have to answer. In the building on Ashley Road, St Paul's, someone downstairs is mixing records. Dionne Warwick's wistful "Trains And Boats And Planes" floats across a brick-hard hip hop beat. Everything falls into place.

This eerie combination of opposites says more about Rob Smith and Ray Mighty and the output of their Three Stripe label than anything. The sound of Bacharach and David, gifted tin-pan composers of the Sixties, colliding with the raw power of scratchy breakbeats and bass-heavy reggae rhythms is really the key to an age-old underground sound. This sound has recently been translated for mass consumption through Norman Cook's Beats International, Soul II Soul, Sybil and a whole posse of others, like Kicking Back With Taxman and Innocence.

Clubland is moving slowly away from the hyper-groove of house and towards the mellow subsonics of new-age steppers. As house is absorbed into the mainstream and legal checkmates threaten this summer's rave scene, the club underground takes two steps back. Smith and Mighty's breathtaking translations of Bacharach and David's "Walk On By" and "Anyone" predate any of these new groups aside from Soul II Soul, whose underground history – from house parties to clubs, from sound systems to records – parallels their own.

But this year's underground is next year's overground. Soul II Soul have already stated the case for London, with platinum-plus sales of their "Club Classics" LP both here and in America. The success of Smith and Mighty and their Three Stripe stable of artists will soon make the case for Bristol, and show the city's undeniable influence on the strangely subdued sounds taking over your radio.

But on radio, you won't hear it properly. On radio, you'll never get the point. This is a music of treble highs and oceanic lows, a deeply sexual slow groove best experienced at a smokey blues party. This is a music made in the giant shadow of Jamaica's melodic but rootsy Studio One sound, a music where Dionne Warwick's "The Look Of Love" is pitched against the subsonic heartbeat pulse of a microchip kick drum. It's hard to articulate the tension created between the robotic pulse of a beatbox cranked up to ten and the sweet flow of a human voice tackling a melody your mum and dad would appreciate. But it's no good asking Rob Smith and Ray Mighty about it. They can't see what all the fuss is about; they just live it.

Smith and Mighty, or Rob and Ray as they are affectionately known to Bristol bassheads (the inference is musical not chemical), have just joined the circus with ffrr Records. For almost three years now, they've propelled their creations into the world through their own Three Stripe label. Ray was part of the city's Three Stripe sound system which lives on through the label and through the surviving giant bass speakers most Smith and Mighty tracks are mixed on. "We know when it sounds good on them then it's right," says Ray.

Rob Smith is a product of Bristol's once healthy live scene. The pair met playing in a band called Sweat in 1985. Robe believes the group was "well ahead of its time. A lot of what we do now was there then. A lot of what we were trying to do then we can do now because the technology is cheap and available."

They began recording together almost three years ago, making music they wanted to hear themselves. "We still work like that; we'll come from a party or a rave fired up, ready to do something. When we do remixes, the only aim is to build something that will rock the places we go to," says Ray. Such remixes are raw to the core and strictly for the underground. From Neneh Cherry to Fine Young Cannibals, a Smith and Mighty treatment puts the rhythm upfront and the bass in your face. Rapper Krissy Kris has watched them work and describes their methods as "weird". "But what they come up with is really special. It just has a flow. They give you the right spaces and drops. They just know."

Even a chance encounter with the Smith and Mighty sound is likely to convince you that all this is worth worrying about. They mix spooked-out electronics with breaks dropped into space; disappearing before you've noticed. There's a melancholic feel to their melodies that Burt Bacharach and Hal David would understand; dub gymnastics Lee Perry would understand; a bass your body will understand.

To those who go to the right clubs and the right record shops they are almost heroes. But Rob and Ray have had no real money to speak of and, most heartbreaking of all, their equipment is falling to bits. "Whatever happens, we'll always make music, but we need money to build a studio to get the sounds we want. We've made music for three years now on nothing." This is the reason they've signed a major record deal which gives them the freedom to create when, where and with who they want. It's a deal that, this year, will enable them to release three albums of their choice out of Bristol and into the mainstream, the first being an album by sweet-voiced singer Carlton.

Charlie, who collaborates with the pair on some of their music and works as part of the rap unit TCP, reveals that they're recording junkies – only really happy when sitting in front of a mixing desk. "Recording is just a day-to-day thing," he says. "Some days we'll get up and it'll be a house groove we get into. Whatever happens, there's always music around."

This I can't argue with. Everywhere we go, during the course of interviews in various locations, people experiment with sound while they talk. It's like they think they'll die if the rhythm stops. At a house bordering the moneyed Clifton area of the city, I talk to the Fresh 4 (who turn out to be six, but who's counting?). Their "Wishing On A Star", a top five hit produced by Smith and Mighty, typifies the real sound of the underground, a mix of mellow soul and funky beats. As he listens to me, Fresh 4 member Flynn can't stop cutting between two copies of a Stezo tune. This man has a musical problem. "You just wake up in the morning and you hit the drum machine. And if it's a slow beat, it's a slow beat, and if it's a fast beat, it's a fast beat."

Rob and Ray are equally obsessed. Having joined the circus they are expected to jump through verbal hoops for the benefit of intruders like me. Polite as they are, it's clear they'd much rather be messing about with a mix than talking to me or anyone else. This day excursion to their St Paul's base they see as part of the price of moving to the next stage. "No offence," says Rob quite genuinely, as he refuses to have his picture taken. "But we don't see the point. Who wants to know what we look like? You're either into the tune or you're not into the tune. Nobody cares what Jah Wobble looks like now: they just buy his records if they like them. We don't want to be recognised."

Rob then proceeds to play through some recent, unfinished tracks as Ray skins up, inhales and closes his eyes as the room reverberates. Rob listens, preoccupied, obviously putting things right silently. He looks almost sad, as well he might. The music sparks with originality and an instinctive rhythmic understanding which connects effortlessly. Eugene Manzi, press officer for ffrr Records, nods along in the knowledge that his employers have bought into a West Country goldmine.

Smith and Mighty have no chance of remaining backroom mystery men – a romantic notion they seem to have set their hearts on. When this gets out, the world and his wife will want to know everything. Already Smith and Mighty are the Stock, Aitken & Waterman of the Two Step scene, producing music that is ideal for all-night house parties, blues dances and underground sound system raves. When the sound goes overground with the release of Carlton's first single, "Do You Dream?", Rob won't even be able to go out for a Rizlas packet without being chased by autograph hunters.

Of course there's a history to all of this. A sound this strong doesn't appear from nowhere. Bristol, with a culturally-aware black community, has always been a reggae stronghold. Even when the sound fell from favour, St Paul's was still pulsing to the beat of Kingston's drum. When hip hop arrived, it seemed a natural progression. Instead of moving from one to the other, Bristol's sound systems mashed it all up.

The Wild Bunch operated from the early Eighties, a multi-racial posse of DJs and rappers who earned a reputation through their eclectic mixes of rap, reggae and smooth soul. Their "Look Of Love", inspired by the version mania of reggae, was the first Bacharach/David cover. Rob Smith admits it was the inspiration behind their own reworkings of "Walk On By" and "Anyone". Created as a one-off dub plate for their own use, The Wild Bunch would blast this as the centrepiece of their sets. Ray mighty remembers his first hearing it and thinking, "'What the fuck is that?' It blew me away." This was released as a B-side two years later by Fourth And Broadway.

The Wild Bunch would play records before and after sets by local reggae band Restriction, and Rob and Charlie were both members of the group. Nellee Hooper of The Wild Bunch would look after the sound at Restriction gigs. Nellee later went to London with his bag of tricks and joined the Soul II Soul posse who'd been working along similar lines in the capital – a sound system with an attitude and vinyl ambitions.

Though the Three Stripe crew may be pissed off with Sybil's recent top ten version of "Walk On By", an idea obviously stolen from Rob and Ray's idiosyncratic treatment of the classic tune, they have no bone to pick with Jazzie. "They were doing the same thing at the same time. It's just an underground vibe. It's probably happening in most cities in Britain. But the Sybil thing was annoying. I know we don't own the tune, but the treatment was a bit close to say the least."

Rob and Ray are used to having people dip into their bag of magic tricks. It's only the fact that they seem to have so many more ideas to work on that stops them getting really upset. That the producers of Sybil's "Walk On By" did nothing new with the record is of more concern to Smith and Mighty. "The appeal of 'The Look Of Love' was that it was a real stripped-down version of the tune. When we tackled 'Walk On By', it was natural to us to play around with the structure of it." Similar dub tactics are employed on most tracks they produce, a sound that also appeals to the house crowd and was popular at last summer's raves. "It's mind-fuck music," says Rob. "It's all about ridiculous treble and massive, massive bass. That's the one thing we have in common with all the people we work with. They're all into bass."

So we pack into their newly-acquired Citroen Familial, a big estate car bought too late for last year's summer raves. We meet most of the Three Stripe artists, bass addicts all. From the young True Funk Posse – a rapper aged 12 and a DJ aged 16 with a combined talent which makes them more than an ageist novelty – to a Fresh 4 shirty with success, everyone is keen to tell you what Rob and Ray have done for them.

It's clear that Bristol is a village. Rapper Krissy Kris tells me, "If you're doing the same thing, you end up bumping into like-minded people." The more people we talk to the clearer it becomes that Three Stripe is a self-supporting family. A London connection for Smith and Mighty means that everybody else gets a piece of the pie. "We know what it's like to be ripped off because it's happened to us," says Charlie. "We want to try and help these people so they don't have to deal with the fuckers we've come up against."

At the end of our day of interviews, an after-hours party is organised so we can chill till the dawn. So the press contingent books into the Bristol Hilton to return to St Paul's later. We order a cab after midnight to get back there, but the cab driver tells us he doesn't go to that area and we're stuck inside our £81-a-night pristine paradise. On the other side of town, the underground rocks regardless •

34   ONE LOVE

JULY 1990

The Stone Roses at Spike Island by Simon Dudfield

SUNDAY MAY 27. By 10am in Manchester, Piccadilly bus station was filled with 13-year-olds with wide bottomed jeans and Stone Roses T-shirts. In Dry, the Factory bar, the band's dancer, Cressa, shared breakfast with Bez of the Happy Mondays, and older fans filled up with croissants to soak up the night before. By 2am that day, a crowd of 30,000 had descended on Spike Island, an unremarkable park in the middle of an industrial estate beside the Mersey.

A few Christians with placards protested that the Sabbath should be kept holy, earnestly arguing their case with a group of drunken Inspirals fans. Men wider than any of the trousers on show were selling "spare tickets" and Stone Roses posters that bore a striking resemblance to Glen Luchford's full-page portrait of the band in January's FACE. Somewhat unfairly, soft drinks and sandwiches were confiscated at the gate, leaving the crowd inside at the mercy of the on-site caterers, and those outside enjoying a hurried picnic to avoid losing their supplies. The police looked bemused, but generally happy. "It's double time today, the sun's shining, and they seem like nice kids," commented one PC. "But why here?"

"For some reason we wanted to do a gig on an industrial estate or an island," says singer Ian Brown when cornered with the same question. "Our manager found it, and because it was cut off and had been used for the Widnes Carnival before, it was spot on. Plus we wanted to play in the north west, and because Spike Island was in the middle of Manchester and Liverpool, it was perfect."

And walking amongst the crowd, when DJs Paul Oakenfold and Dave Haslam were sprinkling magic in the air, when everyone was smiling and dancing, and the maddest had their heads shoved right inside the massive speakers giving it plenty, you thought it looked that way. You realised you had to be there when seasoned clubbers rubbed their Koshino-clad shoulders with 12-year-old schoolgirls in tour T-shirts and didn't mind; when the sun was shining and "Step On" blasted out and everyone cheered and got up to dance.

But if this was going to live up to expectations – the first big rave of the summer – then Oakenfold and Haslam shouldn't have left so early. "The DJs we wanted to play weren't given long enough," explains Brown. "We thought it was in our hands until the actual day. The promoters should have done more for the people; there wasn't enough prepared."

There had been problems for weeks before: "200 people signed a petition to stop us playing, barges tried to knock the bridges down, and the drinks licence was taken off us two days before we did it. The chief of police gave it back though, so we must have friends in high places."

So instead of dancing, you stood there and thought about the enormity of it all. If the first summer of love was in small clubs, and the second took place in fields and aircraft hangers, then the third – if the ecstasy doesn't give way to apathy – is going to be massive gigs and festivals like this one. And then you got scared because people were sitting down, the main entertainment was watching those without tickets storm the bridges and fences, and it all looked pretty bleak. You tried hard to believe New York DJ Frankie Bones when he announced that it was "house music all night long" but you knew it was ending at 11 o'clock. The crowd looked restless, looking at their watches and asking when it would start.

It already had and it wasn't happening; Paul Oakenfold's slot was cut from two hours to 40 minutes to make room for a session from Frankie Bones. "I didn't say anything because I'd already been paid," said Oakenfold. "The Stone Roses made it hard on their fans because they didn't announce anything else was going to happen. So you had kids turning up at 2pm expecting them to be on, yet they had to wait until 9pm. And they're basically indie kids, so they don't want Frankie Bones playing house. It was a bit embarrassing. Parts of the band's set was brilliant, but the day could have been better."

With a huge crowd out on the field and everyone from Smith and Mighty to Ian McCullough in the guest enclosure, the band had a right to be nervous. If I was Ian Brown, my guts would have been on the floor seeing all those people waiting for him to do the business, expecting him to put the day's wrongs to rights. "Nah, I was 100 per cent relaxed. If all these people had come to see us, they wanted it. So why should I have been nervous?"

Because by the time The Stone Roses came on the atmosphere was sour, people were well pissed off, and they needed to be at their best to put something in the air. They were and they did; the night ended with spectacular fireworks, the crowd shuffled home happy, and if Brown can help it this summer will be as special as the two just past: "We're going to do London again because we were a bit disappointed with our gig at Alexandra Palace – the sound was shit. We want to do a massive venue where no one has played before and where we can come on as late as possible. We want to get away with as much as the British licensing laws will let us" •

35　THE END OF THE BEGINNING

The Beloved by Sheryl Garratt (excerpt)

...THESE DAYS, EVERYONE'S looking for the next big thing, I say. They're scared of missing out. A fleeting mention of a new band in The FACE these days – especially one with a Northern accent – leads to a barrage of calls from record companies and other publications eager not to miss out. "It's impossible to have an underground any more," agrees Jon Marsh [of The Beloved]. "The reason the whole acid thing had time to grow was that everyone was so busy writing about rare groove that nobody noticed that there was a whole group of dodgy geezers in south London going completely mad.

"The best thing about it for me was watching all those people cross the river – it was brilliant, everything was going on in Streatham and Bermondsey. Paul Oakenfold's club, The Project, started off in Ziggy's in Streatham, the sort of place we wouldn't have been seen dead going to five years earlier. Now you've got Raid relaunching in Soho with Oakenfold amongst the DJs, and it's £10 to get in – it's gone far away from whatever it set out to achieve. It's become the old school of London clubbing, just as The Wag was three years ago.

"But it wasn't possible to stay underground. When it started, there was a three-year back catalogue of black American music that nobody in London had bothered to play before, but now a DJ has got maybe a month with a record before it goes top 40."

Like most of those involved in the early acid scene – from the Shoom regular who gave up his job to become a poet to the bands whose music changed direction, or numerous new designers, stallholders, fanzine writers and T-shirt bootleggers – The Beloved credit the clubs for their inspiration. "It made you rethink, take a 90 degree turn." But unlike many others, they are also tired of nostalgia. Now even Brookside's Barry Grant is organising acid parties, and you either accept that the scene has widened, or you move on.

"After the first few weeks of Spectrum, we never went anywhere else but Shoom, because after you've seen something that's brilliant, everything else is a load of old wank," says Marsh. "And that's the problem, coming to terms with that now. But I'm fed up with people saying, 'It's not like it used to be'. It was only a nightclub. It was really important to me, but if you spend Monday through to Wednesday getting over it, Thursday and Friday just getting ready for it, then you're missing out on life. People got so spoilt two years ago that they can't accept that for a while it won't be so great. The way things go in cycles, it's just not possible for things to be brilliant all the time."

But for some people, it's only just beginning. You can't deny the same excitement to the ravers at Liverpool's Quadrant Park, or to the young crowd at the last Raindance, a legal occasional all-night rave in a non-residential area just out of central London. The latter is brilliantly organised, I enthuse, the way all raves could and should be if they were made legal and properly monitored by the authorities: a separate parking area with free buses to take ravers to and from the site quietly and efficiently. Polite but thorough searches at the gate eliminate drug dealers. There's a fun-fair, sweet shop and coffee stand, a huge marquee for dancing, and sensitive security staff who gently pick up those who are overwhelmed by the occasion and take them to an on-site medical tent to receive attention.

"But the matter-of-fact way you're talking about having to pick people up from the floor is terrifying!" interrupts Marsh. "When I was 16, it was maybe some speed but usually getting paralytically drunk. I'm not saying that's a good thing, but if you start getting into really heavy drugs at that age – it's like, what is there after that? You've got to get used to the idea that everything can't be permanently nice because life isn't like that. You have to treat it as an every now and again type of thing" •

36   THE ALTERNATIVE ALTERNATIVE

JANUARY 1991

Flying by John Godfrey

WITH A PONY-TAIL that stretches past the nape of his neck and a smile as generous as his girth, Charlie Chester looks as though he could easily follow the career path of his comedian namesake. When he grins, his face erupts in ruddy goodwill, his arms out-stretch and you can almost feel the benevolent vibes. But then, Charlie has good reason to be happy. In less than a year he has become one of clubland's most adventurous entrepreneurs, often following his dancefloor rather than business sense, but always managing to emerge with his wallet and reputation intact. Currently running two of the best clubs in London (Flying and Gosh), organising The Farm's UK tour, and oversee-ing the running of his record shop Flying Records in Kensington Market, Charlie Chester is as prolific as Paul Oakenfold's remixes. Even after the Ibiza '90 trip in the summer, which transported 500 itinerant clubbers to the Balearic island ("the biggest club trip ever," Charlie will remind you) and almost became an organisational nightmare ("those people who complained just don't know how to enjoy themselves"), Charlie Chester's club/promotions empire has widened its horizons even further to include a record label. Like Boy's Own, he has created a club identity out of the "alternative" club scene which wields an influence that belies its size, and also like Boys Own, Flying is a family affair.

"It just happened – we all knew each other, got on with each other and wanted to do the same things," explains Charlie. The core of Flying is Charlie and his girlfriend Karon Dunn, and the DJs Rocky, Diesel, Dean Thatcher, Phil Perry and Glen Gunner. Between them they run the shop, a record mail-order service and the clubs, make and remix records, promote gigs and, now, run their own record company and release their own records. It's an energy that, according to club lore, usually gets dissipated in the inebriated nights and late mornings, but one that was initially inspired by the desire for an "alternative" to the overkill of the rave scene.

"It was a reaction to all that – it was about getting back to small clubs and slowing down the music," recounts Dean Thatcher. "It was something that we had to go through to get to where we are now." And that's exactly what Flying is about – now, of the moment, running against the grain. Even though the "alternative" scene was largely based around London, its sentiment found an echo in the rest of the country, but it wasn't until late last year that the alternative/Balearics ethos was exported wholesale. Essentially a broadminded policy of playing anything and everything, it had an affinity with bands such as Flowered Up and Saint Etienne, influenced dancefloors from Scotland (Slam) to Manchester (Spice), and consequently incurred the wrath of soul purists. London's "radical" radio station Kiss FM even went as far as breaking Saint Etienne's "Only Love Can Break Your Heart" on air.

"Kiss is shit and the musical policy is diabolical," growls Charlie. "Apart from Danny Rampling and Bob Jones' shows, it's as if they're trying to define what dance music is. You hardly ever hear a European record and you don't often hear a good British dance record. There's so much brilliant British stuff from The Sound Of Shoom to Fluke that is just not getting played. They should be more open-minded."

Being open-minded is Flying's raison d'être, and this month they're hoping to persuade Nottingham that good dance music can be anything from This Ragged Jack and Eve Gallagher to acid house classics. After two excursions to Nottingham's Venus club, Flying is now going to open on a regular basis, and they've even started playing acid house (again). In fact, on some nights at Gosh or Flying, you could be forgiven for thinking that the Summer of '88 never ended. "It may sound corny, but I think it's purely 'cause of the Ibiza '90 trip," enthuses Rocky. "For two weeks every DJ in London was over there and the atmosphere was so brilliant that we wanted to recreate it in London. And anyhow, alternative isn't alternative any more – it's in the charts, it's mainstream."

For Rocky & Co, this year's expedition was their first visit to the Summer Of Love's spiritual home, and is proof that Ibiza's ability to influence UK club culture from 2,000 miles away has still not waned. But if Flying are the latest in a club lineage that stretches from Oakenfold/Rampling to Boy's Own, they're also the most organised. "We've built all this almost without thinking – and now we've found ourselves in the driving seat, so to speak," states Charlie.

Few people would quibble with that. In a scene where more effort seems to be put into complaining about the state of affairs than trying to do something about it, the Flying Collective are the exception rather than the rule, or as Charlie says, "proof that clubbers can get off their arse" •

37   QUEER BASHES

FEBRUARY 1991

The Nineties' new gay club culture by Sheryl Garratt

"THE NEW GAY CLONE is wearing Duffer," says David, gesturing at the young, mixed crowd dancing through the dry ice and strobe lights of FF, a Sunday night club open (legally) until 5am. He is wearing a T-shirt that looks at first glance like an Inspiral Carpets design, but which is even more likely to get him arrested for obscenity: the words read "Queer As Fuck". Another clubber's slogan proclaims "QWA – Queens With Attitude", and one would-be entrepreneur declares he's thinking of printing shirts with the defiant slogan: "We don't die – we multiply." "There's a new mood now," he explains. "We don't want to hide any more."

As attacks on gay men increase at a frightening rate, the gay community is starting to react angrily to police indifference and take the offensive itself. In New York, vigilante group the Pink Panthers patrols the streets to keep gay areas free of queerbashers; in San Francisco, direct-action group Queer Nation is calling for violence to be met with violence; in Britain the OutRage activists are organising kiss-ins and fighting outdated laws which hold displays of affection between two people of the same sex to be illegal.

It's a new mood that is also reflected in the clubs, with a new generation of eclectic, funky, and positively gay clubs with names like Spunk, OMO, Queer Nation, Trade, Attitude and FF. With the same mixture of humour and defiance, one young DJ has been holding house parties he calls "queer bashes", and there is even talk of a huge benefit bash in London with attractions such as the lesbians who abseiled into the House Of Commons.

The early acid/Balearic scene was an amiable mix of gay and straight, and stories of Millwall fans stroking each others' tattoos in bouts of Ecstasy-inspired affection became part of club lore. Disillusioned with the bland Hi-NRG fare of most discos, Spunk promoter Wayne Shires began going out to Shoom and later to Charlie Chester's Sunday afternoon Queens club in Slough. Surprised by "the warmth these suburban, heterosexual types showed to us", he began a Sunday night in a London gay venue for that crowd to move on to after Queens closed at 5pm. But, then, as dancefloors became more dominated by pony-tailed aceeed lads, it evolved into the overtly gay Spunk, which may soon open up on a weekly basis, but at the moment relies more on one-off, unlicensed parties: "Suddenly we were attracting a crowd who wanted to listen to decent, upfront music in a venue with an edge to it, not a tacky West End disco."

"I always thought there was an irony in a gay club like Heaven hosting a rave night such as Land Of Oz with hundreds of straight men hugging each other and saying 'I love you, matey'," laughs Patrick Lilley, promoter of Queer Nation – named after the San Francisco group in a link he describes as "more emotional than political".

Lilley opened his Sunday night club in Covent Garden after High On Hope – the much-loved garage one-nighter he ran with DJ Norman Jay – finally closed down at the start of this year. Inspired less by the house boom than by the gay clubs that have helped revive New York's flagging club scene and produced groups like Deee-Lite, his Sunday night at the Gardening Club in Covent Garden aims to revive the spirit of mid-Eighties clubs such as The Lift – a mix of gay and straight, black and white, all attracted by the friendly ambience and by DJs playing the best in cutting-edge dance music.

"People are getting tired of Hi-NRG or Kylie and Jason," says Breeze, DJ at Queer Nation and at Spunk. "They go to the straight, alternative clubs and they want to hear that in their own clubs too."

Julia, DJ at the Brixton Fridge's long-running Tuesday-night Daisy Chain, agrees. "The scene is more mixed now – there are more girls, it's not as heavy as before, and the music is more varied."

A return, perhaps, to smaller, more intimate clubs with more of a family atmosphere, the new scene also reflects a new generation of young gays who are harder, more assertive in attitude: "We're saying that we're a force to be reckoned with," says Wayne Shires. "We're here, we're not going to go away, and we're not going to hide at home full of self-pity – we're going to enjoy ourselves" •

38   COME DANCING

SEPTEMBER 1991

A directory of modern dance steps by Gavin Hills

GET DOWN. GET out. Get funky. It's time to move your body – this is the Dance Generation, and wallflowers are wilting everywhere. There was a time when you could go down the local hop, drink a few pints of Tennent's Extra, eye up the spare, and the nearest you'd get to dancing was a quick fumble with a fifth-year when they played the smoocher. The only physical exercise you'd get was in ganging up and chasing the small twat who supported Crystal Palace. Now, if you get the chance, you dance. Everyone is doin' it. They're struttin' their funky stuff, they're swinging their pants, they're shakin' their good thang, they're er... just what are they doin' exactly? Truth is, no one's sure.

It used to be easy. In the early years, you lindyhopped, you jived, you jitterbugged. If you didn't know how to, you went down the local youth club and slavishly learned the moves. Then it got easier. There was the Twist, the Mashed Potato, the Locomotion – I mean, these dances had records spelling out just what was expected. Every moron can do the Twist – it was the "Agadoo" of its day. Disco had Travolta films to emulate, and if you couldn't suss the pogo then you really were punk. Even breakdancing and bodypopping came with their own WH Smith wallcharts. Now you just... do your own thing? Please!

Ideally, dancing should be like sex: something you just do. But a lot of people out there quite clearly shouldn't be doin' their own thang. Their own thang is a source of great ridicule and embarrassment. We're not all Michael Clark; some of us aren't even Bonnie Langford. We need clues. Whole nations are afflicted. Natural rhythm does not exist – Milli Vanilli proved this.

It would be a great help to left-footed groovers everywhere if we at least had some names for new moves. So let's get up off the wall, y'all. Don't be tame, don't be shy, come on girl, come on guy.

Do the...

TECHNO PUNCH. This little baby has been around for quite a while. Usually a male affair, you wait until the bassline kicks, then climb on to something. A podium or a stage will do, perhaps a tractor – improvise! Put your feet together and point your toes out. Shuffle feet in and out to the beat while swaying slightly. Now, with your leading hand punch the air above your head in a Eubank fury. Ideally, you should be wearing round sunglasses, have a hood, and be shouting something meaningful like "Yeh! Let's go!", "Hardcore!" or (lest we forget) "Mental!"

SPREAD YER LEGS. Favoured by skimpy-topped Deee-Lite dollies and post-Pan's People Top Of The Poppers, this dance is supposedly "horny" (it's about as horny as a tube of Anusol as far as I'm concerned). Place your feet as wide apart as possible and squat your bot down a bit. Proceed to wave your arms back and forth then up and down in a seductive manner.

RIDING THE WHITE HORSE. As above, but lips must be pouting, groin bouncing, and arms stretched out as if riding Desert Orchid to his third Gold Cup win.

THE DIALLER. A real Ted special, this. Click your feet in and out and bounce your legs. Stick your lips out as if giving a frenchie to a water buffalo. Bring your right arm out and make circles with your pointy finger as if you were "dialling" a phone. A crazy cat/annoying bastard sort of dance.

WASH THE WINDOWS. Another Ted special. More appropriate for spacious outdoor venues. Skip on the spot in an almost "Moonstompin'" manner. Imagine your hands are chamois leathers. Wash the windows on the right (use both hands), then the windows on the left. Every so often, hop around a bit. To do it properly, you need a shaggy bob if you're a bloke and a Karen Carpenter cut if you're a girl. When cleaning windows, make sure you're wearing a Grandad Bloggs flannelette nightshirt.

HELLOING. A downmarket version of vogueing. Strike a pose there's nothing to it. At all.

THE BALEARIC SHUFFLE. A lot of people too cool for their own good are now championing this, which is done by Michiko and Richmond-clad clubbers who stand just back from the dancefloor. They want to dance but they don't want to risk ruffling their togs. Sway your body. Jig arms a bit. Nod. Shuffle around. Stop. Repeat. Also known as The Milk Bar Mambo.

Credit where it's due. A couple of hot moves have really put the dance in indie dance. Here's to…

THE BEZ BARNY. Get wasted. Stumble on stage with a well-known Northern band. Move around like Bruno in a sixth round like Tyson. Shake a maracca. Wave a tambourine. Stumble off stage. Get wasted.

THE MOONCULT STRUT. Named after Barry Mooncult of Flowered Up. Get on stage with some Camden renegades. Strut around like a poorly chicken. Fall off stage. Insist the whole audience gets back on stage with you. If the bouncers complain, get your lead singer to deck them. All this should be accomplished while wearing an all-in-one size-six leotard.

THE PESTS CONGA. One trend I thought had died out in '88 seems to be on the return. A dance for three or more, you'll never see more than five joining in. It occurs in the early hours when a few novices find each other and bond after one half too many. Wide-eyed "friends" form a neck-chaffing buddy chain and proceed to do an upright version of the "Oops Upside Your Head" dance. They smile and pester everyone to join in. Shake their hands and pass them some battery acid to rub on themselves. How's that for an all-over buzz?

If these tips aren't enough, watch *Dance Energy*. Study ragga gymnasts getting down. However, if you ever get good enough to appear on the show, it does mean you have to be the only one in the country who forked out for a pair of British Knights or parted with £200 for a Troop tracksuit. Damning details like the fact that you come from Hemel Hempstead may be splashed on the screen. It's not worth it. Being a wallflower isn't too bad, and some places still serve Tennent's Extra. Some even finish on a smoocher (although don't dance with a fifth-year unless you want the police called). If you're really forced to dance, try to remember some of The Wombles' better steps. Keep them guessing, they might think you're at the thrust of the avant garde. I mean – there was a time when Martin Kemp was considered a bit of a mover •

39 WHATEVER HAPPENED TO THE LIKELY LADS? DECEMBER 1991

Did acid house kill the football hooligan? By Gavin Hills (excerpt)

IT'S IMPORTANT TO realise that by 1988, the traditional local communities that soccer clubs drew support from had changed. When you knew everyone in your street, and went to school with everyone on your block, you became territorially minded. Soccer gangs were often a local-based hardcore, swelled by ranks of commuters. Some of the more notorious firms came, not from the bigger football clubs, but from tight local communities. The reason why only 30 West Ham fans could run half the country was because they knew what they were doing, and they knew each other. But the privatisation of council houses and the speculative property markets changed the social structure of many cities. London boys moved east into Essex, south into Kent, and west into places like Slough. You can't put an advert on the telly if you want to form a gang; they had to evolve at a local level. So by 1988 attitudes, places, and people had all changed.

Then along came that smiling matey acid house and the boys found a new buzz. But, in any case, the soccer casual and violence thing was already over. It stopped because people were fed up with it. Some were too old, some were just bored, and others realised the damage they were doing to soccer. Also, the stakes had got higher. Knives had become commonplace, a good biffing was now a good gassing and the loss of several pints of blood. You could do a firm one week, only to find them waiting for revenge at 8.30am at Euston the next Saturday. Firms started to know each other not just by sight, but by name, address and telephone number. The police got to know everyone and arrested en masse – the need to be "seen to be doing something" led to many a fit-up. It wasn't fun any more, it was just sick.

Acid house was a nice little rescue ship that came along when HMS Casual sank. Before, there were only two sorts of nightclubs: the ones where you dressed up in smart clothes, went out, got down and got incredibly drunk to the sounds of whatever Capital Radio jock happened to be playing; or the trendy clubs which you were never allowed into. The dawning of rare groove and warehouses attracted a lot of chaps with a more urban soul boy/jazz-funk background. They started to attend clubs with good music, good draw and no violence. Some north London boys even started to get DJ slots at places like the Wag. When the doors of the club scene broke open completely in the '88 "Summer Of Feeling Nice", the remaining bulk of hoolies romped in. Happy to swap their designer thug image for the more positive identity of acid house, many a sworn enemy was to be seen OD-ing together at Spectrum, Clink Street etc. Raving was proving more fun than that wet awayday to Newcastle could ever be. A comfortable little full-stop was placed on casual.

Had all the lads become loved-up? No, this wasn't a cure for violence. Nasty pieces of work remain nasty, no matter how jovial they seem. It just meant the fashion had changed. The "thing to do" was to go out and get on one, not meet at Finsbury Park at eleven o'clock. People conformed to happiness and peace as much as they conformed to hatred and violence. The guys who did enjoy the violence in the first place weren't changed. Some did mellow out a bit, become bouncers, that sort of thing. A few with good organisational skills started their own small businesses. For some this meant a chain of gardening services, for others drug dealing and door-to-door intimidation. The ICF (InterCity Firm – always the best name, don't you think?) became a kind of East End IRA without the politics. Some run their own raves, others own clubs. The Government must be well pleased with the entrepreneurial society that's sprouted.

There are a few nutters who still go to have a whack-a-bout at Saturday soccer. I guess they can't break the habit. All the last few years have meant to them is that they're drugged up to the eyeballs with dope, charlie and E. Many of Millwall's minor away-game incidents from Bristol to Newcastle have been caused by some old die-hards with a couple of doves inside them. Ecstasy will not prevent you from fighting; it will, however, make you enjoy it more when you do. A couple of old faces have taken one trip too many and killed themselves. Unable to come to terms with things, a bullet through the head was the honourable option for one prominent Eastender, while the England team still attracts a few of the country's criminally unstable. At last year's World Cup, they were occasionally in evidence. The rise of soccer hooliganism on the Continent has meant that there were plenty of foreign dogsbodies to have a biff with if so desired. It takes more than drugs and dancing to cure hardened psychos; the medical profession has known this for years.

Raving has achieved something, though. The inheritance of soccer violence has been halted. Schoolboy story-tellers are replacing terrace tales with tales of manic all-nighters. It may be that they will colour them with Moss Side drug mayhem or Sobell Centre stabbing, but still it's a slight advance. They listen to Flowered Up, not the Cockney Rejects. But bad boys will never stop being bad boys. A need for power, excitement and profit see to that. But now, though, there are new heroes for them to emulate. They're still smartly dressed (still in Chevignon in a lot of cases!), they DJ now and then, get the squeeze at the clubs that count and they've got a pocketful of herbs and chemicals. Every now and then they wash'n'go the pony-tail which hangs flaccid from the back of their head. It's still a mug's game, but at least they don't want to kick the shit out of each other so much. These aren't flower children. They're just kids with a bit more of a clue.

It's all too close to call at the moment. The appeal of violence won't die. Not unless machismo goes out of fashion. Who'd have thought that 15 years after mods and rockers battled it out on Brighton beach, the next generation would do it all again? By 1995 the population of young males will be on the increase again. That means more naughty boys per square inch. What will these new lads be doing? The advances of football and its supporters over the past few years give some hope that it will avoid further scares. Minor incidents will continue to occur in the football league and at England matches, but fashion currently dictates that these incidents will remain isolated.

Given the choice between spending money on football and spending money on drugs, nine out of ten ex-hoolies choose drugs, though there still could be major trouble abroad. "Big games bring out old faces, with old scores. All it needs is one important fixture in a country with its own hooligan problem. Even if it's not us who starts it, no one likes getting run!" commented one retired gooner. The surrounding publicity to such an incident could blow things open again. Fashions have this horrible habit of coming back – look at Kickers.

Today, though, there are new career opportunities for bad boys. How about "urban rioter" for a start? Now, when two or three are gathered together a bit pissed off about something, they can spend an evening setting cars alight and chucking bricks at the bobbies. When two Newcastle joy-riders died after being chased by the local constabulary, all the local lads got together and caused three days of hell for them. Ten years ago they wouldn't have known how to. They could have invaded a pitch, though, that had been on the telly before. A new tradition is developing. Did you really think you'd ever see riots in Oxford? I guess they were just all desperate to be local heroes. What if this becomes the fashion, the "thing to do"? Will it still involve shopping in South Molton Street? Will it herald another Kickers revival? Will they be purple? We should be told.

But for those likely lads of '81, the last ten years have been a remarkable education in life. When you've stood in the middle of a full-scale soccer riot, with everything going off around you. When you've stood, rushing off your head in a packed field of friends dancing, and watching the sun come up. That's when you begin to know how confused the line between love and hate is. It's all just a buzz. This may sound wanky – it is. The whole thing is too recent to give a real perspective.

Perhaps in five years' time people will want to forget the whole house scene just like they want to forget hooliganism. Judging by all the lost souls you see around town, this could well prove to be the case. Guilt fades. The most obvious thing to happen is that the rave scene will get the "Swinging Sixties" sanitisation treatment. Our kids will be collecting the Panini "Great pitch invasions of the Eighties" sticker collection. They'll send off to K-Tel for a video CD of *Those Smiling Lucozade Days*. We'll develop false memories and start spinning tales. That's our fate, I guess.

Our culture is like that of the great civilisations. We soar and build with great enthusiasm. We peak. Then, with a loss of faith, the barbarian hoards set in. The next civilisation builds on the ruins. It's lack of faith, not the hoards that are to blame. Tracksuits, trainers, and InterCity trains; now turntables, trips, and techno...

"'How did it go last night?' 'Great, I sold about 40.' 'I was talking about the party!'"
Flowered Up: "It's On" •

40   I CAN'T GO ON! OR CAN I?

DECEMBER 1991

The future and possible lack of it: a reader writes

THE FOLLOWING LISTS, written after the style of Camilla Deakin's popular Six Of The Best column in The FACE, were contained in a letter sent to us by a reader from Middlesbrough. The Ecstasy feature mentioned refers to a story by Mandi James, which was one of the first to warn against possible dangers associated with taking the drug. The writer, incidentally, appeared to have succumbed to optimism: they signed themselves as simply "Keeping The Faith".

Six of the best reasons for thinking it's all finally over:

1. Everywhere north of Manchester seems to be either kiddies' corner, techno city or *Top Of The Pops*.

2. The sight (and smell) of 1,000 mad Geordies, some of whom have taken to wearing cyclists' smog masks filled with Vicks.

3. Getting to a club to find the DJs on the flyer were never anything more than that.

4. Feeling past it at 21, in a club where the average age is five years younger.

5. When the attitude of "It's not where you're from, it's where you're at" is replaced by "It's not where you're at, it's what you're on".

6. Reading the Ecstasy feature in the latest FACE.

Six of the best reasons to keep the faith:

1. Making eye contact with a member of the opposite sex and exchanging a knowing look or a hug.

2. Making eye contact with a member of the same sex and exchanging a knowing smile or a hug.

3. Talking utter shite with complete strangers in the loos.

4. Feeling as if you're in on the best-ever secret when you look at students, townies or parents.

5. Just letting go.

6. Standing under the DJ box at The Haçienda and feeling the sheer energy hitting your body as the whole club puts its arms in the air to K-Klass' "Rhythm Is A Mystery" •

41 BHANGRAMUFFIN!

MAY 1992

The changing face of Asian dance by Vaughan Allen (excerpt)

A NIGHTCLUB IN Bradford, complete with lasers, video screens, and blinding lights. Tonight's crowd is predominantly Asian, here to watch three live bands and to dance. Vigorously, sometimes violently, they throw themselves around to the beat of the tabla, the thud of the dhol. High-pitched Punjabi vocals fly over the top of the rhythm, fading with the Indian instruments but then returning over a chattering hardcore techno bassline. The crowd dance on, unfazed. As the night progresses, so do the mixes, throwing Punjabi tunes together with drum machines, house beats, reggae rhythms. And the crowd keeps dancing.

Bhangra is nothing new, of course. Traditionally the music of Punjabi harvest dances, it was taken up by British-based bands like Alaap and Heera, who introduced Western instrumentation and developed a hybrid that was simultaneously pop, dance and folk. These original bands were usurped by a new generation, and the sight of Pardesi smashing up guitars on stage, or of Achanak's early promo videos, created a sense that bhangra might adopt Western posturing to complement its appeal, and go mainstream. "A lot of the younger generation just couldn't relate to people like Heera," explains Mick Chandsoor, a DJ with Bradford's Sunrise Radio. "But the bhangra scene was the only real part of their culture that they could relate to, so they took it and adapted the sounds."

And now yet another generation is coming through, influenced by rave culture and adapting the tabla- and sitar-oriented sound with the three Ss: synth, sequencer, sample. The word bhangra is now being stretched to cover a wide variety of sounds, and there have been cross-over experiments involving most current dance styles. Bands such as Shaktee and Intermix play a heavily-synthesised dance music, in which only the vocals and drums are recognisably Asian – and even here, with everyone from George O'Dowd's "Jesus Loves You" to The Grid borrowing such sounds, the two are growing closer together.

The rave scene has been the crucial influence. "A lot of the DJs have started mixing in bhangra stuff and rave music," says Puriwal, a DJ and promoter on the Bradford scene. "People come to gigs to see the bands, but there's always room for DJs to play in between them. And as long as you keep that beat, you can mix in anything. The cross between bhangra and ragga has brought a lot of black people into the scene, and toasters and DJs are working with Asian artists. And now white people are starting to come in too."

The publicity attached to the post-bhangra scene has started to mirror that of the commercial rave sector, throwing up name DJs and mixers. Some of these – like Bally Sagoo – have made their names mixing bhangra styles and ragga. Others – X-Zecutive Sounds, Back To Basics, Fresh Beats Inc – haven't stopped there, but have thrown together Asian sounds, ragga, house and hip hop. Meanwhile, Apachi Indian, from Handsworth in Birmingham, has blended bhangra and ragga, and, after topping the reggae charts with his independently-released singles, has played to mixed Asian and African-Caribbean crowds.

At the Bradford event, clubbers react enthusiastically to the suggestion that there's a natural connection between the bhangra house being played and mainstream commercial dance beats. "I like hearing traditional sounds, but when you come out, this mix is just right," says a dancer called Sonia. "Everything's in here: reggae and house and bhangra." Her friend Zorina, whose flowing red sari seems made for dancefloor exhibitionism, agrees. "I love to dance, and this is all great to dance to. It's like our own version of the pop on the radio" •

42   PUSSY POWER

JULY 1992

Ladies with an attitude by Sheryl Garratt

"I LIKE TO LOOK good when I'm going out," says DJ and promoter Lisa Loud, "but there's no use not having a good time. I'm up for getting in a mess, having a giggle. There's no denying the looks help, but I wish sometimes people would look between the ears and see the brain. That's what's important."

Women have always worked in clubs: some of those in this feature on these pages have been involved for up to a decade, and they are just a fraction of the country's female DJs, promoters and venue managers. But the attitude they embody has never been stronger: these are women who dress up and have a good time without caring what anyone thinks. Strong, sexy, and not at all passive, they don't feel the need to apologise if they end up rolling round the dancefloor, though you'll often end up apologising to them if you don't join in.

Perhaps the short-lived Night Of The Living Ultravixens club night tells the story best. The brainchild of Josephine White, aka Pussy, and her partner Bunny Vixen, it existed for only ten weeks but caused a splash with its dress-to-kill theme nights and welcome sense of fun. Records were played by The Cleavage Sisters, who painted their nails between tracks as a dig at the current cult of the DJ, while the crowd were organised to play games – men did the ironing or fertility chants, while women did press-ups and arm-wrestling. "We get men to do feminine things, and women to do fake air guitars onstage," says Pussy. "Everything we do is an exaggeration, tongue-in-cheek. Men always run to the front to ogle, but then they shy back because we're not acting like they expect – we're strong women, vixens. We want women to see they can be glamorous and powerful, and use their sexuality in a positive way to make them feel strong and in control of their lives."

Though they have pulled off some spectacular parties, since appearing on Channel 4's *Rude Women* programme Sara and Farika of the Pussy Posse are probably best known as the girls who demonstrate how to put on a condom with your mouth. Starting out with the double intention of promoting guilt-free female sexuality and safer sex, they ultimately aim to move from parties to more ambitious projects like a safe-sex hotel. Working "like art installations", their nights have featured an entrance fashioned like a giant vagina, kissing booths, massages and trays of free condoms. The idea is to provide an arena where talking and flirting can once more take place; at Pussy Posse events, the emphasis is anywhere but the dancefloor. They are often misunderstood, they say, but it is not a real problem. "Who gives a shit if people take us seriously or not? It's a way of weeding out people who are never going to understand what you're trying to do. We're looking for a really rich, funky heiress to work with!"

After the house boom, in part started by their own now-legendary night Shoom, Jenny and Danny Rampling's club Pure Sexy was among the first to put flirting back on the agenda. Now, they're re-emphasising that other F word – fashion – with their current night Glam. "After Pure Sexy, every club copied the idea," asserts Jenny. "Some were really tacky – and condescending to women. Some of the images on flyers were really embarrassing, degrading. So we started Glam. British people are reserved on the whole, but if they dress up, it's like they're allowed to go mad on the dancefloor."

Dismissed by some as merely Danny's wife – a problem shared by many women who help their partners run a club only to be dismissed as the promoter's girlfriend – Jenny is nonetheless one of the most feared doorpersons in London. It's a reputation she relishes, and though many have complaints about not being allowed in, no one disputes that her careful choosing of the crowd rarely results in a duff night.

Security, for many female promoters, is a constant headache. Pussy claims that the only trouble they had on the door of Ultravixens was down to a male bouncer installed by the venue's manager: "He didn't like having a woman on the door: he didn't trust her to be able to stop trouble. But the only trouble we ever had was when the bloke he'd put on got drunk and started getting to one of the customers. A woman would never do that."

Roxy Deluxe, organiser of London's Sign Of The Times parties, has had similar problems, but on the whole she finds her gender an advantage. "The quality of clubs has got to go up, and women are better at looking after the details. Men are good at concentrating on the music, but they don't take any notice of the decor, the little things that make the night. The music's always good, but the atmosphere can be too macho."

"I'm not part of that competitive DJ scene," says Rachel dismissively. "People take it too seriously. You're entertaining people – you've got to have a sense of humour and not try to play all these records no one has ever heard of." Like many of the women interviewed here, she has a strong gay following, and it seems that gay clubs – or clubs boasting a mix of gay and straight clubbers – have often been the most receptive. "There are less prejudices and hang-ups," explains DJ Vicki Edwards. "Some men do have problems with women who look good, are confident, and are bloody good at their jobs, but in gay clubs that's not a problem."

She ends with a warning: "There are more of us than ever now, and the new women are getting credit for it – they're proud of what they're doing and who they are, and they draw a lot of attention to themselves. It may just be a fashion thing now, but because of the nature of the women involved, they're not just going to go away."

"We're reclaiming the glamour back from transvestites, using it to attract men, ensnare them, then ultimately dominate them" •

43   THE DREAMS OF CHILDREN

OCTOBER 1992

Soft crusties by Richard Benson

IN A DUSTY VICTORIAN town hall in the East End of London, I stumbled down the steps to the exit, and left half of young, disaffected London dancing and laughing in rooms decked out like candy-striped pleasuredome marquees.

"Size Of A Cow" was playing, the long, brown hair was a-swaying, and young London was wearing washed-out T-shirts, batik waistcoats, face paint, Indian cotton shirts, Uzbeki hats, old Miss Selfridge frocks, holey leggings, black canvas trousers, plaited wristbands and DMs, DMs, DMs, DMs, always boots, mostly black, and often daubed with ohms, stars, and yin and yangs, sometimes just sprayed gold or silver, and threaded with laces, purple, red, green, yellow, pink and striped. This young London, happy tonight to be among its own kind, sometimes dangled a polythene bottle of cider by the neck, laughed at itself for acting crazy on the dancefloor, and now and again tried to look thick, or stoned.

I could have found exactly the same clothes and expressions anywhere in the United Kingdom that night of course. While you lovely nouveau beatniks, Eton-cropped dancers, workwear groovers and full-effect ravers were holed up in a handful of chosen niteries, these suburban salopes, these soft sixth-form crusties were out everywhere, going forth nationwide and multiplying. These children that you taste-fully spit on have, for months, been spreading like mould on muck, and yet, and yet – no one knows their name. There have been no articles in the Sunday papers to keep the grey-templed liberals in the swing. No one causing a scene at the *NME*. Not so much as a sociology essay, or an urban character sketch in London's *Evening Standard*. But there they are, mid-teens to twenties, neither crustie nor indie, po-faced, well-spoken and in every good school, office and higher education campus that you're unfortunate enough to visit. What is all this ?

I don't know any more than you, but curiosity was killing this cat, and I wanted their measurements. So there I was at the Whirl-Y-Gig, which is a New Age club much favoured by the Haight-Ashbury set. It plays world and indie music, it has face painting and babies, and, if you're interested, it's held in the Town Hall in Shoreditch on Saturday nights.

Were they from Camden communes? Or maybe long-haired bohemian bivouacs on the edge of town? I asked Sarah and Mouse, who, as it turned out, were from Slough. Sarah had her hair in plaits, and Mouse had his in a ponytail. She was a graduate and worked in a record shop; he was doing a law course. Did they like the Whirl-Y-Gig? They did not!

"There's too many rich kids 'ere," said Mouse, taking care to drop his aitches. "It used to be really anarchic, but then all sorts of casuals started wearing yin and yang on their hooded tops because it was trendy."

Sarah was staring away, looking distinctly unimpressed. So I asked her why she wore those clothes (a green cotton dress with its hem coming down, holed leggings, and uncared-for DM boots).

139

"What?" she said.

Well, were they making any statement about herself, perhaps?

"No," she said.

So why wear them?

"It's not a religion."

I'm sorry?

"I just wear what I want."

But why do you want those things?

(Pout) "Comfortable."

Progress! Had anyone ever taken the mickey out of her because she looked untidy?

"Fuck off," said Sarah, and walked away laughing with Mouse.

Well, hippies – they told us never to trust them, didn't they? I bought a little carrot cake, watched someone juggle, awoke from the consequent torpor, and collared a mixed tatty flock lounging at the edge of the dancefloor. They were thin (soft crusties always are, unlike their ancestors the goths, who wore those loose black garments to conceal their lumpy bodies – you fooled no one, goths!) and they worked as publishers, temp secretaries, or, in one case, as an articled clerk at a firm of environmental lawyers. Did they feel something in common with the rest of the Whirl-Y-Gig clientele?

Everyone looked at everyone else, except for Zoë the environmental lawyer, who was as eager as your dad's new girlfriend.

"Obviously there's something or we wouldn't be here. But I think you have to say the club's just not as much of an event as it used to be. There's loads of kids who are just fashionable London types, and they're not into it."

It? What was "it"? Coca-Cola?

No, no, the idea of something communal and spontaneous, she said, which sounded like the "it" of any other bag you might be into. Was there, I enquired, some spirit or belief I was missing? What if, I said, they were just playing at being drop-outs?

A ripple of life went over the face of Mark the publisher's assistant. "Nah, 'cause you don't have to drop out, like, completely. The Sixties' people, right, or the crusties or whatever dropped out, and that didn't change anything, but you can change things, sort of, from the inside."

Now I knew why there were so many badly-written books – Mark was proof-reading them. But what was he changing?

"Aw, you can't put it like that, in that exact way," he said. "You just change yourself, and don't put up with the crap."

The crap?

"Well, you know, like... like there's exploitation of people, politicians, racism, all that shit, you just don't want to be a part of it."

So, politics then? Nope, no takers here, comrades! All the parties were the same (such cynicism from our beautiful people, I thought) although, someone droned, "Maybe anarchy would be all right if you could make it work." Lord! I sighed, and I despaired – and then Zoë, bless her pent-up, tie-dyed heart, came back in:

"People just don't want to be part of a world that doesn't have compassion, or spontaneity, where playfulness is just limited to football and sex! You look at a so-called adult world," she said, "and people just behave ridiculously. So you want your own thing. The trouble here is that these kids just don't understand it."

Truly, there is nothing worse than a world-weary hippie, and nothing more strictly self-superior than the elders of the benevolent-beat-bohemian class. Without humour to camouflage themselves, they give themselves away every time, and when Zoë said "adult world" and "these kids", then, suddenly, I had them, by the scruffiness of their necks! I saw then that Zoë, and the Whirl-Y-Gig, and the whole soft crust of young Britain were just scared to grow up.

They hated the kids who, being kids, wanted to try this buzz for laughs rather than love, and they hated the"so-called adults", rotten with self-importance. But they daren't take on the decisions and responsibility that would allow them to make their own alternatives, and to drop right out. Life was just a little too sweet. They just wanted everybody to be nice, like they're nice to you when you're a kid.

Now to be fair, the dilemma was there as the whole soft crust thing got going on 10 November 1989, when the fall of the Berlin Wall gave a prop of plausibility to the caring-Nineties media-schlock and to Rifat Ozbek's baggy Kleenex-vagabond numbers. For a month everything was beautiful and inspired, and you could believe in the innate and irresistible urge towards freedom and fellow-feeling that would take care of political nastiness, or of the crap, as our eloquent friend might have put it. But deep down you also knew that it couldn't be so simple. Sooner or later some crap and a lot of nastiness would have to be dealt with, before Europe could come together. Sadly it was sooner, and it spoiled the whole party.

It wasn't long after the ball got rolling, together with the heads of the Eighties opinion formers, that it got going in the wrong direction. In 1990 the commercial success of the Wonderstuff and Ned's Atomic Dustbin started drawing in the disaffected. The desire to be Miles Hunt soon led to an admiration of Carter, and Carter led to the Levellers. (Nirvana and grunge are really sideline interests for the soft crust, who like a good melody with their nasal, mockney invectives, and hence favour bands who are, at heart, folk groups.) By 1991, the Levellers, then without a chart hit to their name, were said to be the fourth most bankable live band in the country. And in 1992, having been mere space-fillers in the music press, the Levellers had a top 20 single.

The Levellers. What do they say in their most famous line? "There's only one life to lead, and that's your own." If that's not a summary of failed inspiration, failed compassion, and the failed dream that would bring us together, then the Levellers are the next Sex Pistols. It is simply a footnote to the failure of people who can't focus their displeasure, and who anyway are scared of acting upon it. In short, it is the soft crust itself: Eastern mysticism and compassion, sealed with a sulk.

When you see them as grown-ups who'd rather not grow any more, you realise that even their clothes resort to childhood in the face of responsibility and decision. There is no disgusting crusty dirt that doesn't care if it loses its job; instead there are the big boots and frocks of the playground dressing-up box, the scruffy jeans and last year's trainers like the ones set aside for playing after school. The soft crust thinks the rotten so-called adult world shops at Next, and it takes itself too seriously (like any sullen delinquent) to explore the groovy games of style, experiment and enterprise played by the "kids". All it can do is say "I hate everybody and it's not fair". On behalf of their inarticulate owners, these clothes say "I'm not playing!" and then sit on the sidelines (so you can see how upset you've made them), and wait for the world to be nice.

It won't last, thank the Lord. Wanting to remain a child becomes unfeasible even to the most stupid old beard at the age of about 35; they eventually give up and accept they were born to be schoolteachers. If you want to change, you create something you can pass down to the young. Irresponsibility, spontaneity and hedonism are the primary colours of any youth movement worth its sweat, but they are not world-changing legacies and they never have been. That is why hippie, in all its shabby, flabby, dope smoke-yellowed mutations from beatnik to gothic, always, always, always FAILS. Reality overtakes it and it hasn't the reserves to claw back. It gets old: ignore it and it goes away.   141

There are no Sunday newspaper features, no *London Evening Standard* sketches, no *Def II* interest because we need to label things only if they challenge the status quo. A name means we understand, and it allows the press to encourage or denounce, depending on whether the subject threatens or bolsters things as they are. The soft crust, by its own sullen admission, does neither, and so – nobody cares. Not even the music and style press, who ought to at least register their existence, can find a good word for them.

Although they could try "failure" •

44 WONDERLAND UK

JANUARY 1993

Why people take drugs and go to clubs by Gavin Hills (excerpt)

CURIOUSER AND CURIOUSER. Another year on and the dancing isn't over. A few summers ago most of us thought the explosion of drugs and dance music which formed that four-letter word rave would wither and die like so many youth cults before. Usually such things shoot up like a rocket from a milk bottle, sprinkle in the sky with starlight glory, then quickly fall to earth in a burnt-out shell of their former selves. But something funny has happened with house music and the drug culture it spawned. Instead of burning out it has spread out, sprinkling its pixie dust across our country. Whether it's Sunday afternoon football or shopping in Dixon's, the music is there, harmlessly thumping along. And drugs have taken their place alongside TV, video and satellite as part of our entertainment system. Youth culture is now in the public domain.

With age no longer restrictive, we are seeing a future where drug use becomes endemic and youths never grow up. Kevin from Wood Green explains: "The Es around now are vile, and I keep deciding to stop. But then I hit the real world and realise I'm 28, I live with my mum in a shitty council flat, I've got no money and no chance of earning any, and every time I have sex with someone new I'm scared I'll catch something that'll kill me in eight years' time. And suddenly monging out on a crappy rhubarb-and-custard seems quite attractive, actually." The horrible truth is that we're living in a country where the only real prospect many people have of a decent future is to retreat into wonderland.

After 12 years of Conservative government our society has become disparate, cocooned and cold. One of the few communities that remains today is that of the networks built up around clubs and drugs. However flawed and fake they may be they exist, and provide one of the few support systems some people have. While trying to live in a world of constant hedonism may be an admirable enough goal, you have to ask where it will all end up. When is it time to stop? There must be more to life than new Stone Island jackets and cocaine habits. How shabby it all seems.

There was a time when youth had no culture. When youth slaved for pennies in dark mills and their way forward was a roof over their head, enough to eat, and a fair day's work for a fair day's pay. With this dream in their hearts they trudged onwards. And every inch they moved forward, every battle they won, moved us that much closer to these: our glorious days of triumph.

From the Fifties onwards the young people of this country have benefited from the changes in society which gave us a bit of cash and a bit of leisure time. This small but significant empowerment gave us the lot: teddy boys, Cliff Richard, mods, purple hearts, "Rubber Soul", Slade, skinheads, Captain Sensible, Seditionaries, New Romantics, Wham!, casuals, and house music all night long. Forty years of youth culture all hinge around the fact that the social struggle of those who went before us gained our status as creative consumers. Sitting in your bedroom listening to Nirvana or lying face down on a nightclub floor thinking you're a goldfish may not seem like one of the great triumphs of the working classes, but it is. The only way to enjoy such delights before these times was to break into the cliques of bohemia.

Drugs and dance music are nothing new, only the sheer scale of those who are indulging is novel. Warehouse parties were around in the Twenties. Published this month by Lawrence & Wishart, Marek Kohn's The British Drug Underground offers an excellent account of the moral panic that led to the criminalisation of drugs. (They haven't always been illegal. You used to be able to get cocaine from Harrods and opium from the chemist's, and squares impregnated with both were advertised as ideal gifts for the boys at the front.) After the Great War a combination of jazz, cocaine and female emancipation led to a booming London nightlife. There were parties in "unlit buildings in foreboding neighbourhoods. Costing two pounds entry and filled with young dancing girls who were underdressed, perpetually seized with hysterical laughter, and ogling foolishly," according to a Daily Express report of the time. Sound familiar? How about "gum being chewed to stop involuntary teeth-grinding"?

Gurning flappers aside, the moral outcry of the time was due to the horrible idea that young white English roses, who obviously knew no better, were being fed drugs by "gentlemen of colour" who sought a bit of deflowering. This was the fear that led first to the criminalisation of drugs in 1916 and later to campaigns in the papers against "dance dens and drugs". The concern then, as now, was not borne from any deep-rooted worries for the health of individuals, but from panic about the erosion of a prejudiced conservative order. Despite such moral forces, this century saw pop music and recreational drugs slowly drift away from bohemian cliques. Beatniks, mods and hippies were all propagandists for this winning mixture. Yet it has taken until now for there to be universal acceptance of such excesses as the norm.

What has occurred is a certain loss of innocence. Primary schools hold junior discos, 12-year-olds skin joints; life's little joys now come ever earlier. Job prospects are bleak, decent housing eludes most of us, as does the responsible rationale of adulthood. For mods in the Sixties there came a time when they sold the Lambretta, got married, had kids, and saved for dream houses in the suburbs. Even with hippies, when the acid got too much to take, the drop-outs dropped in again, nursing their broken dreams of love and peace. Now there are no such full stops, no obvious ends to youthful glory days. With the sham of Eighties enterprise culture lying bankrupt all around, the sons and daughters of the suburban dream house will not give up Tennent's and Ecstasy for the promise of lower mortgage rates and the hope of shares in a privatised coal industry. That simply isn't progress •

45   SAFETY FIRST

FEBRUARY 1993

Manchester City Council's Safer Dancing campaign by Chris Sharratt

----

UNDER THE SLOGAN "Safer Dancing", Manchester Council has launched a code of practice for club owners and promoters, the first of its kind in Britain. Produced in association with the Lifeline drug agency and Manchester University's Department Of Social Policy And Social Work, it aims to make clubs as safe as possible. "Our over-riding objective is to help prevent any further accidents or deaths from dance drugs like Ecstasy and whizz," says councillor Pat Karney. "We prefer people who come into Manchester not to take drugs, but it is a fact of life that thousands of people are making private decisions to do so." The code suggests that up-to-date information on drugs should be available at clubs, and that temperature and air quality should be monitored. Adequate chill-out facilities are also promoted along with free water and an end to the practice of cutting off the cold-water supply in toilets. A leaflet and poster campaign is under way, while a Safer Dancing Hotline has been opened for disgruntled local clubbers to complain to. "It's a commendable idea," says The Haçienda's Paul Mason. "Switching off the cold water taps is a disgusting practice. Any club caught doing it should have its licence revoked immediately." Aspects of the code may cause problems for smaller clubs who cannot afford expensive alterations, but the campaign aims to educate the club trade rather than close them down. But that doesn't mean the council won't flex its legal muscle. Says Karney: "If certain clubs continue to break health and safety regulations, they will jeopardise their Music And Entertainment licence." Decoded from council-speak, that means the music will have to stop •

TURN OFF. TUNE OUT. DROP DEAD

APRIL 1993

Drug bores by Mandi James

JUST SAY NO, right. We've been warned how drugs can play havoc with our health, but nobody ever told us about the dangers of drug bores to our social life. These are the people who live every weekend like it was their last, spend all their excess cash on popping pills, hoovering lines and knocking back narcotics like it was going out of fashion. You'll find them slumped in corners in clubs, draped over bars or locked in your toilet at post-club sessions. They don't want to dance, they don't want to get to know you, they don't even seem to want to enjoy themselves any more. They just want to flake out and forget. One weekend merges into another, and weekdays are for recuperation. Friends are people you see through bleary eyes at the weekends, conversations are centred around who's got the best deals and who takes the biggest doses; sex is something other people do; and relationships take second place to weekend trivial pursuits. Excuse me while I crack my jaw yawning. I don't mean to paint a vulgar picture but, let's be frank, drug bores are a depressing sign of the times. A gripping recession means most of us now live for the weekends, and five years of hedonism are bound to claim a few victims. But what a way to go. There are, of course, still pockets of euphoria and enthusiasm dotted round the country in such places as Birmingham, Belfast and Glasgow, party people who manage to go for it without losing the point and purpose of what they're doing. It's the ones who were there when it all kicked off who are starting to look really tired. Dedicated clubbers, the ones who haven't already burned out, grown up or moved on, new either save themselves for one-off parties, or have grown more moderate in their old age, sick of being palmed off with horse diuretics instead of MDMA, having learned that abstinence makes the heart grow fonder. Necking or nibbling or whatever took your fancy was supposed to enhance your big night out, not dominate it. At least that's the way I remember things. Wasn't club culture always about allowing freedom to party, not freedom to puke? Wasn't it about dressing up, showing out and fooling around, not freaking out your friends with regular fits from over-indulging? Wasn't it always about looking forward and being one step ahead, not forever moaning about the good old days and how dire things are now? Drug bores have lost the plot in every way. Wake up! Get a life! Get back to reality! Clubbers have always experienced ebbs and flows of enthusiasm – familiarity breeds contempt and sure, it's easy to take things for granted, but you don't get nothing for nowt in this game. While drug bores slump in a corner, trying to blot out the stresses and strains of – oh no – going to the same club every week or seeing the same old crowd, the rest of us gather our strength for the next inevitable assault. Pockets of people are slowly crawling out of the woodwork and beginning to stretch their social life into week nights. Conversations are actually manoeuvring above and beyond dissecting events from the weekend before. It's a positive move in the right direction. Club culture's great, but there is life above and beyond it. Rejoice or be dull and be damned •

47   FREE SPIRITS

MAY 1993

DIY and the free party network by Mandi James

HISTORICALLY, DIY EVOLVED out of protest. Ripped off too many times at parties such as Biology and Amnesia, they decided that if you're going to do it, do it right, do it yourself, and do it for love, not loot. Chronologically, DIY kicked off with irregular dawn-raid house parties, which had graduated into a regular club night at Nottingham's Kool Kat by early '89. Ideologically, DIY clicked into place the following summer at Glastonbury when they hooked up with the Tonka sound systems in an acid house free-for-all. Since then DIY have aimed to engender a community through regular free parties and the common bond of body language. As hapless and hippy as that may seem, DIY put their money where their mouth is. The free parties are funded by ventures such as Bounce, their regular Friday night in Nottingham, and travelling sideshow DJs Digs and Whoosh. Their events attract dedicated disciples from all over the country, and are enthusiastically championed by the likes of Andrew Weatherall – a regular fixture behind their decks – and 808 State's Graham Massey, a regular fixture on their dancefloor. The music is cutting-edge, tripped-out, revved-up and devoid of trends, with hard hip hop sitting beside dub disco. As a result, they attract a wide cross-section of clubbers. Tattooed babes rub shoulders with balearic beatniks, funki dreds share spliffs with short back 'n' sides, while everyone cheers intros, stomps over breakdowns, and sweats in unison. The only people not dancing are ones left standing in the queue outside. Hooked on the altruistic idea of "big outdoor, naughty parties", DIY started off with two decks and a box of well-worn records, and have evolved into a groove corporation devoid of greedy corporate ethics, an ever-growing gang that's fast becoming a clan. They have a label, Strictly 4 Groovers, their own radio show, in-house designers, close links with Nottingham's Time Recordings, and a single, "Hothead", out on Warp. They also had six members of their posse up in court in April, facing a possible jail sentence for "conspiracy to cause a public nuisance" for their part in the Loxton Summer Solstice Festival last year. If DIY aren't paying for your entertainment in one way, they're paying for it in another. "As you can probably tell, we don't want to be this month's thing; we don't want to be seen as some movement," ventures Harry, who, he adds, isn't the spokesperson, simply the first to pick up the phone. "We've been doing it for longer than that; our commitment goes a lot deeper. We want to service our community. You will make that absolutely clear, won't you?" •

48   THE SWING THING

JULY 1993

London's swingbeat scene by Lee Harpin

IF THERE IS ONE genre of modern dance music that has consistently provoked general disagreement in British musical circles, it is swingbeat. Hardcore rave may have had its doubters, but in this country at least, Teddy Riley's "New Jack Swing" experiment seemed at times to have fewer friends than George Graham's Arsenal football team. In America, Riley's own group, Guy, enjoyed huge commercial success, as did the LA and Babyface-produced Bobby Brown. Swing, with its amalgamation of tough hip hop beats and R&B vocals, rapidly emerged as black America's modern-day pop form. And perversely, even in Britain, where swing was frequently attacked as a "manufactured", "soulless" nonentity, a host of swing cuts sold well enough to dent our national top 40. The likes of Keith Sweat's "I Want", Pebbles' "Girlfriend" and Bobby Brown's "My Prerogative" may have rubbed the purists up the wrong way, but someone out there was buying them. Even Teddy Riley expressed surprise at the ecstatic response Guy received after their first live London dates in 1991. But by then, London's underground swing scene was already well established.

Starting in 1988, for three years Legends hosted the phenomenally successful Wall Street and Bounced nights, run by Digger, an expat American currently working at leading London dance music shop Wild Pytch. "In America you may have 25-30 million black people supporting their music, but as with ragga and hip hop, London's always had a big swing following," he explains. And perhaps most importantly, alongside a wealth of pirates, London has two legal dance music stations.

Kiss FM's Steve Jervier was one of Britain's first swing pioneers. "For me, swing's appeal has always been centred around its use of the song, coupled with the production," he says. "People didn't understand it at first, because we had the house fad at exactly the same time as swing started to come into its own. It was far easier for people to make records with one hook at 120bpm. A lot of people ignored the fact that real songs will never die."

Likewise, critics of the music have also discounted its growing strength at club level. "This is the healthiest the club scene has ever been," says Steve. "And significantly, with clubs like Mutiny (regularly turning away 200 people each week), Brazil and all the big one-off concerts, many people are only just beginning to realise what's going on."

Equally important has been the role of London's other legal dance station, Choice FM. "I guess we saw swing as the modern-day equivalent of the Motown R&B era," says station boss George Kaye. In the past year, choice has brought over the likes of Jodeci, Father MC and Boyz II Men from the States. Every show has sold out, despite little or no outside publicity. "What bothers me is not that people seem to want to ignore this fact, but that they don't even notice it," says George.

As American swing acts have continued to enjoy success here, a new generation of London DJ crews has emerged, the Boogie Bunch and Rampage among them. With their roots in sound-system culture, the Boogie Bunch have drawn on a diverse selection of swing, rap and Seventies and Eighties boogie, playing alongside live acts or at clubs such as the weekly Stateside night at south London's Podium. "The swing stuff has definitely become more popular recently," says Boogie Bunch member Brian. "It's slowed down in tempo and become easier-listening."

Nowhere was this better illustrated than with the recent British chart success of SWV and Jade, both with prime examples of catchy, poppy swing. For JM, head of club promotions at Kiss FM, it's this wealth of new material that's really fuelled London's swing scene over the past year. "Because there's so much good swing out now, it's certain that the scene'll be fresh and happening. It's a scene that's always been strong, but since the recession the club market's collapsed, giving the opportunity for more swing clubs to open. It's highlighted the music's appeal and also allowed it to widen."

Could swing's current popularity lead to the emergence of new British acts? Steve Jervier certainly thinks so. This month he releases a compilation of ten artists signed to his own Street Hype label. "I've made sure all my acts don't sound like Jodeci or Mary J Blige," he says. "It's British swing with a slight change of feel, a slight difference in the way the songs are written."

But Choice FM's George Kaye believes there is still widespread resistance towards swing among British record companies. Of homegrown talent like the Epic signing Rhythm & Bass, he says, "They're four talented guys, but I don't think they've been allowed to find their direction. I think Bryan Powell will be the biggest name in this field. He knows his direction and hasn't swayed from it."

But with fair debuts recently released from other British acts like Kreuz and D-Natural, there's undoubtedly a wealth of developing talent. "A couple of years ago you couldn't get arrested with a track like SWV or Jade," says Steve Jervier. "The dance music we've had over the past couple of years has been diabolical. Swing is about to blow up. It's our future pop." He might just be right •

49   PARTY POOPERS

SEPTEMBER 1993

Club culture under attack in Glasgow by Mandi James

"THINGS AIN'T WHAT they used to be," is a perennial clubland gripe, although Glasgow revellers have more reason than most for misty-eyed reminiscences. As International City Of Culture in 1990, it boasted some of the best nightlife in Europe. Three years on, a rigorous curfew has been imposed on the city centre in a bid to curb street violence and amend drinking habits. Drastic changes to licensing laws now mean that clubs close at 2am and unless revellers are inside before midnight they are refused entry. "The council has drawn up further proposals, including a ban on bottled beers, and umbrellas being confiscated at the door," says Calvin Bush, a Glasgow journalist and club disciple. "There are so many anomalies – Victoria's, a handbag disco in the city centre, still opens until 3.30am – that you can't help thinking there's some kind of concerted attack on Glasgow's club culture." Local DJs and promoters are equally appalled. Orde Meikle, half of the Slam team, comments: "It's an infringement of civil liberties. Slam have been lucky that our Friday venue, The Arches, is a theatre complex with a 3.30am dance licence. We're beating the curfew. But we've still seen figures go down as people adapt to the midnight restriction." Ironically, far from curbing street violence, the restrictions mean every weekend hundreds of disappointed clubbers are being turned away from venues and left with nowhere to go, and there have been numerous local newspaper reports of trouble. Strathclyde Police headquarters denies knowledge of any incidents, however, and Licensing Board chairman James Coleman claims: "Newspapers are probably getting their information from the Disco Owners Association, who are mounting a very active campaign to try to get the legislation changed. But the information we're getting direct from the police is that there is now no queuing, people are leaving pubs earlier if they want a night out, and reported offences are going down quite dramatically." Fears that Glasgow, once at the heart of Scottish club culture, will become a shadow of its former self appear to be well-founded – there have already been signs of an exodus to Edinburgh clubs such as the frantically fashionable Carbolick Frolick and the disco pogo of Pure. "Unfortunately local councillors are not interested in our plight," concludes Orde. "Their solution to the perceived problem, rather than making provisions to allow people freedom of movement, is actually putting people off visiting Glasgow or even going out. It doesn't make them feel safe, only frustrated and restricted" •

50   GIVE THEM JUST A LITTLE MORE TIME

OCTOBER 1993

Junior Vasquez and the Sound Factory by Tim Jeffrey

HEARD DAVID MORALES or Frankie Knuckles on one of their recent UK dates? Wondered what all the fuss is about? After all the hype about these New York DJs, their UK performances often disappoint. This is not because Morales and Knuckles are no good. They are brilliant, and deserve the acclaim they receive. The problem lies in the way clubs in the UK are run. Outside a few big cities, most nights are still restricted to a 2am finish, which hardly gives any DJ room for manoeuvre, let alone New Yorkers who are used to playing for four or five hours. Venues that do have late licences insist on crowding as many DJs on to the decks as possible. The byword is quantity not quality. DJs often play for as little as an hour and very rarely for more than two, and few are likely to take a chance with new music and ideas when the DJ that follows will bang out all the latest big tunes and steal the glory. Those that do dare to be different risk their place on the gravy train of highly-paid guest spots. The result? Long nights of banging house with no subtlety, no imagination, no change. When did you last hear a hip hop track or something more alternative at a "name" club? Promoters of course blame the punters, who, they say, won't turn up unless there is a long list of DJs. So it's no surprise that when the likes of Morales and Knuckles are caught up in this absurd treadmill, we are let down. On a recent sweaty night in New York, I was given a stunning reminder of how it should be done. Junior Vasquez's set at the Sound Factory was astounding. In nine hours, Vasquez takes you on a roller-coaster ride of rhythms that's impossible to get off. He has some significant advantages – a truly hedonistic 1,500-strong crowd and a sound system that makes UK clubs sound like jukebox halls – but it is his supreme ability that puts him in a league of his own. For the first few hours, he builds the atmosphere with smooth-sounding garage grooves, teasing his crowd, preparing them for the aural onslaught to come. From around 6am, he unleashes a bombardment of rhythms that will rise and then drop to just hissing hi-hats for several minutes as the crowd is kept teetering on the edge of a musical orgasm. Favourites like The Fog's "Been A Long Time" and Xpress 2's "London Express" are worked for over half an hour with Vasquez mixing in his own beats and breaks to create inspiring "live remixes". And just when you least expect it, he drops in unusual records or even turns the music off to play classical music or swirling sound effects. If the UK club scene is to avoid stagnation, it must invest less in huge line-ups and more in creative individuals. Sadly, Vasquez's fear of flying means we are unlikely to experience his skill here. But with the right conditions there's no reason why the UK can't produce DJs of equal imagination •

51 THE INSTITUTION

DECEMBER 1993

Norman Jay by Sheryl Garratt

HE NORMALLY IGNORES people we bring in to interview, but this time, the man in the café near the FACE office is impressed. "Are you Norman Jay?" he asks. "Why did you leave Kiss, man?" It's a question that's been heard in the capital again and again since the DJ, a mainstay of London's "radical radio" since its heady pirate days, resigned on air last month.

But characteristically, Norman isn't out to dish the dirt. "I wasn't happy with the music direction the station was taking," is about all he'll say. "I felt it had lost the plot, really. The ideals we founded it on were being eroded day by day in pursuit other things, including profit."

The £28 specialist DJs were paid for their two-hour shows was not enough for him to compromise his principles, he says. So, when asked to move from his Sunday evening slot, he left. The support was overwhelming: hundreds stood outside his club at The Bass Clef the following night, unable to get in but wanting to pass on their regards anyway, while a few weeks later a warehouse clash between Soul II Soul, Mannaseh and Norman's Shake 'N' Finger Pop crew attracted a crowd almost 3,000 strong.

But then, ask clubbers around the country to name their top ten DJs, and Norman Jay will feature somewhere in most lists. A man who has taken in most movements from jazz-funk and reggae to rare groove and house, he's welcomed in guest spots across the country. Able to play in gay clubs, acid jazz clubs, soul sessions and sweaty house nights, Norman Jay is more than just a DJ; he's a clubland institution.

Like most DJs, he started out as a fan – buying the records, reading the magazines, going to live shows and clubs. Football helped too; Norman would travel round the country to Spurs matches, staying on to check the local clubs before hitching home for the Sunday sessions at clubs like Crackers in Soho. Celebrating his 36th birthday this month, he's a living history of British clubland. Northern soul sessions, the Caister weekenders, his brother Joey's conscious reggae sound system, shebeens in Brixton and Ladbroke Grove, the early punk clubs, the white funk scene at Le Beat Route – Norman went to them all.

He recalls with a laugh being mistaken for a rent boy in seedy dives in Soho, or meeting Sid Vicious and Johnny Rotten at the Sunday-night funk sessions at Ronnie Scott's, where they came to buy weed from one of Norman's friends. Or Jaws, a Saturday-night soul session deep in east London in 1976 that ended at midnight. If he missed the last tube home after, he'd walk back into town, and sleep in a tree in Hyde Park because he was too exhausted to go any further.

"Very early on, I was part of a group who saw themselves as different to the mainstream. I never went as extreme as my white friends, but I did have a ginger streak in my afro, used to wear clothes that gay men wore, just to be different," he says. "The first time I went to Wigan, I was the only black guy in the place, and I was offered drinks all night. I was like a pop star! There was a gang of us – four black guys, three white guys. We'd bundle into my Mini and just drive all over the country. We were known as The London Mob. We'd pick up Blues & Soul, and crash in there with our rowdy cockney selves."

He recalls being in New York on a family visit during the height of the disco boom and being admitted into the now-famous Studio 54 because he had an English accent. He also remembers being refused entry into the legendary Essex club The Lacey Lady on his 21st birthday because all the friends he was with were black. It was this kind of experience that led him away from the clubs as a DJ, and into the first generation of soul sound systems. As Shake 'N' Finger Pop, he would play instead at house parties and warehouses, building a scene that eventually became so big that legal club venues had to invite them in.

"If you believe in what you're doing, sooner or later those who rejected you will cross the street to see what you're doing," he says. "Black music is littered with that. They'll always snatch a bit of your culture and interpret it their way. America especially is very creative – just as you thought disco was dead, they came up with electro, then hip hop, then house. It doesn't matter if, as soon as you lay the egg, they snatch it, when you have the power to go lay another egg. That's how I know I'll survive. I'll always be part of something creative, just by being true to myself."

But staying true has not meant sticking with one type of music and defending it to the last. While never rejecting his history, Norman has always embraced the new. While some DJs on the rare groove scene became dinosaurs overnight when acid broke, he glided effortlessly in, his High On Hope club becoming a Thursday-night garage/house heaven. "It wasn't like house was completely new," he shrugs. "I was always going to like it because I'd liked the disco records it came from. I can always find the soul in whatever it is. That's what punk taught me – don't be dismissive of anything, don't be scared to go against the grain.

"I still have the same enthusiasm in 1993 as I had in 1973. Perhaps more so, because I understand it better now. There's no better feeling than suddenly becoming aware that you're part of something, and watching it evolve, grow and reach its logical conclusion. Wicked! That's the kick I get out of starting and running clubs. I'm still a punter, I'm still a fan. I've never lost that."

And with that, Norman Jay, clubland institution, is back on his lovingly-restored Chopper bike and is off into the night •

52　BUG-EYED, BLOODSHOT AND FULL OF LOVE

AUGUST 1994

Berlin's Love Parade by Gavin Hills

I CAN NOW CONFIRM that, no no, no no no no, no no no no, there's no limits. None at all, bar overdose. The acid/house/rave/techno scene has spanned the globe and snatched the souls of the world's reckless. It reaches every corner of what we call the West and happily entertains those in the Third World who are at economic liberty to indulge in such follies. Apolitical, agnostic and asexual, this particular brand of hedonism has taken modern computers and pharmaceuticals then plonked them together with dances and beats as old as our species. And what a great success it's all been. Now it even has its own annual festival. The Berlin Love Parade draws huge crowds from all over Europe and beyond. It's a celebration of house music, of peace, love and tolerance. It's a coming together of the world's youth in a spirit of, er, togetherness. It's also a damned good excuse to dance and take lots of drugs.

For years the town of Munich has paid host to regular beer festivals. People gather from this planet's furthest corners, all to celebrate the old god alcohol. Now the city of Berlin has provided a rival session for the young. Here, in the first weekend in July, the Love Parade pays homage to the new idol Ecstasy. At only six years old, it is a pretty young tradition. But with over 100,000 people attending this year, it's a date that looks likely to have some longevity. This much fun doesn't disappear overnight.

The Love Parade was one of those six-in-the-morning ideas, an abstract concept set up by the city's camp club crowd. They just thought it would be a laugh to nut around town proclaiming their love for fellow human beings. Originally an odd mix of the Notting Hill Carnival and Gay Pride, it's developed rapidly into the march of the rave generation. This year's event started at 4pm on Saturday July 1. This was a very reasonable time. Left-wing activists tend to do things at about 10am and eco-warriors think dawn raids are a good idea – trust clubbers to get things right.

Having had only two hours sleep in the 48 hours prior to my arrival, things were already looking messy. But my own folly was put into context by the other English in attendance. Various DJs, club promoters and party tourists had made the journey. Most of these ne'er-do-wells had, quite literally, crawled off the aircraft, lost their luggage, necked the duty free and were only being kept together by continual downing of the essential medications they had brought over by the truckload. Announcing "Suck my stump!" to the customs officer is not my idea of endearing yourself to the locals, but remarkably all on board our flight were waved through.

Call me a lightweight, but after a couple of days on the go I find a kip in a hotel can do more for my party perkiness than one up each nostril and a bottle of Dom Perignon ever can. However, one must keep up appearances and these days if you're not bug-eyed, bloodshot and barely comprehensible there's obviously something completely wrong with you. I find sleeping in lifts gives one a similar look and has none of the nasty after-effects. Anyway, after spending the morning gaining an optional 40 winks travelling between the basement and the sixth floor of my hotel, I made my way to the 4pm kick-off at the Wittenburg Platz in the centre of what was – and I suppose still is – West Berlin.

At first I couldn't really work out just what was supposed to happen. All down the main high street and right into the platz everywhere was jam-packed with clubbers. They were cheering, whistling, pinching arses and indulging in manic water-pistol fights. It was all good fun, but I didn't really get it. Then, from the back of the platz, the drums were heard. A faint beat drifted over the horizon and ignited the crowds into motion. Over a lake of bobbing heads and waving arms I saw the tip of the first articulated lorry. Smothered in dancers, sound system blaring, it entered the crowds and pied pipered the awaiting mass further into the city centre. It was the first of 30 floats put together from clubs, record shops and various groups from abroad. They banged out the tracks and set every building thumping. The city hadn't taken such a pounding since World War II.

A jolly mix of trannies, straights and gays then paraded their love around town. And what an attractive love it was. Tight Adidas outfits do something for our passions that fishnets provoked in previous generations. Oh, for a leggy blonde in Lycra now that summer's here! There is no crusty element on the scene in Germany and things seem far more united than they could ever be here. Even your average Mr and Mrs Schmidt seemed happy enough to sit at the many pavement cafés, drink a beer and clap along to the throngs of dancing *jugend*. What police there were confined themselves to a few traffic duties. It did occur to me that a similar event in Britain would have resulted in a fair few stabbings, looted shops and acid-spiked drinks. Still, we Brits like a good laugh, don't we?

After strutting down the strasse with the sun in my hair and sweat on my forehead, a strange thought occurred to me. Germany's actually a really nice country. Actually, knock me down with a brockwurst, but the Germans even have a sense of humour. After all, you can't drop two Es, then march down your main street dressed in frock while holding a large blow-up duck without seeing life's more mirthful side. Even the Japanese had their own float and were wiggling with the best of them. Why, I almost found myself becoming uncynical; dancing away a weekend has its purposes. As a result, I got to know the German people particularly close up by crawling around their gardens and fish ponds at seven on the Sunday morning. (Fair play to the *fräulein* who fished me out, incidentally.)

The parade was a kind of Poll Tax riot in reverse. After the last sound system drove off into the sunset, everyone was left buzzing with excitement and headed east to the city's numerous clubs, most of which were initially squatted when the wall came down. Berlin has a plethora of dandy nightspots. E-works, The Bunker and the legendary Tresor all provide the head-strong with a far more banging soundtrack than you hear in the UK these days. Clubs all over town were jammed, but Tresor was particularly insane, as well as baffling. I'm not used to grown men showing me their cuddly toys, and I'm not sure if I approve. "Handbag" is not a genre that has reached Germany, and to be honest I don't really think it will catch on in a country where practically anything with lyrics is considered disco. Gabba and hardcore provide lads' music in a lot of the clubs, and the quest for a bit of piano proved an elusive one. But at the Tresor it's still techno, techno, techno. This sound is still the erratic heartbeat of the city that was once the centre of the Cold War world. Despite the thaw, Berlin remains unique. And for the young, the Love Parade still gives it the edge on a lot of Euro destinations. For all concerned, it is a particularly mad, unusual, barmy, bonkers, bender of a weekend.

After a weekend of prime Berliner abuse, my vorsprung had lost its durch technik. I crawled out of the lift and into my hotel bed and took notes, trying to make sense of what had gone on. This unique event, this weird music, these happy-go-lucky people – this strange nothingness. In a bizarre attempt at drugged-up self-analysis, I took out a pen and preposterously started to look for meanings and concepts to explain what's happening to us all on planet party. It was tempting to write that we live in world so remote, so fucked up, that pure hedonism is our only escape route. Or perhaps attempt to justify it all not as submission, but as a strong force for empowerment, a push for a liberal agenda of equality, tolerance and freedom. Trouble is, I'm not so sure of anything, certainty being what it is these days. I threw the pad to the floor, raided the mini-bar, skinned up and put on the television. CNN is the only channel in English, so I sit and stare. It's Larry King Live. Guess who's on? Noel Edmonds, pushing Mr Blobby to the Yanks. "I don't get it," says Larry. "All he says is 'Blobby, Blobby, Blobby'. How do you know what he's going on about?"

"It's obvious," replies Noel. "Blobby is on a mission to save the world."

Bingo! Inspiration. Follow me, if you will, away from Berlin and into our vaguely collective psyche. Blobby, Blobby, Blobby: techno, techno, techno. Read what you like into it. Can it save the world, or is it complete nonsense? All I know is that it leads our lives out of the mundane. The vacuous feeling of Monday mourn has little to do with what has gone before and more to do with the future we face. With our souls on slide and our hopes dashed, maybe things can only get better, maybe there are no limits. Where will the Love Parade lead us? •

53 "BECAUSE EVERYONE'S SEEN THEIR MUM WITH A WHISKY IN HER HAND GETTING GUTTED TO FRANK SINATRA, HAVEN'T THEY?" DECEMBER 1994

True adventures in the easy-listening underground by Kate Spicer

----

MADAME JO JO'S ON a Tuesday night, and the transvestites in the usual cabaret have a night off to go clubbing. Instead the Soho piano bar has been taken over by Indigo, an evening of floorshow, dining, and exotic easy listening. Unemployable Sohoites, besuited professionals in their early thirties and fashionably dressed students (there's even a few leathered-up bikers around) all cram together on the plush red banquettes, craning their necks to get a view of the act on the twinkling stage.

The Mike Flowers Pops and his Sounds Superb Singers come to the end of a medley of Prince songs à la Burt Bacharach, played by the 12-piece orchestra of brass, strings, Latin percussion, electric harpsichord and two Hammond organs. Mike Flowers – bad nylon toupee, just-too-tight suit – gives a little Terry Wogan chuckle, turns to the audience and asks, "Who said the popular song was dead?" Pinching his conductor's baton, he moves on. "And here's a number from another child prodigy, a li'l lady called Björk," and he's off into an arrangement of "Venus As A Boy".

Standing at the bar, a devotee of the scene encapsulated by Indigo explains their style. "The clothes are notable in that there's a certain lack of taste, and plenty of man-made fibres." Daywear for men might be a cream Yves Saint Laurent jacket, shot with mustard, green and orange, finished off with the flourish of a yellow flowery cravat. Hair is bouffed, moustaches waxed, shoes gleam. "We call it the power pensioner look."

A man in a gaudy polyester shirt puts the whole scene more succinctly. "Everything's so wrong, it's perfect."

Indigo was set up by 29-year-old musician Count Indigo and 24-year-old "retired scientist" Felchley B Hawkes. Neither had promoted a club before. "I just wanted somewhere to go," says Indigo. "Clubland was alienating, the places that were more sympathetic to people being with people tended to be exclusive. I wanted something more democratic." Hawkes was an ex-thrash metal-head, who had been converted three years ago when, rifling through his parents' record collection, he chanced upon an album by crooner Andy Williams. That was it – he had been caught by what he calls a "disease"; easy listening. He started DJing on hospital radio, moving on to pensioners' coffee mornings, and then, naturally, to Indigo.

As the most recent attempt to formulate a club alternative, Indigo's ingredients seem horribly wrong. The club plays the kind of records to be found dog-eared between the old Pinky And Perky albums in your local Oxfam: movie soundtracks, instrumentals, old stereo showcase albums. It puts on cabaret acts ("Makes the evening an event," says

Indigo) that are a cross between pretentious art-school revue and the pure showbiz of Las Vegas. And there's not even a dancefloor. Yet in the seven months since they started they have watched a regular following grow. New faces appear every night, and when someone like The Mike Flowers Pops play, they are packed to capacity.

Easy listening has been played in smaller London venues for the last three years, and has long been collected by a quiet clique of music lovers who didn't want to talk about what is popularly seen by them as lobotomy music. In the louche opulence of Madame Jo Jo's, those disparate threads started to pull together and something like a Nineties lounge scene started to appear. Its unwitting pioneers are the Karminsky Brothers, James and Martin. The two DJs met each other six years ago in their early twenties in Southend, when they were both rare groovers with similar tastes in music. James says they only started getting into easy listening "by being broke, really poor. Rather than spending £15 on a jazz record, I'd spend £1.80 on an easy listening album because of the weird cover". To his surprise, he found tracks "that you wouldn't believe were easy listening – you might think it was some obscure funk track. So much of the music is so damn groovy; really, really groovy."

By 1991 they had amassed so many records that they started playing easy listening tracks at their rare groove night, Espresso Espresso at the Brixton Brasserie. More lost sounds than schmaltz, their collection also covered the stranger elements of jazz, Latin, mambos, and film soundtracks like Mancini's "Breakfast At Tiffany's" and "Barbarella" by the Bob Crewe Generation Orchestra. People liked it, and The Karminskys continued doing small nights with evocative names like Holly Go Lightly at the Alpine Ski Lodge, and The Tender Trap in Soho.

When they weren't languishing in the beat lounges of Karminsky nights, the small, polite crowd that had gathered around the music tolerated, as one follower called it, the "here's the Sixties and Seventies dumped in your lap" retro-kitsch vibe. At clubs like Smashing and Leave My Wife Alone people danced to everything from disco pop to rare grooves, an eclectic mix which celebrated the history of the dancefloor rather than the comfort of the living room. Easy listening aficionados would sit patiently at the bar, metaphorically nursing their pina coladas, waiting for a DJ like Smashing's Martin Green to drop in the occasional class track or for the Karminskys to play their guest slots.

They were an unintentionally cliquey set, who took those occasional novelty tracks seriously. At the housey/Seventies babefest of Discotheque in '92, the Karminskys had a room downstairs called The Bamboo Curtain. "You'd see people put their head round and then just run upstairs because they were scared." Not just because of the strange music, James Karminsky explains. "We tend to dress up – in leisure suits, a polo neck, a nice Casino Royale look. Sometimes there are people dressed entirely in furs. That's not something you see in a house club."

The music they play has become more avant-garde. Current favourites include "Exciting Sounds Of Tomorrow" by the Pete Moore Orchestra, and "Hammond Stereo Sounds To Spoil You" by Roger Conlan. Their collection allows them to cater to specific audiences at the different clubs they play. At Indigo you'll hear safe soundtracks and pop easy listening; downstairs at the massively popular Blow Up they play the strange end of Sixties dance music. It's at their own night, the Sound Spectrum in the cosy chalet environs of Soho's St Moritz club, that they get to play the "complete array of sounds" they get such a buzz off – from soundtracks to Moog music and surreal cover versions.

In Camden Town, DJ Fred Leicester likes his listening cheesy and is not ashamed to
play it. At his club, Cheese, at the Laurel Tree in NW1, he concentrates on the crooning,

showbizzy elements and a less surreal nostalgia than swinging Sixties movies; "Because everyone's seen their mum with a whisky in her hand getting gutted to Frank Sinatra, haven't they?" The same, if more earthy, come-together sentiment of the other easy listening clubs is there. Cheese, he says, "is about getting drunk and singing along to 'New York, New York' with your arms around someone you've never met before".

Exotic bon vivant and dubious lounge lizard Sal Volatile has been running private parties and trips to lifestyle meccas like Portmeirion and Broadstairs for the last three years. Like Fletchley B Hawkes, he left rock behind to "gnaw at its own kneecap" and has turned to easy listening. Again, the diversity and freshness of the music coupled with its image drew him to it. In the New Year he hopes to open a late-night American-style bar in a London hostess club. "It'll take a direct line from the LA exotica bars, that whole Heffner-esque, Bunny Girl/bachelor idea, a place where you expect to see a young Dean Martin or Sammy Davies sliding along on an oil slick of pina colada." All very un-PC for the PC Nineties. "Exactly – that's the entire idea, a complete turnaround. A return to a time pre-Seventies, a more innocent, romantic time when people dated, knew the roles to be played, knew what to do."

But there's also a cynical twist to the Nineties Martini. The music's dubious original uses – the rendering of pop culture saccharine, and, as Volatile says, "as bachelor pad music, a part of the whole softening process" – have been turned around. Lorraine Bowen, a regular performer at Indigo, sings ironic odes to domestic bliss, accompanying herself on a Casio keyboard perched on top of an ironing board. Mike Flowers, performing the music he genuinely loves with proper musicians, is after more than just laughs. "I'm interested in being iconoclastic, doing the Prince, doing the Nirvana, 'Smells Like Teen Spirit'. I'd love to do a U2 tune – the pomposity of it; you want to deflate it a bit, a take which in turn draws people to a kind of music they would not normally consider."

None of the people mentioned here are using the term kitsch or camp. "It makes it look like people like Danny Baker and Jonathan Ross are in control, that easy listening is just another parade of old artefacts on show," explains Sal Volatile. "People aren't into it for that – this music is scintillating stuff" •

54 BABES IN BOYLAND

JUNE 1995

Time for the baby doll to grow up by Laura Craik

EVER SHARED A MIRROR with the sort of sunbed-kissed, chasm-cleavaged babe found at your average happy house night? It's not a bonding experience. Have you seen the evil looks these munchkins give each other? Like contestants in a provincial beauty pageant, they're all too busy checking out the competition to get on with the act of enjoying themselves. Some smart-arsed economist once said that competition increases efficiency. Bollocks. It increases inadequacy, which is then filtered out in a thin green arc of venom on to the nearest female who triggers the emotion.

Why can't things be more like they are in the bird kingdom, where the males are brightly feathered and the females hide their souls behind muted browns and greys? It's much easier to warm to Justine from Elastica than the two Plumstead puffballs from Shampoo, because La Frischmann doesn't set herself up for a pasting by walking around wearing knee socks, ruffles and plastic hairclips. In these days of in-yer-face-ness, it takes more style to slouch out in a loose denim number than it does to bare all in the latest baby-doll. It shows you're not competing. It shows you're comfortable – in your clothes and in yourself. Women don't feel as hostile towards androgynous women as they do towards fluffy, flauntsome babes. Seeing sex on a stick glide past your eyes makes you doubt your own powers of attraction.

It struck me in Fat Cat Records. As I hovered kind of apologetically by the Hard House A-J section, I felt an envious pang towards the row of loose-limbed blokes leaning baggily over the record counter together. I say "together" because they didn't know each other; although they had only been thrown together by chance and a shared desire to purchase anything obscure by Andrew Weatherall, they were united by a camaraderie I've only felt amongst my own sex after six years of senior school and several hundred shared hangovers. Not for the first time, I wished I had a willy. Blokes don't put other blokes through a ten-point vetting process to determine whether they're OK to associate with. Blokes have a liberal attitude towards other blokes, even when they're eyeing up their women. Blokes don't have as great a propensity to cast evil looks or to "accidentally" spill drinks over your dry-clean-only skirt.

Try to articulate your female-induced paranoia to your boyfriend and he'll stare at you blankly. Men just don't get it. Why would they? Brought up to be valued for their brains rather than their beauty, they feel no need to flaunt their skin-deep attractions. Clothes don't maketh the man, but they certainly maketh the woman. The "wacky" apparel of Chris Evans doesn't translate in the same way to Katie Puckrick. He gets respected; she gets derided. Women can't wear what they want and get away with it.

All fashion is tyranny, but babe fashion – the act of squeezing into a teensy pink T-shirt and a micro mini – is especially cruel. New Men aren't new after five pints of beer, and dressing like a dozy 12-year-old means you're likely to be treated as one. Irony isn't best understood during last orders, when words come fast and loose and tend to be peppered with insults. It's hard enough for a woman to be treated as an equal, even without a "come and get it" slogan across her chest. Wouldn't we rather men read our lips than our tits? Fashion magazines like *Elle* have recently claimed that feminism has progressed to such an extent that women can subvert their own sexual identity. But any article which suggests we are now sufficiently confident about our gender's role in society that we can play games with it by dressing up as bimbos is talking absolute gobshite. Maybe when it's safe to walk home after dark in red high heels I might believe you. Until then, journos, I only hope your cab fares are on expenses if you practise what you preach •

55 METAL GURU

JULY 1995

Goldie, jungle and the true spirit of B-boy by David Toop

GOLDIE THE METALHEAD, in repose, on the floor, supine in Stüssy, bleached head etched with lines. Caps on the wall, pinned in neat rows, graffiti on canvas, club photographs. The massive Massive – half pit-bull, half mastiff – stretches out on top of him in a docile, besotted heap of muscular dogflesh. "Killer dog," chuckles the manager. Mobile phones shrill incessantly in the electronic rainforest; Goldie contemplating the city through his eighteenth-floor picture window. Pollution haze creeps up London's buildings in grey asthmatic mist. Down below in the rat runs, violence entering a periodic upturn: stabbings and shootings all around, racial tension, mob attacks, riots on the brink.

"I'm always looking out the window," he says, words tumbling in a rush, "thinking I wanna be part of London, I wanna see what I can do. I didn't think I'd be doing this. Switch off, look at these paintings, look out the window. It really is part of that landscape that I'm surrounded by. That's why I love this place so much. It's such a nice vibe to be here and have the space to be able to get away from it all."

A few weeks earlier, I clocked Goldie's brief appearance in *Death By Bass*, Harsha Patel's short film about in-car bass fetishists. The people who go boom. The people who vibrate street air with mobile bass pressure, shop windows exploding as they pass, old grannies folding at the knees in bass shock. "To me it represents aggression," he said, gold-laminated incisors bared, slow-motioned in pit-bull growl. "It represents being part of the street. It represents anger and it represents being able to say what I wanna say in sounds, you know wha'mean? We've said all we can say and nobody listens anyway so fuck 'em, we just give 'em bass."

Soundbite culture. Is drum & bass reducible to the repressed black youth theme, then? Today Goldie is in expansive mood. But Goldie is always in expansive mood. Pity the poor film editor who has to select one simple, short, sharp message, for Goldie talks high signal to noise flow, complex, contradictory. Constant paradox in his feelings, his aesthetic, his life. Like Escher, the artist who created paradoxical yet apparently logical images, winding stairs that go nowhere but somewhere.

I interviewed Goldie last October, again in May. Both occasions he threw Escher into the conversation, comparing those image puzzles (always popular during periods when certain drugs are abroad) to fourth-dimensional graffiti and fourth-dimensional breakbeats. "It doesn't exist but it can exist. All those impossible angles. That four thing again."

I can hear Escher in the music, I say, thinking about 4 Hero's remix of his "Inner City Life", remaking Marvin Gaye's "Trouble Man" for the psychedelic harsh Nineties, crisp drums in one brief section spiralling away into nothingness as if sucked up by JG Ballard's sound Hoover. "You will do," he replies, "because it's disguising things. Illusion of sound. Sound is going fourth dimension. It is opening up. A couple of years ago when I started experimenting with all that shit, it hadn't really been done, it hadn't really been fucked about with except prior to that in the Sixties, with guitars and stuff for live acoustic sound."

Illusion of sound. Goldie talks about music in terms of visual images, or breakdancing, or trainer fetishism, or hip hop attitude. Old school. "I wouldn't like to say jungle," he says, so we won't. We go back, instead, to some of the frontline spermatozoa that seeded this movement that Goldie describes, with pride, as the first true UK subculture.

The Metalheadz album, "Timeless", will be anticipated as an important test tone for this subculture. The one that will continue to be called jungle no matter what. Those voices are speaking again, through subsonic vibrations, fluttering moth-wing hi-hats, eroded soul fragments, rattlesnake snare drummers of the apocalypse. Speaking, but not heard with clarity, so fiercely defensive, protective, fanatical in self-definition. Almost a secret society, in fact. Goldie examined this theme back in October by distinguishing the drum & bass lifestyle from UK hip hop.

"The things what happened in hip hop for me," he says, "what got fucked up with it, the UK imported it. They all wanted to be the bad boys. They wasn't even living in the social conditions to wanna be bad. When you're talking structurally, socially, New York and Miami, you know what I'm saying? Please! The thing about this culture as far as the hardcore thing's concerned, is that it is the underground culture of the UK. The darkest drugs are getting taken, the darkest people are meeting. It's like going to the South Bronx, a real hip hop jam, or a block party.

"There's always gonna be a situation within that – your drug dealers, the people who are doing shit, the people who are doing nothing, the people who are trying to make an impact. We called it dark because it was unnoticed. It was winter. It was dark nights. Things weren't happening. We called it dark many years ago and people said it was demonic. It was dark because it was on the scene, it was unheard, it wasn't in the limelight. It was the equivalent of blues in the Sixties. What we are trying to do is to do with the positiveness of it, musically, taking things forward."

So "Timeless" will be judged by that yardstick. A very long album, the title track topping 20 minutes, two others breaking the 10-minute barrier, this mix of ballads, jazz solos, lush synthetic strings, soul vocals and ferocious digital-Escher percussion riddles may be dismissed by detractors who figure hardcore has gone softcore, dignified and "progressive". Equally, it may be rejected also by a general public who cannot deal with 4D sound illusions so intensely focused, so microscopically tracked, reversed, X-rayed or magnified, repeated until your head spins.

The first four minutes of "Jah The Seventh", for example, inhabit an aether domain of corkscrew vapour trails and pummelling beats. Then Goldie drops the strings and you feel you have opened that eighteenth-floor window, find yourself soaring down to the aural cataclysm of death valley below. "Timeless" was produced with Rob Playford, engineer, programmer and boss of the Moving Shadow label. "Metalheadz, it's another world," Playford told me last year. "Programming it is a bit of a nightmare."

Programmed drum loops are the core of the hardcore but "Timeless" opens out into musical areas which are an archaeology of Eighties soul boy/B-boy lifestyle. "State Of Rage" samples and dissects Maze's "Twilight", a moody, minimalist near-instrumental produced in 1985 by Frankie Beverly in the twilight of Maze-mania. "All-dayers," says Goldie, and suddenly we're talking Change, Loose Ends, Mantronix, Barry White, MC Shan's "The Bridge", all the tracks, the nights, the clubs, the breaks that filter through into the Goldie/Playford version of hardcore. Alongside vocalists Diane Charlemagne and Lorna Harris and jazz-blues keyboard-player Justina Curtis, jazz players such as Steve Williamson and Cleveland Watkiss perform on the album.

In one breath, Goldie will talk about the adrenaline charge of 160, 170 beats per minute, comparing the job of cramming structural necessities into a land-speed-record vehicle to the rush of painting a train quickly, furtively, under cover of night, or making analogies with breaking. Learning to move fast, flip, backspin, get on the good foot. All that stuff once dismissed as a juvenile fad or "ethnic vernacular art" but now revealed as essential homework for a future career in electronic creativity. "Eighty, 90 bpm is like a stroll in the park," he says. Then again, he downplays the importance of tempo. "It's not the speed, because let me talk about jazz." So there are influences from jazz guitarist Pat Metheny's "First Circle" in there, and a period of study at the loudspeakers with Miles Davis' "Decoy".

Yet when there are jazz ballads, the image is slightly out of register. "Adrift" features Watkiss and Williamson, sounds a little like Luther Vandross on acid, and indeed, as Goldie confirms, explores the comedown phase. Inconveniently for those who would freshen up beleaguered youth culture, Goldie discusses the relationship between drug use and his music with disarming candour. I mention churning sounds that grind in the catacombs beneath those technorama string sounds on "Timeless". "It's very dark," mutters Goldie, darkly. "It's undercurrent. That top surface cannot work without that. It's fierce but it's not harmful. That's very much that drug movement. What I've taken. I couldn't do that without experience. It's not saying, 'Listen guys, taking drugs is the best thing to do,' but that is all part of that culture of me growing up. There's a certain amount of escapism in that. I could get a fix off that."

William Burroughs, not a man to necessarily practise what he preaches, believed that certain drugs required only one try. After that, the effects could be recalled and exploited through art without a depressing onset of compulsive behaviour. Goldie likes this idea, talks in detail about timestretching, pitchshifting, square sine waves, distortion-free distortion, software writing and other technicalities of perceptual manipulation, ending up back in the fourth dimension, via passing analogies to Adidas shell tops and the drying time of spray paint. Phew, drum & bass.

But Goldie's no pot head pixie. "I met Kase 1 with the one arm," he says. "You see Kase 1 in Style Wars [Henry Chalfant's graffiti documentary]. Real freaky story, I met Kase one year, hero, hero, and then within a year I saw Kase again, in a tunnel on 116th Street. We were painting a train in the middle of the night and Kase was there, cracked out, looking for paint. It's like realising Father Christmas ain't real any more."

He also talks about Heathtown Estate, Wolverhampton, home for him after growing up fostered and in care. People he knew, on their way to achieving something, even something disreputable, now reduced to shuffling the streets in their pyjamas, no shoes, Golf GTi sucked into the maw of cocaine need. "I used to live next door to the gambling house," he says. "Crack fucked it. The graffiti's still there on the walls, decaying."

Wolverhampton Council members still remember Goldie from his days of bombing Heathtown walls with spray paint. I first came across him in 1986. Film-maker Dick Fontaine asked me to write music for a graffiti documentary. Bombin', made by Fontaine with photographer Gus Coral for Central TV, tracked Bronx graffiti artist Brim through London, Oxford, Wolverhampton, Bristol and Birmingham, filmed Afrika Bambaataa, Lisa Lee, Red Alert and The Wild Bunch in session and took Goldie to the source of his inspiration in uptown New York City. At the close of the film, Goldie paces through the walkway maze of Heathtown, a public gallery for his own paintings. "When I was a kid," he says on the audiotrack, "I didn't have nothing to look at, man. I was looking at people in care and I was looking at care assistants. All these feelings I wanted to portray... I've been able to go outside my head. As far as I live my time in town I'm just gonna paint. There's nothing else for me to do."

Those raw, derided attempts to emulate American graffiti, breaking, rapping and electro were formative elements of jungle breakbeats; the UK techno of LFO, Black Dog and Bandulu; the so-called Bristol sound of Massive Attack, Nellee Hooper. That "nothing else for me to do" was short of the mark, but then how many of us know where we are going? Logically, it might have been possible to look ahead in 1985, like some kind of supercharged William Gibson, and imagine how music could turn out if you combined the technological sound of "Planet Rock" with live B-boy mixing, reggae sound systems, soul all-dayers, warehouse funk parties and the kind of sounds emerging from Paul Murphy's jazz rooms. Even then, you couldn't imagine Madonna's "Bedtime Stories", Björk, Tricky or "Timeless" in your wildest dreams.

Goldie's drive still runs on old school hip hop idealism: artistic collaboration, mixed media, social arts, public art, props where they are due, integrity, the Zulu Nation. "If you've got everybody collaborating on a mass scale, you can't be stopped," he wrote in *Spraycan Art*, a book by Henry Chalfant and James Prigoff. "You can do anything, man. You can move mountains. If all the kids in this estate were piecing, can you imagine what a beautiful place it would be?" Even when he said it, back in 1987, half of that feeling must have been shadowed by a bleaker awareness. Sink estates can't be cured by graffiti.

Yet mini-industries have grown out of all that spraycan, breaking and turntable wildstyle. Metalheadz, Nellee and Massive Attack are one side of it; gallery exhibitions of streetwear and breakdance photographs represent the other. What the survivors learned, the ones who evolved rather than imitated, was how to create and survive under pressure.

"To me, this music is the B-boy move," says Goldie. "It rocks my head more than all this jive hip hop shit coming out of the UK. What kicked me as a B-boy was going to a practise session and breaking for three hours, just having breaks looping. That was the whole point. That kick going into battle. Doing it. This is what makes it move for me. I'm hearing these people going, 'Yeah man, did you hear that fucking loop, did you hear that 2 Bad Mice break, fucking hell, ripping it up.' All that friendly rivalry paid off. It think it gives me more of an insight, the way I shaped my life and what I wanted to achieve with it. The music side of it's purely accidental. I realise now, from living in Miami, the whole multi-cultural side of it – Hispanic, black-American, black-Jamaican, the Haitians – you start realising what hip hop did for American culture was it gave a universal medium, a language of style. The development of that laid a ground rule down for a whole lot of different people."

When times change beyond recognition but nostalgia still exerts a pull, then fleetness of foot is a must. Goldie designs fonts on a Macintosh now with Gus Coral, dreams about meeting software writers, talks about Neville Brody as easily as he talks about DJ Fabio or Grooverider. "Now, with modems and information, you know," he says, "I just turn on MTV on a Saturday morning and you're in New York. You can get there. If you wanna go and buy Puma sneakers you just go down to, like, Office, or you can go to Oxford Street. The play's been taken out of that." Must be distressing for some. Doesn't appear to bother Goldie. You seem very content, I suggest. "I just feel I've got it sussed," he says. "I've finally got it sussed. I'm content" •

56   ALL BACK TO MINE

JULY 1995

Problems with the post-club home soirée by Robert Newman

NO MORE MR ALL Back To Mine. It's always the same. You think it's gonna feel like your birthday party, but by the time you get back to yours there's somehow only ever two people you actually know, and ten loser, druggie scumbags sizing up your gaff and drinking all your liquor. And because you're in a flat full of strangers, your own home doesn't feel like home any more. The other night, while informing one of my guests that alas, no, I didn't have any Alcan foil, but would he and his friends, however, care for some tea to go with my last bottle of Famous Grouse, I was suddenly aware of the browbeaten expression on my face; it was the hangdog, fucked-over expression of a Salford publican when the local gang have forced an impromptu lock-in on him. Happy days.

As these low-life wasters refuse to take the hint that you'd like to retire now and would they like hackney-carriages summoned, your conscience hands you a Polaroid of the room. Up till now you've been thinking that if a picture were taken of the scene in your front room it could be entitled something like "The Great Artist As Truly Comprehensive Soul Able To Mix With All Walks Of Life". But the picture you see is "The Lost, Wasted Years Of Bullshit, Druggy Conversations. Soul In Ruins. Cushions Fucked-Up. Freefall".

Clearing up the next day you're struck by the impersonality of the litter. It's different when you've had your own, actual, proper friends round. When tidying up after your friends, your flat becomes a scrapbook. You think, "Here is the cassette box Martine was holding when she came up with that excellent joke about Brett Anderson. Here is the ice-cream Sid spilled before coming up with the phrase 'I've totally chocolated me strides'. Here are the splinters of the wine glass I was absent-mindedly chewing while my ex-girlfriend phoned her boyfriend, but the morning after the all back to mine... well, this could be the floor of the Electric Ballroom after an Angelic Upstarts gig. And looking at all the many empty bottles of wine and spirits (dark butt-ends dissolving in the last stale dregs), you remember how carefully you chose the wine because it was intended for when the woman you love next came by. You remember that that crate of Kronenbourg was what you were storing up for when your friends came round to watch the Umbro Cup. What I'm trying to say is that the most depressing thing about an all back to mine isn't that all your liquor has gone down the gannet gullets of ungrateful, tedious strangers. No, the most depressing thing is to do with what those empties symbolise. It's this; your future has been drained of all the intimate, cosy or celebratory occasions in which those bottles were to be a part.

What were you thinking? Why did you behave like a kind of loved-up Travis Bickle: "All the animals come out at night: whores, dopers, junkies, sick, the scum, the filth. Hey everyone! All back to mine!" What made you say "All back to mine"? Think back. The lights came on and you felt like your flat was a bully waiting to give you a hard time if you went home alone. Better to face that bully with some friends or whoever. It turns out, contrary to your plans, that it's whoever. Next morning, of course, you feel just as empty. The only difference, you realise – as you notice a hi-fi-shaded patch of slightly lighter wallpaper – is that now the flat feels strangely empty too. Two smaller patches of new-looking wallpaper form an outline the size of speakers, and on the floor, under those lighter shades of wall, is a neat dust-free square.

There is, of course, another, more shameful reason that prompts the cry of "All back to mine". You think some women might come back too – I mean, it's the law of averages, innit? Maybe the same women who found you unappealing or completely invisible in the club will see you in a new light back at yours just as soon as they see that clip-framed Secondary School Watermanship Certificate 1975. ("One width of the pool, then one in pyjamas, plus being able to tread water for 20 seconds, girls.") But no, for some reason the all back to mine is as oestrogen-free as Supergrass. There may be a girl necking with her boyfriend, or that other denizen of these occasions… the absolutely terrifying loony woman. (She has a full pint-glass in her handbag. She has vomit in her teeth. She wants to phone her brother.) But mainly the chilly air hangs grim with testosterone.

And oh what bollocks is spoken! One of my guests (of the "I thought he came with you?" "No, I thought he came with you" variety) took 40 minutes to tell us the plot of a Stephen King story. Forty minutes of this: "And then… the man… or was it the woman? Anyway… they go into this house… No, they don't, they leave this house, oh no that's not them that's someone else." At every interruption from bored, tired, broken listeners he would a) say "but it's got a brilliant ending, right, a brilliant ending," and b) double the volume of his voice. As dawn broke, he finally said: "Here it is, right, this is the brilliant ending right, this is brilliant right… Oh what was it now?… No, it's gone… Sorry." They leave. You turn in. You wake up in a skip that once was a home. Oh well, you may have been bored but at least you weren't lonely, you think. Then you notice a Watermanship-Certificate-shaped patch of wallpaper that's a shade lighter than the rest of the wall •

Ecstasy testing in Amsterdam by Andrew Smith

STEPPING INTO HALL ONE at Digital Overdose on Saturday night is just... indescribable. We poke our heads into the large techno room, check out the ambient and jungle spaces upstairs. Then we follow the line of people across the corridor, drift innocently through the doorway and here we are: standing, staring – not sure whether to turn tail and run or succumb to the unbearable urge to giggle like infants.

The place is about the size of Wembley Arena, with steel balconies at either end. Vast video screens are running macabre footage of natural disasters and the like. Crammed on to the generous dancefloor below are hundreds – no, thousands – of young men, boys even, wearing gaudy shell-suits and shaven heads. They're jumping up and down and wiggling or kicking their legs very fast. It looks like an aerobic lesson for recently decapitated chickens. I realise for the first time just how little a bald pate and adolescent features suit each other.

This is Gabba (pronounced "habba"), an invention that the Dutch claim for their own, the story being that it began in Amsterdam and spread south to the industrial port of Rotterdam, where it got harder still (there's always been a rivalry between the two cities). The DJs have names like Gizmo, Weirdo and Darkraver and there are PAs from Neophyte and Ultra Violence, who hails from Nottingham. ("Yeah, there's a big Gabba scene in Nottingham – in my bedroom.") The factor common to all is the skull-shattering, almost martial, 4/4 or 8/4 beat, which never drops below 170 bpm and is frequently nearer 210. Labels such as Mokum, Rotterdam and Thunderdome Project claim sales of up to 200,000 apiece for these records. "Techno and house," opines DJ Weirdo, "is too soft for people here." Beyond that, there isn't much, just some background rumble and white noise. It's very white, very male, frighteningly asexual.

Some of the tunes feature a single, shrill, vastly sped-up phrase, often sampled from another record – it might be "I'm not in love" or "Born to be wild" or "Tear that fucker up" or "Ecstasy love" – which loops away for the duration. I later learn that this is Happy Hardcore, a new offshoot which was designed specifically to soften things up. "The government was starting to show concern," one of the Dutch DJs confides. "In Rotterdam, the E-taking was becoming like a sport: people were taking ten in one night – and speed." Pseudo-political parties were also starting to show interest, like the (and I kid you not) Nightmare Rotterdam Fascists.

In the adjacent Hall Two, the techno's playing and the Safe House tables are under siege from dozens of eager punters waiting to have their pills tested. The four-man team are working hard to keep pace with demand. When they started doing this, their job was relatively easy, there being only three or four different types of "Ecstasy" pill. Now their records cover more than 500.

To identify one, they run the chemical test, measure its circumference and depth, then note its colour and markings. They have lists of known specimens – pages and pages of them (the one I'm perusing runs to nine pages and it covers only blue tabs from the last four months), with the details compressed into a 13-digit code. When they find one which corresponds exactly, they know what they're dealing with.

At this stage, Herman and his colleagues can tell you what you're about to take: "This is MDMA 90 milligrams," they might say, or "MDEA 120" or "MDA 120" – in which case, of course, they would strongly advise you not to take it. Most of the time, the tabs turn out to be what the ravers expected, MDMA, though as I watch, several fail to provoke a colour change in the acid, which means there's no way of knowing what they are. Someone turns up with a new type of pill, on which there is so far no lab report. Two others arrive with capsules containing powder. It would be a bad idea to take any of these things, but Herman doesn't put it that way. He merely states the obvious truth: we don't know what this is, so if you swallow it, anything could happen or not happen. This is much scarier than someone telling you not to take something. In each case, the punter tosses the mysterious tab on to the floor.

By midnight, the crowd has increased dramatically and, judging by the saucer-like dilations of many pupils, some of these people are already making their second or third pass. I notice that, if a man and woman are together, Herman talks to the woman. That way she can tell her partner not to take it if necessary and he doesn't have to feel a sissy – just a beleaguered male like any other, which is easier to live with. Herman maintains that he can intuitively tell what someone's on. Though he can't say precisely how, he's seldom wrong. When a client is clearly overdoing it, he might ask them if more is a good idea, but won't try to persuade them. Some people have to learn by falling on their faces, he says.

"You usually find that they had a good Ecstasy experience a month ago. They take a pill and that feeling doesn't come back as they remember it. So they take another. Still not there. Another one. The truth is that you'll probably never get that feeling because that was then and those circumstances will never be the same."

Herman will never say whether a pill is "good" – despite being asked the question repeatedly – simply because its effect can vary from person to person and time to time. When August de Loor (whose name is above the door of the Adviesburo because he started it and is the political and administrative head) asks me to join him in the Red Cross room, where a girl is in trouble, I begin to understand how true this is.

We arrive to find a young woman lying on a bed being soothed by her boyfriend and a woman wearing the uniform of the Red Cross. The eyes of the women on the bed are rolling, her jaw is working furiously and she's fidgeting compulsively. She looks in a bad way to me. "No, she's playing games," August smiles. She's had three MDMA 90 tabs, but she's OK. "You see, I teach the workers here to create an atmosphere of trust and safety. You cocoon whoever's in trouble, so that you can help the kids gently back down. The thing is that the cocoon is a nice place to be and sometimes they don't want to come back out, so they play games. Then you have to kick them out." A boy who's sitting on a chair in front of me looks over at my T-shirt, grins wildly and says, "Is that Jimi Hendrix? He played with The Doors." I vow never to take any drug ever again.

A few moments later, August has been summoned to the other Red Cross area, where another girl is on a bed, this time clinging, as if for dear life, to a Red Cross worker. The untrained eye says that she's flipped. No, more game-playing, whispers August. She's only had one pill. They know what it was and it's nothing out of the ordinary. How did she get like this, then? "Maybe she's menstruating – that can make a difference. Or maybe there's a problem between her and her boyfriend... who knows?" Her boyfriend is sitting by her bed, eyes like saucers, smoking a fag, trying not to laugh. She's got her back to him. He's in his own world, not even noticing. Yeah, maybe that's it. In half an hour or so she'll be fine.

The warning sign everyone here is looking for is an uneven pulse. If they detect that, the ambulance is called straight away. Otherwise, treatment is as undramatic as possible. "Not like what I've seen of the UK, where they take your name and then jab valium in your backside," August comments drily. "The thing is, we know what drugs are out there, because we've been testing them all night."

When he negotiates with promoters, the first thing August does is persuade them to let people keep any Es they've brought for themselves. That way, they avoid creating an internal market, which might allow shit into the system. As soon as anything dodgy is discovered, he has the authority to stop the music and make an announcement, advising people to identify and eject the dealer.

Returning to the Safe House table, I'm lucky enough to bump into Franz, the man who came up with the acid test for Ecstasy. It became a "mission" for him eight years ago, when someone spiked his 20-year-old daughter's drink with LSD. She was in between college courses, he says, living in New York, working as a model and hanging out with a singer from a well-known British band. She'd flown back to London for the launch party of their world tour and it was at that party that the "accident" happened. Not normally drinking or taking drugs herself, her body couldn't handle what was put into it. She was permanently brain-damaged. Franz is stoic about it, but watches the testing with a peculiar intensity.

Three in the morning and the Gabba hall is in full cry. The men are shirtless, the women are in their underwear and many have given up even trying to dance. Instead, they're hanging from the platforms, staring into space. The music by now sounds like a swarm of 40-foot high, very angry bees, flying at you at speed. Sampled chants and cheers provide the only focus, along with the occasional Mickey Mouse clarion call: "Fuck me – ye-ah!" It's surreal.

But something has changed. About an hour ago, someone offered me an E. I gave him 25 Guilders (£10) and I watched the small white pill get tested. MDMA 130 – strong, but manageable. Then I went up to the jungle room and stayed there a while, occasionally decamping to the bar.

It was nice, vivid and intense and I thought how lovely it was to know precisely what you've taken. Eventually, there came a peak and the mellow slide back to normality started. At this point, something drew me to Hall One, and as soon as I arrived, I realised why. The nearest thing I've heard to what's going down here is the blunt scrap the likes of Spiral Tribe used to hammer out. When the more creative DJs start spinning in other stuff, I briefly hear echoes of a Junior Vasquez set at the Sound Factory – but that's minimalism; it invites your imagination to fill in the gaps. Subliminally, it swings. Gabba mugs your pulse. It is totally utilitarian. Music is not the point. My high, which was on the wane, comes flooding back.

But it's not until the lights go up and the records stop that it becomes clear just how weird this scene is. As the music subsides, people on the platforms start jumping up and down, staggering their rhythms so that it sounds very much like what's been blasting from the speakers all night. And the people below are dancing again.

In the next hall, Herman and his pals have finished packing up. I realise that I've never directly asked what his own attitude to Ecstasy is. "People should use what they want to," he offers, "but in such a way that they don't get into trouble. If they use drugs to make them more up and alive, OK. If they use them as pain-killers, as with heroin and sometimes alcohol, then that's a shame."

He freely admits that he's tried most of the things we've discussed. "But people make drugs too important. The way people talk, everything depends on the pill. If the evening was nice, it's because the pill was nice. Bullshit. You can take the same pill 100 times and 100 times it will be different... and that's beautiful! Accept that – it's life! Yesterday was yesterday and today is today. Have no expectations. Just be there, live in the moment. Don't say, 'All I need is this one last thing, a pill, and I'll be happy...'"

And you know, he's right. All our existential crises elegantly encapsulated in a little pill. One to ponder, as the sun rises above us, on the way home •

ANORAKS' PARADISE

NOVEMBER 1995

Learning to be a DJ by Gavin Hills

ANYONE WHO CAN PLAY chopsticks on the piano and knows how to work a Gameboy can be a DJ. All you need is some sense of timing and a few basic technical skills and you too could be on a grand a night. This all became clear to me after spending a day at the DJ Workshop – the first event of its kind, held in September by the British Record Industries Trust School at London's Royal Festival Hall – a splendid occasion where the massed ranks of DJ wannabes were taught how to cut it with the best of them. This was a day's training at the school of hardcore and the acid university.

My first class was an admittedly rather mild learning-curve into the world of techno. Or rather "Techno Techno Techno", as the sign on the door so proudly announced. Teacher was T23. An unusual name for a lecturer I grant you, but he did have the wit to let us call him Trevor.

Pupils had arrived at the South Bank from all over the country, travelling from as far afield as Norfolk in the east to Aberystwyth in the west to Edinburgh in the frozen north. They consisted of a typical club crowd of obsessives, nerds, nutters and pseudo sophisticates. All were eager to learn.

Trevor likened a Technics desk to a potter's wheel. He proceeded to throw his records of clay on it and produce the unmistakable form of a "tight set". To prove a point, others were allowed to attempt the feat and all stumbled like the classic senile buffers on *The Generation Game*.

Then Trev gave the game away. He explained what all the knobs do. He showed how to line up the perfect beat and how to adjust the speed of records. He showed that with a bit of savvy and a lot of practise any mug can mix records together. Basically, the "art" of DJing is about finding some nice records that sound the same and then fine-tune. Eager faces watched him at close quarters.

This was a Rave Anoraks' paradise: we were all allowed to stare over the DJ's shoulder, rifle through his record collection and even listen in on the headphones. I sat watching music. No one danced. No one indulged in decadence. We were there to learn. It worked. Soon I was fluent in DJ spiel. From the basic "whackin-it-in" (cutting straight to the next record) to a "slow blend" (gradually mixing one choon with another). Then on to advanced DJ, or "getting cocky".

Top disc jockeys from London's sassy house pirate Girls FM got into the intricacies of cockiness. Ms Crazy D explained how to "phase" (play the same record on both turntables so the breakbeats cancel each other) and how to mix with acappella records by counting the bars. She also got down to the burning topic of the day – looking for a screw.

Everyone who turned up was obsessed with the search for a screw. Just a little one mind you. One that lives at the bottom of a Technics deck if you're mug enough to pull it apart. Apparently, adjustment of the screw can increase your speed by 16 per cent. Why you'd really want to do this was never really explained. But, like most
things during the day, it was nice to know.

My only musical training up until that point had been banging three bits of a glocken-spiel during "Jesus Wants Me For A Sunbeam" at Leatherhead Primary School's harvest festival. But by the end of the DJ workshop I was well on the way to remixing "Jesus Wants Me For A Sunbeam" into a jungle classic.

I've always admired DJs. Anyone who can make people dance all night has got to be rated. After eight hours of intensive house training, though, I've come to the conclusion that the whole thing is an absolute racket.

In the field of music you have your architects and your builders. My little education has proved a dangerous thing. I've realised that we are being short-changed. Ninety per cent of DJs wouldn't even qualify for a City And Guilds in plastering.

I'm baffled that clubs fork out so much for top-name DJs to do a couple of hours of shoddy work when they could just stick on their "best set ever" tape for a fiver. It's not like they are up for taking requests or anything. Most punters wouldn't give a toss, especially if the money saved went on cheaper drinks or even adequate bog-rolls in the loo. What amazes me even more is that the majority of DJs get paid more than the people who make the records. I've learned someone somewhere has got a screw loose •

59   SNIFFING GLUE FOR THE SOHO SET

FEBRUARY 1996

Disco Pogo by Johnny Davis

WEST LONDON, DECEMBER 1995. The afternoon after the Christmas party the night before. Tom, the Chemical Brother most resembling a sedated Afghan hound, is drunk. Ed, the other one, is grappling with both his hangover and his pigeonholes.

Ed: I think our music's funk. I hate it when it's described as "rock music for dance heads".

Tom: I don't see anything wrong with rock'n'roll.

Ed: I'd prefer it to be described as funk.

Tom: It's not rugby music.

Ed: It does upset me when we're associated with that big, thuggy hands-in-the-air male thing. And I don't like being associated with amyl nitrate.

The, ahem, Chemical Brothers are about to find themselves without a choice. "Brit Hop And Amyl House", a compilation album released this month, is the first (and not the last) to gather together the like-minded bust-up breakbeat sounds of Richard Fearless, Emmanuel Top, Justin Robertson and, indeed, The Chemical Brothers. "I think it's the worst title for a record I've ever heard in my life," says Ed. Tom doesn't agree. "Brit Hop And Amyl House" is, after all, released on his girlfriend Vanessa's record label, Concrete, and was mixed (despite insistences that "she's a good mixer, my girlfriend") by him.

Brit Hop? Amyl House? You would be forgiven for envisaging genre-fretting journalists and unit-shifting record companies alike engaged in a new year round of backslapping over the fabrication of yet another spurious scene. Remember New Wave Of New Wave? How about Fraggle rock, Lionpop or Krautrock? Well, the news is that this particular turn of fashion's fickle wheel is actually pretty grand. Reflecting the roughness of early-Eighties electro and hip hop, your typical track combines walloping looped beats, scuffed-up samples and acid 303 squawks with a verse/chorus structure alien to most techno music. In short, the notion of The Song is put back into a genre (at times) obsessed with chin-stroking cleverness and a belief that Hard + Fast is in direct proportion to Quality. Which is why Josh Wink is on this album and Carl Craig isn't. And if you think this sounds like a recipe for It All Sounding The Same, then you're right. But, as Tom once sagely noted, that's a bit like complaining that Stone Roses records always have too many guitars on them.

Keen music genealogists will point to The Chemical Brothers' genre-defining "Song To The Siren" single in 1993, since which a number of similarly inclined acts (Daft Punk, Monkey Mafia, Death In Vegas) have started to surface. "Obviously you go to record shops and you hear tracks you wouldn't have been able to hear a couple of years ago. But when we were making our records we were copying bands like Coldcut, Renegade Soundwave and Depth Charge," says Ed. "That's how dance music has always progressed."

The Chemical Brothers story is one you probably know. Manchester 1989: two Chaucer students discover their mutual passion for over-indulgence at the Haçienda.

They befriend club-running and Eastern Bloc-working DJ Justin Robertson and find themselves behind the decks and clueless at his club nights Spice and Most Excellent. Encouraged, they start their own night, Naked Under Leather, mixing Mantronix with the Happy Mondays, The Beatles with Ravesignal III and prompting epidemic overuse of the adjective "eclectic". Taking the name The Dust Brothers – later changed to Chemical after legal moves by US producer duo The Dust Brothers – Ed and Tom famously decide they haven't got any records loud enough and vow to make their own. Using an S1000 sampler and a Hitachi hi-fi, "Song To The Siren" is created in Tom's bedroom. A pre-Sabres Of Paradise Andrew Weatherall hears and champions the single. Record deals, fastidiously cool remix offers, hitching up with Heavenly Records via the Sunday Social and a top-ten album all follow by natural progression.

Herein, however, lie not only the origins of the music but also of the club culture that has grown alongside it. For intrinsic to the notion of "Brit Hop" as a genre are the lager-fuelled, jump-around shoebox clubs like Athletico, London After Midnight and the Big Kahuna Burger Co (most usually the basements of tawdry pubs) to which it is best suited.

A decade ago, when Marshall Jefferson, Steve "Silk" Hurley and Farley "Jackmaster" Funk span old Philly records over Roland 808 kick-drum patterns, they realised that the beat had become the focal point of the music: the most significant sound since punk was born and the rest is history. But in 1996 when your identikit silk shirt and Soho crop has become more important than the music that moves your feet, it's time for a rethink. And action and reaction breed change.

"Spice and Most Excellent were about variety," explains Justin Robertson with reference to his old Mancunian nights. "When house became so big that it moved to large venues it lost its intimacy. The 'eclectic' nights sprung out of the tradition for playing chunky hip hop stuff at the end of the night. Those were the records people went the maddest to."

If Spice and Most Excellent have found themselves reduced to mere footnotes in the chapter of Clubland History entitled "Balearic", it's doubtless due to the overshadowing presence of one club. And that club is the legendary Sunday Social. So legendary is the legendary Sunday Social that it's almost never referred to without its prefix "legendary". "Basically we ripped it off," enthuses Heavenly Records' Robin Turner, who runs the club. "We ripped it off from a lot of clubs. There was Full Circle in Slough, Disco Pogo and a pub called The Swan in Windsor which was free on a Sunday night. It's a formula that works. It's for people who feel isolated by techno and glamorous house clubs, for people who were bored of hearing Richie Hawtin play 'Spastik' for 20 minutes and wanted to hear songs, have a beer and get a bit stupid again."

Listen to any of these Brit Hop tracks and you'll discover a vitality, humour, energy and soul (soul doesn't stop at Aretha Franklin) lacking in so much "dance" music. Look around any of these pub-clubs and take in the punters. At the bar Northern Soul fans spotting B-sides, by the DJ booth liggers and B-list indie pop stars vying for attention, on the dancefloor kids on drugs, dolled-up glamour girls and dressed-down students. You know, like, variety. Life. Something a bit different. It's probably not the future of music, dance music, clubs or even Saturday night but at least – and this is the important part – it's spontaneous fun.

As the effortless successes of Gilles Peterson and James Lavelle's That's How It Is, Goldie's Metalheadz and Paul Anderson's The Loft illustrate, a new climate has broken that's seen intimate, midweek clubs as a stalwart alternative to predictable Saturday nights. "It just works a lot better when it's a small crowd. When people are crammed in they've gotta dance," says Ed. "Smaller places are like being at a house party when you are 14."

And not unlike those teenage house parties, the Sunday Social also managed to capture something of the joys of youthful hedonism. There were tales of blow-jobs behind the decks. Dancing on the tables and along the bar was *de rigeur*. Nights would reliably end with a communal shout-a-long to The Beatles' "Helter Skelter". And then, woeful reader, there were the amyl nitrate stories.

"This flaming shoe came past us while we were DJing," reminisces Ed. "Someone dropped a bottle of amyl and their leg went up in flames." "People used to do amyl circles," nods Tom. "And then dance in a burning ring of fire. We've seen some pretty strange things." Bizarrely, the wholly unpleasant act of sniffing poppers has become something of a Brit Hop institution. Sordid folklore dictates that Heavenly's Robin regularly had to dispatch someone from the Sunday Social to the sex shops of Soho in order to replenish supplies. "Most Excellent used to be held in a gay club and they sold amyl behind the bar," suggests Justin Robertson. "Perhaps it's a throwback to that." Tom: "It's grim. It's seedy. It's sniffing glue for the Soho set. But it's quite funny isn't it? I wouldn't call a record 'Amyl House', though." Heavens, no.

The true measure of the impact of This Music Known As Brit Hop, however, is its infiltration into the lives and record collections of previously disparate groups of club-bers and music enthusiasts. House and techno heads have latched on to its big beats and wailing samples, while your traditionalist rock fan has seen the likes of Paul Weller and Noel Gallagher show up to endorse the Chemical Brothers' sets personally. The Chemicals themselves are particularly enthused by rock music (check the titles – "Leave Home" lifted from the Ramones, "One Too Many Mornings" from Dylan, "(The Best Part Of) Breaking Up" from Phil Spector), they prefer reading the *NME* to dance magazines, and say: "We tend to remix rock records and indie records because there are sounds that we have no access to. On dance records there aren't going to be that many sounds that we couldn't have made ourselves." Meanwhile, pop fans can witness Brit Hop's erstwhile chart success via the likes of the Chemical Brothers and Josh Wink. And there will certainly be others. Those who proffer the elitist argument that this is merely whiteboy hip hop – a lame, Happy Shopper version of an authentic sound – should be directed to the Chemical Brothers' sledgehammer reworking of Method Man's "Bring The Pain" included on his "You're All I Need..." single.

Where the analogous successes of the Chemical Brothers and the Sunday Social have led, others have followed. Newer clubs taking up the Social blueprint have appeared like the Big Kahuna Burger Co in London. "What happened with Dan and Jon [Big Kahuna's founders] was brilliant," enthuses Robin Turner. "They were people who came to the Social and were inspired. When we had 14 months off they wanted to do it for themselves. It was that total get-off-your-arse attitude, total DIY culture. They built up a following by DJing last, like the Chemical Brothers, and trying to make the audience freak out to them."

(An aside. And some wise words of warning for potential DIY enthusiasts. There's more than a little method in the eclectic madness that lies at the heart of the success of these clubs; a new night recently took over the old Sunday Social site and, on a Sunday, promised anything-goes abandon and promptly mixed up The Cure with A Guy Called Gerald, Ozric Tentacles with The Pop Group. The result? Audio hell and audi-ence horror. "It's really easy to abuse and the whole thing becomes pointless. Taking over the same night, the actual place. It wasn't really on," reckon the Brothers.)

The new big-beat faces are coming, too. Many have been knocking around a while, others are a debut single away. And they've all got proper pop star names, just like the old days. Daft Punk ("More like *NME* cover material than anyone else," says Robin Turner), Death In Vegas, Lionrock, Depth Charge, Mekon... the beat is, indeed, on.

"Tom and Ed have started something because people relate to them. They've got an outlook on things and an opinion. It needs something for people to latch on to. The whole point of being young is being in a gang," reckons Justin Robertson. And when you're in a gang with thousands of other paying househeads in a disused aircraft hangar, any ideas of youthful rebellion seem a bit laughable. Things are getting smaller, more intense."

Jon Carter, the man behind Monkey Mafia (about to unleash a scratch-up frenzy follow-up to his "Blow The Whole Joint Up" single), agrees. "I can't hack going to house clubs any more. Total respect to the Chemical Brothers. They came first. They've changed people's minds and opened people's minds up to it."

So what does he make of all this Brit Hop and Amyl House business? "Well..." he muses for a moment. "Dodgy name, isn't it?" •

THE DREARY DAIRYLEA PROCESSION

JUNE 1996

Club mix CDs by John McCready

THAT THESE THINGS are popular is beyond question. Mix CDs sell and we aren't here to dispute that. I'd simply like to call time on the idea that they are in any way a creative form. Mix CDs are yet another sad example of the greed and patent lack of nous of the former house republic, now an ugly monarchy. No amount of coloured cardboard, rubber or tin packaging can disguise the fact that a dreary Dairylea procession of all the latest intros and breakdowns does not equal the soundtrack to a generation. Mix CDs are direct descendants of cash-in compilations like "Top Of The Pops" in the Seventies (which had better sleeves) and "Now That's What I Call Music" in the Eighties (which had better music). As a technical point of order, most of the names cluttering up the flyers on a bar table near you couldn't mix a bag of cement. Some of these jokers claim their mixes are "live". Take it as read that they have spent a week starting over and over again. So far, the only CD by people to have even scratched the surface of this much-abused art of mixing two records together was Coldcut's recent contribution to the "Journeys By DJ" series. The rest are too busy having their pictures taken for the cover or recovering from "'avin' it" over the weekend. Having an opportunity to express yourself creatively over the length of an LP and instead using the time to Sellotape together all the promos you got in the post last week won't wash. Don't waste your money on something you will end up giving to Oxfam in five years' time. Buy yourself a C90 and go and do something more interesting yourself instead •

61   MOVING HOUSE

JULY 1996

Cream's promoters on their attempts to break away from the superstar DJ circuit and the superclub market. By Richard Benson

----

SO, CREAM. We note a conspicuous absence of the old techno graphics, and a conspicuous presence of James Lavelle's name beside those of Nick Warren and Paul Oakenfold on your club's new mix album...

Darren Hughes (promoter): Well there's a reason for it, you know, which is to do with the way we felt by the end of last year that the whole so-called superclub market had become a joke. We even looked at ourselves and said this is a joke...

Why?

James Barton (promoter/DJ): Because it got to the point where there was nowhere left to go, except maybe to start again. We had too many DJs turning up five minutes before they were due on, having played in a few other clubs on the way, and going on and just playing records, as opposed to DJing.

The difference being?

JB: The difference being that a proper DJ turns up early, with a lot of his records, listens to what's being played, and then plays to the crowd's mood, and in continuity with the last DJ. Someone who just plays records only brings between 60 and 90 records, and plays a pre-planned set. At least 20 of the top house DJs currently are not sticking to their original principles.

But you're still putting on "top house DJs".

JB: No, you'll find that us and a lot of promoters like us are now cutting the ones I'm talking about. Who? Just anybody who's playing three times a night, take your pick. I know that by giving star billings to DJs, Cream has in the past helped to create stars and star followings. But that time when people could just rely on their name is over now. A lot of promoters are saying that...

These people are, of course, notoriously dear. What's the most you've ever paid?

JB: The most we've ever paid is £5,000 on New Year's Eve for Sasha, Jeremy Healy, Danny Rampling and Roger Sanchez. Our DJ bill can reach £25,000 a month now.

DH: But he [James Barton] was voted Cream's favourite DJ when we did a survey, which was interesting because he was a resident, not one of the big DJs. There's my hope – the 2,000 who come for the music, and not just because Pete Tong's on and he's telling everybody about it on the radio.

How come you're still booking Jeremy Healy then?

JB: 'Cause Darren likes him.

DH: "Jeremy Healy" is like a catch-all phrase for cheese at the moment. But his DJing is actually really good; I think that the people who slate him don't listen to him   179 play. It's because he's put himself up for that superstar role that he gets criticised.

A lot of people think his DJing is, to say the least, inconsistent.
JB: He's not my type of DJ, but he is a great entertainer. It's funny actually... In my opinion he made one big mistake last year and that was doing so many gigs that he never had time to buy records. He knows that. I think he knows he now has to start playing.

You've got James Lavelle on the album, and you've had the Heavenly Social and Logical Progression DJs on in your new room lately; some would say you're trying to buy into something a bit more underground to add a bit of life and credibility.
DH: Well we don't buy in ideas... we don't put anything on unless or until we like it. The point is that James Lavelle is in a totally separate standard of dance music, and to have a long-term strategy for our business, and to keep liking our business, we need to present new, emerging music.

But James Lavelle's not new and emerging, he's very well established...
JB: He's established in his field. But to a load of kids who come to Cream on Saturday night he *is* new. Kids don't come to Cream to listen to DJs like that, but they might be interested if they do hear them. It may be that we have to have rooms half-empty and lose some money, but... that way you're giving people a chance to hear different music, and giving those DJs an audience and a system and facilities they might not otherwise get. I'd make a point about drum & bass. A friend of mine at Deconstruction was saying to me that drum & bass will never ever be as big as people think it could be until it gets a presence in the North. Until that point it will continue to be regional. Of course I'm not saying we can break drum & bass in the North-west, but I think if we can open up new music to people in our catchment area we're going in the right direction. So, you know, we put LTJ Bukem on, and the people who go to Cream who wouldn't normally hear it – and the people who just come to hear him, maybe snobbier people who would look down on house music – will also get to hear the best house played on a good system. That excites me.

Does this mean that clubs like Cream now become big umbrella organisations for dance music, jukeboxing the underground to a more mainstream audience?
JB: I don't know about other clubs, but it was always our ambition in the first place to have lots of different kinds of music playing under one roof at the same time...
DH: We want to represent the whole culture...
JB: But I don't know about talking about the "underground" or buying credibility anyway. When we had Logical Progression, the room was rammed, and the Social DJs were the most popular thing on the night they played. Those DJs are commercial.

So you're big and successful. What more do you want?
JB: I'd really like Cream to be something that proved it... that proved the culture isn't all about gangsters and drug dealers like some people think, that it's a legitimate way of life. The funny thing then, of course, is that it'd be normal, like everything else, so what would you have achieved? It's weird to think about that, isn't it? •

62   SATURDAY LOVE

AUGUST 1996

Tribal Gathering by Miranda Sawyer

AT FOUR O'CLOCK the normal world seemed very very very far away. Far away from the mad lad in the big E T-shirt, waving his neon wands to the tune of the fairground bumper cars; from the post-Leftfielders, stumbling out of the Starship Enterprise tent to lie flat out beneath an almost-full moon; from the bungey nutters, rubber-balling between heaven and earth; from the dancers, the chancers, the chemically enhanced-ers; miles and miles away from all of us. It was out there, somewhere, but far beyond our ken. And as for Ravey Davey, waving at the future with his £5-a-pair luminous white gloves... he was on a planet of his own design.

Yet, 12 hours later, tucked in under the normal world's everyday duvet, it was like nothing had ever happened. We waited so long for Tribal Gathering '96, and it came and went in the blink of a wide-awake eye. Now it feels as though you could never find your way back; and if you did, there'd be no evidence remaining, not a crushed beer cup or ripped Rizla to prove that, yes, there were 30,000 of us and, yes, we had the time of our lives.

The Sunday papers, even the Monday ones, despite their recently acquired house-happy attitudes, gave no more than a hands-in-the-air picture and a few lines of review. These last were muted, rather disappointed. They bemoaned the Gatherers' good manners and queuing ability, clearly wondering why they weren't sticking knives into one another or dying from overdoses or robbing or rioting or at least showing the camera their liberated, photogenic chests. "The E-generation," sniffed the *Guardian*, "are polite, suburban and luvved-up": and then went on to review the live acts as though they were performing in the Astoria. The verdict? These DJ types have no stage presence. Duh.

Perhaps you can't blame the papers for feeling let down. Without Glastonbury as the cartoon-fest du festivals, without the backstage star hobnobbage, the beardies, the weirdies, the dealers, the didgeridooings, the media is stuck for a big summer youth story. So it runs between The Who and Luton Hoo, comparing corpo-rock with get-down-on-it get-on-with-it dance culture, searching for the angle, spoiling for a fight; hoping that someone will cry, or at least try to fly, before they get cold. When no one does, they damn youth culture as boring. But they've missed the point.

Tribal Gathering, despite its bongo-bothering name, was never searching for astral significance. It didn't have to smear itself in woad and stick bells to its toes and slop lentil offerings around in order to give itself a sense of purpose. And it didn't want to call anyone to revolution, or to vote Labour, or to be a Tomorrow Person, or to stutter stuff about the generation gap. In an era when even Noel Gallagher uses stage-time to tell you to support Tony Blair, this is rare and, frankly, restful.

What else didn't Tribal Gathering do? It didn't have comedians; it didn't do massage; it didn't make a special feature film to show during performance; it didn't refuse to   181 move on when everything closed; it didn't even complain when it couldn't get out of the car park. All that happened was that everyone turned up except Underworld and the poetry tent; everyone got mashed and happy and danced till dawn; everyone went home.

And in a way, that was just as much of an achievement as a twatted Take Thatter gatecrashing Glastonbury. There were plenty of obstacles for the Gathering to negotiate: not least the cancellation, a week before its scheduled May kick-off, of the licence for the festival to be held in Oxford. Traffic problems, apparently: though no one worried about central London being held up by 150,000 Hyde Park road-ragers.

According to Paul Shurey, Universe head honcho and man behind the Tribe, the only reason why TG '96 went ahead was luck. "Another organisation had already applied for a licence on the Luton site, but they hadn't managed to get it together," he explains. "They hadn't any track record of holding big events but they'd still managed to get a licence – so we went in on the back of that. It was a one-in-a-million chance."

Never mind one-in-a-million: the odds were incalculable that the partygoers were going to make it, let alone all the acts and DJs. Yet just a handful of tickets were returned, and only Underworld, of the headliners, couldn't alter their commitments. Leftfield played the Roskilde festival in Belgium, then hopped on a plane to London to strut their stuff hours later in Luton. Everyone made the effort. As DJ Rap was later to pronounce: "Well, you're a sad fucker if you miss it, aren't ya?"

It's more than that. If you miss it, it's not only you that's sad – everyone else is too. Not literally, not broken-hearted but, as Dr Cliché says, the difference between a rock event and a dance one is that the former is all about the stars; the latter, the audience. If you, the ticket holder, don't turn up, it's everyone's loss.

You could see this when Black Grape played. At a rock gig or festival, the point is to see the band: push to the front and sweat it out with the big mosh boys or you're a part-timer. At Tribal Gathering, people were dancing outside the tent and having a top time. What mattered was not how close you were to Kermit's toes, but who was around you and how good you all felt when Shaun got his melons twisted round "Pretty Vacant".

So was Tribal Gathering a festival, or just a one-night Brownie camp for DJ worshippers? Over the last few years, festival culture has warped out of all recognition. Neil "Old Man" Barnes from Leftfield can provide a potted history of sorts.

"Well, I used to go to Bracknell Jazz Festival and Womad," he recalls mistily, "just because of the diversity of music you'd get there. But coming from a punk background, festivals went out of favour for a long time. You know, Glastonbury was seen as just a hippy thing. It's changed now, of course."

Of course. The homogenisation of guitar music has meant that bands like Oasis, Ash, Skunk Anansie, The Manics, Radiohead, plus solo acts like Alanis Morissette, are straddling the music/generation/denimwear gaps that have gaped between indie and rock for years (proof? Oasis choosing to play at Knebworth, for Jovi's sake). These days, "alternative" bands see mainstream as something to be proud of, and festivals are big business. Frankly, where there's muck, there's buckets of brass. With Oasis rumoured to be insisting on the installation of dozens of temporary cash machines at Loch Lomond so the punters have enough notes to spend on merchandising, the only difference between their gig and The Who's Mastercard moneyspinner is the age of the scooters they arrive on.

This isn't necessarily a bad thing, just a thing. Music has always been a business. And these days, at least everyone likes music and wants to go to festivals – and everyone's welcome. Even Channel 4. Even Radio One. Even (mother!) Johnny Rotten.

But against this money-machine backdrop, the dance scene seems innocent, inventive, diverse, to die for. It's mainstream all right – look at The Prodigy, Orbital, Massive Attack; Oakey, Sasha, Carl Cox; Tricky, Portishead, Björk – but on most levels it's more independent, more creative, less crass, less in-yer-face-up-yer-nose than its guitar-wielding loadsamoney contemporaries.

Worries that the reports about Tribal Gathering's licensing problems would lead to too much publicity and, horrors, over-commercialisation were completely unfounded. And we're still a way off from a full-blown three-day dance music festival. Though Paul Shurey has named this as his express intention – a long weekend of outdoor sounds, with perhaps one teeny stage for alternative rock, sidelined in the way the dance stage always is at mainstream festivals – police and public attitudes suggest that this is still some time away.

Tribal Gathering, when it comes down to it, didn't really feel like a festival for a couple of reasons. One: everything was under canvas, so there was nothing that could capture the heaven-soaring, all-uniting sensation of a Glastonbury Orbital '94 or Prodigy '95. Two: it was only one night. You need at least two days for that true festival sensation, at least 48 hours to get really down and dirty, to lose the plot and never think of looking for it, to live a lifetime in a night-time, to come home and not recognise the door to your room.

But what it did feel was good. Midnight came and you didn't have to search for a party. You weren't turfed into a separate field to trip over tents and choke on the smoke from students burning plastic bags. You didn't traipse for miles to find the only sound system was powered by bicycle. You weren't harassed by dealers, worried by drug virgins, mithered by chippy crusties, forced to endure bagpipes at five in the morning.

What Tribal Gathering was about, pure and simple, was pleasure. If we've learned anything in the eight years since house music turned us round, it's that dancing till tomorrow with a generation of strangers is just a really fantastic laugh. We're well aware that it's not a political act; at least not in a way that gets transformed into votes or direct action. We've got no time for the pseudo accessories: crystals and hairwrapping are about as intelligent as trying to fly by astral plane. And we know that drugs won't change the world. Of course everyone was out of it: it's just that they weren't making a fuss about it, or telling you about how charged they were. OK, some did.

No one who stayed up all night on June 29 thought that it was going to change their life. It was just part of their life. Thanks to its size and profile, Tribal Gathering provided an unprecedented demonstration that what would have once been strange, underground and exceptional events were now just single nights in heaven, enjoyed not by marginalised demi-monders but by a mass of well-balanced everyday people who believe that having fun is as important as having a baby, or a job, or friends, or your health.

It's this that confounds the media, brought up as it is on hippies and punks and show-offs and big mouths. Not everyone who stays up all night has an agenda. Or a stupid wardrobe. Or a problem with self-esteem. No wonder the reviewers were confused. An event that's about the people there, but the people don't even dress funny? Like the man says, it's not rock'n'roll.

What Tribal Gathering did was to move popular culture on, quietly but significantly, bringing together remarkably diverse strands of dance music, and thus entirely different sets of people, in a way that would have seemed unthinkable even two years ago.

Who'd have thought that jungle could sit so nicely next to happy house? That The Chemical Brothers could shake off their indie boots so successfully? That strangers could hug each other and not think they're government-toppling? No more, no less. In the end it's turned out that 30,000 people standing in a field is an excellent way to feel for the future •

63   PRETEND THAT WE'RE CRED

AUGUST 1996

How big business hijacked club culture by Stephen Armstrong

CLUBLAND HAS ALWAYS been filled with the soft whisper of money changing hands behind the scenes. Record companies pay DJs to plug new releases, dealers pay door-men to let them do business, and pirate stations get set up to promote dodgy drum & bass nights in Peckham. The issue has always been sloshing around in a nickels-and-dimes kind of way, but now there's some big money moving in and the club runners are falling over themselves to get a piece of it. The multinational drink and cigarette com-panies are looking to hitch the nation's youth on to their marketing bandwagon, and big clubs are their latest route.

The corporate logo is everywhere. Earlier this year, Ballantynes Whisky co-promoted a night in Paris with Cream; last year Pepsi backed the Ministry Of Sound Tour; Sony PlayStation paid for a room in the Ministry Of Sound when it relaunched last September; and Silk Cut tied up with Renaissance for the Renaissance Silk Tour promo-tion last month. Mark Ratcliff, who runs youth advertising and research company Murmur, says that almost every big club in the country has contacted him over the last year trying to find a commercial sponsor. "Companies can spend almost any amount of money on these things," Ratcliff explains. "It can range from a few hundred bottles of free booze which are 'prominently placed' in the venue, through the £15,000 that Silk Cut paid for the Renaissance night to the £50,000 that Sony is supposed to have paid out for the PlayStation room at the Ministry."

In some cases it's simply club runners and promoters – who have been grafting for years and paying through the nose for name DJs and obligatory "protection" – who are accepting this sort of sponsorship, because it means they finally get to see some profit. In other cases, greedy and unscrupulous managers see pound signs and till receipts flashing before their piggy eyes and sell out without thinking twice. "It's really the more sophisticated club runners wanting to run a big business who are getting involved," says Paul Morrison, associate director of KLP, who tied up the Ballantynes/Cream deal and the Silk Cut/Renaissance night. "They want a corporate partner to align them-selves with. The brand might pay a licence fee to use the club's name, pay for most of its advertising and have their logo on any associated record label."

The whole deal works because the club economy has spawned its own prolific media with magazine ads, radio ads, compilation albums and flyers, all providing extra public-ity opportunities, while advertisers are desperate for credibility in the sophisticated and cynical youth market.

Mark Ratcliff strikes a note of caution. "Chucking money at a big nightclub says nothing except that you have a lot of money and are trying to be trendy," he says. "To impress people, you genuinely have to give something back, not just line some coke-head promoter's back pocket" •

Five clubbing concepts for the Nineties

THESE ENTRIES ARE TAKEN from a feature called 50 Revolutions Per Minute, which appeared in the 200th issue of The FACE. Written and compiled by various staff and freelance writers, the feature identified 50 new social phenomena that characterised British life in the 1990s.

Hedonism: Blue Tuesday Syndrome
Having it, larging it, giving it loads... House music wrenched nightclubbing away from Curiosity Killed The Cat and gave it back to the everyday party people. Since then, our nation of shopkeepers has been united by that Monday-morning feeling, the tacit understanding that the sniffling, touchiness and inability to concentrate will be gone by Wednesday, and forgotten by Friday, ready for the weekendering to begin again. It starts with a lager-lager-lager shandy and ends in a whirl of powders and spliff: a good night out for soul boys, terrace hoolies, bikini-clad garage babes, jump-up junglists, daddy's girls, posh boys and everyone in between.

Jockey Sluts
The rise of DJ culture and the bedroom boffin has produced some baffling conse-quences for the music industry. The real pop stars are now not the artists but the peo-ple who spin their records, who now also attract their own groupies. Entering the DJ's inner circle needn't have sexual connotations for the aspiring jockey slut, of course, but below-the-decks action and hedonist clubbing goes hand in hand (or cock in mouth), at least according to the new folklore.

Domestic Hedonism
As practised by people who prefer M&S meals and Friday-night telly to eating out and queuing for a club. As leisure opportunities multiply, so does the pressure to go out and enjoy them in all their manifold permutations. From this comes the perverse pleasure of staying in. Why pay pub/club prices when you can get some mates round, stick on a record and crack open a bottle of vodka?

Club Babes
As much a fixture in any large niterie as rude doormen, blocked lavs and dealers selling Disprin, the club babe is everybody's good-time girl for whom sunbeds, alcopops and lime-green strappy mini-dresses are less of a fashion statement and more a way of life. Immune to the sex-appeal exuded by donning a baggy T-shirt and casual jeans, these are girls who let their bodies do all the talking because their minds are empty. At least, that's what they've been brought up to believe. Corrie's Racquel and Gazza's Sheryl are their spiritual sisters; house DJs and club flyers showing half-naked tottie are the agents responsible for validating their "tits-oot" style.

Diffusion Clubbing

Once there were underground kinds of clubs and there were high street Mecca kinds of clubs and that was that. Those clubs still exist, but a big grey area has spread between the two; we know of at least one club in Britain which has dispensed with its DJs who once span SAW records to happy lagered-up Saturday punters, and now merely puts house club mix CDs on. Which says it all, really •

65   BLEEP OF FAITH

Hardcore's second coming by Rupert Howe

BACK IN JANUARY 1992, when "toytown" tunes sampling kids' TV themes made rave a dirty word, Suburban Bass label boss Dan Donnelly released a track called "Hardcore Will Never Die" under the name Q-Bass. While his label soon moved on into the realms of darkcore and jungle, the spirit of that track lives on, in the "nobody loves us but we don't care" attitude of the "happy" hardcore ravers who, despite being regarded with contempt by the rest of the music industry, carried on regardless. And though you may still think it's video-game noise for pre-adolescents, you won't be able to avoid hardcore in the next 12 months. With every other aspect of dance culture sucked dry, hardcore remains practically the only thing left to be snaffled up by the mainstream media. There'll be ads with happy hardcore jingles by summer.

The only thing to change since the early Nineties is that a new generation of teenage ravers waving luminous sticks has joined the white-gloved stalwarts still high on 1992. Even the music has kept the faith. Eschewing the progressive tendencies of jungle/drum & bass, hardcore remains based around a series of tried-and-tested motifs: jittery synth stabs, big piano breakdowns and helium-pitch vocals. These days, even its own perceived stupidity has evolved into a kind of in-joke with tracks like "Toytown" by Hixxy & Sharkey and "Airhead" by DJ Brisk playing it deliberately (and hilariously) dumb.

There are, however, emerging signs of change. The main source of contention is the relentless 4/4 kickdrum which powers the music along in a state of permanent rapture. For a time, the so-called four-beat style (all double kicks and relentless, 170bpm velocity) was converging with the famously uncompromising beats of gabba. Now many of the DJs who championed that sound are looking for a way out of the louder/faster/harder cul-de-sac.

"I think the gabba scene is totally different to the hardcore scene and I know a lot of DJs aren't playing that full-on techno any more," says hardcore/four-beat legend DJ Seduction. "I know I won't. I'm introducing a lot of breaks back into my stuff and I've been hearing more tracks with breaks in. I don't think it will be as heavily breakbeat-oriented as it used to be, but the breaks will be there. Basically, the music will be getting more bouncy."

The result is a fragmentation of what was once one of the most unified of dance scenes. Scotland, for instance, remains devoted to the four-beat techno/gabba pulse. London and the south-east, meanwhile, seems to be turning back to the classic hardcore sound of 1992. "More and more parties are doing old-school rooms," notes Jimmy J, co-author of the happy anthem "Six Days". "Moondance, for instance, put on parties that are pure old school, and they're sold out every time long in advance. In London, they love the breakbeat stuff, but when you go up north they like it bangin'. And if you want the record sales you have to sell up north. So you're caught in a bit of a dilemma. Which is why people are starting new labels, rather than converting the labels they have at the moment back to breakbeat."

Jimmy J himself is on the point of starting up a new label with a more breakbeat-oriented sound. Happy breakbeat might yet merge with the more upbeat end of jungle, although the impetus is more likely to come from the hardcore producers than the junglists – one-time "happy" producers like Nookie and Danny Breaks having severed all connections with the current hardcore cliques.

Yet whatever the concerns of the DJs and producers, the hardcore audience continues to grow apace, a fact not lost on the major labels, which last year finally cottoned on to the fact that happy hardcore was loaded with instant pop appeal when Baby D's old-school anthem "Let Me Be Your Fantasy" went to number one. Besides, few people on the hardcore scene talk about "selling out". For many hardcore producers a return to the halcyon days of 1992, when hardcore records regularly made the charts, would be the fulfilment of a long-cherished dream.

"As soon as someone charts something, the majors will be bringing out all these hardcore tunes," reckons Jimmy, who has recorded a selection of (unreleased) material for ffrr and had a hit in Australia with "Six Days". "At the moment, everyone is waiting to see what happens. It's down to who wants to spend the money to try and promote it and give it the first push.

"This whole industry will probably end up going full circle like it did in '92. It'll start underground, chart like when SL2 charted, and then go back underground again. It just keeps going round in a great big circle" •

Stephen Armstrong is a freelance journalist who writes for The FACE, *Time Out,* the *Sunday Times* and the *Guardian*

Lindsay Baker is the commissioning editor of the *Guardian Weekend* magazine

Richard Benson is the editor of The FACE

Stuart Cosgrove is the controller of arts and entertainment for Channel 4

Laura Craik is the fashion features editor of The FACE

Johnny Davis is an associate editor of The FACE

Simon Dudfield is working on his first book, the authorised biography of Andrew Loog Oldham, to be published in the autumn of 1997

Robert Elms is a writer and broadcaster

Sheryl Garratt was editor of The FACE from 1989-1995, and is now a contributing editor. She is currently working on a book about the past decade of British club culture, to be published by Headline in spring 1998

John Godfrey is ex-deputy editor of THE FACE, ex-editor of *iD*, co-author of *Altered States*, and is now series producer of *Eurotrash* and *Fortean TV* at Rapido TV

David Hill is a feature writer and critic for the *Observer*, and the author of books on football, politics and (coming soon) the future for men

Gavin Hills was a genius, and a wonderful bloke. He died in May 1997, and is missed indescribably

Lee Harpin is deputy music editor at the *Daily Star*

Rupert Howe is a freelance writer

Mandi James is a DJ now working chiefly in Thailand

Tim Jeffrey runs the Loaded and Skint labels, and is a freelance music writer

David Johnson was an eyewitness at enough of youth culture's defining moments to know that the eventual writers of "pop history" screw up because they were somewhere else. He clubbed it (as a verb) for The FACE 1982-4. By day he has worked as a journalist with the *Evening Standard, Daily Telegraph* and, currently, the *Sunday Times,* where he edited *1,000 Makers of Music.* By night, he subscribes to minimal sleep theory

Sarah Kennedy is a contributing editor of *Cosmopolitan*, having previously worked for *Company* and *19*. She is also the mother of two small and fab boys, still chainsmoking 40 a day, and having the best time ever

Sivan Lewin is a photographer. She lives in London

Don Macpherson is a screenwriter who has worked with Terry Gilliam, Jodie Foster, Oliver Stone and Steven Spielberg. His latest film is *The Avengers* for Warner Bros (1998)

John McCready is a DJ and freelance journalist

Robert Newman has spent the last two years writing a second novel, *Manners,* which comes out 1997-98

Deanne Pearson is a freelance writer and editor specialising in complementary health and fitness. She considers this a natural progression from sex'n'drugs'n'rock'n'roll, given the histories of of Lou Reed, Iggy Pop, Boy George et al

Laurie Pike reports on the underground for magazines and television. Most recently she produced a documentary on dance crazes for Channel 4, and directed and starred in a short comedy film, *The Baby Haters*, co-starring Eugenie Vincent and Mink Stole

Paul Rambali is a writer

Neil Rushton is a the owner of Network Records, a born-again Northern Soul DJ, part of Commit No Nuisance! music promotion company, a Birmingham City fanatic, and a club runner with Keep The Dream Alive

Fiona Russell Powell is a journalist, currently working on *Talk Trash To Me*, a collection of her best celebrity interviews

Miranda Sawyer is a contributing editor of The FACE, and serves as token bird on a variety of other publications and radio and TV programmes

Andrew Smith is the pop critic on the *Sunday Times*

Kate Spicer is a freelance journalist

Chris Taggart is a magazine publisher

David Toop is a musician and writer. Author of two books: *The Rap Attack* (1984,updated second edition, *Rap Attack 2*, published 1994, Serpent's Tail) and *Ocean of Sound* (published 1996, Serpent's Tail). He released two solo albums in 1995-6: "Screen Ceremonies" (Wire Editions) and "Pink Noir" (Virgin), as well as curating a series of compilation albums for Virgin ("Ocean Of Sound", "Crooning On Venus", "Sugar & Poison", "Booming On Pluto", "Guitars On Mars")

Lesley White is a feature writer for the *Sunday Times Magazine*, and a columnist for the *Sunday Times*